To Brother Chet

Ismael

Beyond Mainstream Explanations of the Financial Crisis

This book provides a critique of the neoclassical explanations of the 2008 financial collapse, of the ensuing long recession and of the neoliberal austerity responses to it.

The study argues that while the prevailing views of deregulation and financialization as instrumental culprits in the explosion and implosion of the financial bubble are not false, they fail to point out that financialization is essentially an indication of an advanced stage of capitalist development. These standard explanations tend to ignore the systemic dynamics of the accumulation of finance capital, the inherent limits to that accumulation, production and division of economic surplus, class relations, and the balance of social forces that mold economic policy.

Instead of simply blaming the "irrational behavior" of market players, as neoliberals do, or lax public supervision, as Keynesians do, this book focuses on the core dynamics of capitalist development that not only created the financial bubble, but also fostered the "irrational behavior" of market players and subverted public policy.

Due to its interdisciplinary perspective, this book will be of interest to students and researchers in economics, finance, politics and sociology. It will also be of interest (as well as accessible) to "non-expert" lay readers.

Ismael Hossein-zadeh is Emeritus Professor of Economics at Drake University, USA.

Routledge frontiers of political economy

1 **Equilibrium Versus Understanding**
Towards the rehumanization of economics within social theory
Mark Addleson

2 **Evolution, Order and Complexity**
Edited by Elias L. Khalil and Kenneth E. Boulding

3 **Interactions in Political Economy**
Malvern after ten years
Edited by Steven Pressman

4 **The End of Economics**
Michael Perelman

5 **Probability in Economics**
Omar F. Hamouda and Robin Rowley

6 **Capital Controversy, Post Keynesian Economics and the History of Economics**
Essays in honour of Geoff Harcourt, volume one
Edited by Philip Arestis, Gabriel Palma and Malcolm Sawyer

7 **Markets, Unemployment and Economic Policy**
Essays in honour of Geoff Harcourt, volume two
Edited by Philip Arestis, Gabriel Palma and Malcolm Sawyer

8 **Social Economy**
The logic of capitalist development
Clark Everling

9 **New Keynesian Economics/Post Keynesian Alternatives**
Edited by Roy J. Rotheim

10 **The Representative Agent in Macroeconomics**
James E. Hartley

11 **Borderlands of Economics**
Essays in honour of Daniel R. Fusfeld
Edited by Nahid Aslanbeigui and Young Back Choi

12 **Value, Distribution and Capital**
Essays in honour of Pierangelo Garegnani
Edited by Gary Mongiovi and Fabio Petri

13 **The Economics of Science**
Methodology and epistemology as if economics really mattered
James R. Wible

14 **Competitiveness, Localised Learning and Regional Development**
Specialisation and prosperity in small open economies
Peter Maskell, Heikki Eskelinen, Ingjaldur Hannibalsson, Anders Malmberg and Eirik Vatne

15 **Labour Market Theory**
A constructive reassessment
Ben J. Fine

16 **Women and European Employment**
Jill Rubery, Mark Smith, Colette Fagan and Damian Grimshaw

17 **Explorations in Economic Methodology**
From Lakatos to empirical philosophy of science
Roger Backhouse

18 **Subjectivity in Political Economy**
Essays on wanting and choosing
David P. Levine

19 **The Political Economy of Middle East Peace**
The impact of competing trade agendas
Edited by J.W. Wright, Jnr

20 **The Active Consumer**
Novelty and surprise in consumer choice
Edited by Marina Bianchi

21 **Subjectivism and Economic Analysis**
Essays in memory of Ludwig Lachmann
Edited by Roger Koppl and Gary Mongiovi

22 **Themes in Post-Keynesian Economics**
Essays in honour of Geoff Harcourt, volume three
Edited by Claudio Sardoni and Peter Kriesler

23 **The Dynamics of Technological Knowledge**
Cristiano Antonelli

24 **The Political Economy of Diet, Health and Food Policy**
Ben J. Fine

25 **The End of Finance**
Capital market inflation, financial derivatives and pension fund capitalism
Jan Toporowski

26 **Political Economy and the New Capitalism**
Edited by Jan Toporowski

27 **Growth Theory**
A philosophical perspective
Patricia Northover

28 **The Political Economy of the Small Firm**
Edited by Charlie Dannreuther

29 **Hahn and Economic Methodology**
Edited by Thomas Boylan and Paschal F. O'Gorman

30 **Gender, Growth and Trade**
The miracle economies of the postwar years
David Kucera

31 **Normative Political Economy**
Subjective freedom, the market and the state
David Levine

32 **Economist with a Public Purpose**
Essays in honour of John Kenneth Galbraith
Edited by Michael Keaney

33 **Involuntary Unemployment**
The elusive quest for a theory
Michel De Vroey

34 **The Fundamental Institutions of Capitalism**
Ernesto Screpanti

35 **Transcending Transaction**
The search for self-generating markets
Alan Shipman

36 **Power in Business and the State**
An historical analysis of its concentration
Frank Bealey

37 **Editing Economics**
Essays in honour of Mark Perlman
Edited by Hank Lim, Ungsuh K. Park and Geoff Harcourt

38 **Money, Macroeconomics and Keynes**
Essays in honour of Victoria Chick, volume one
Edited by Philip Arestis, Meghnad Desai and Sheila Dow

39 **Methodology, Microeconomics and Keynes**
Essays in honour of Victoria Chick, volume two
Edited by Philip Arestis, Meghnad Desai and Sheila Dow

40 **Market Drive and Governance**
Reexamining the rules for economic and commercial contest
Ralf Boscheck

41 **The Value of Marx**
Political economy for contemporary capitalism
Alfredo Saad-Filho

42 **Issues in Positive Political Economy**
S. Mansoob Murshed

43 **The Enigma of Globalisation**
A journey to a new stage of capitalism
Robert Went

44 **The Market**
Equilibrium, stability, mythology
S.N. Afriat

45 **The Political Economy of Rule Evasion and Policy Reform**
Jim Leitzel

46 **Unpaid Work and the Economy**
Edited by Antonella Picchio

47 **Distributional Justice**
Theory and measurement
Hilde Bojer

48 **Cognitive Developments in Economics**
Edited by Salvatore Rizzello

49 **Social Foundations of Markets, Money and Credit**
Costas Lapavitsas

50 **Rethinking Capitalist Development**
Essays on the economics of Josef Steindl
Edited by Tracy Mott and Nina Shapiro

51 **An Evolutionary Approach to Social Welfare**
Christian Sartorius

52 **Kalecki's Economics Today**
Edited by Zdzislaw L. Sadowski and Adam Szeworski

53 **Fiscal Policy from Reagan to Blair**
The left veers right
Ravi K. Roy and Arthur T. Denzau

54 **The Cognitive Mechanics of Economic Development and Institutional Change**
Bertin Martens

55 **Individualism and the Social Order**
The social element in liberal thought
Charles R. McCann Jnr

56 **Affirmative Action in the United States and India**
A comparative perspective
Thomas E. Weisskopf

57 **Global Political Economy and the Wealth of Nations**
Performance, institutions, problems and policies
Edited by Phillip Anthony O'Hara

58 **Structural Economics**
Thijs ten Raa

59 **Macroeconomic Theory and Economic Policy**
Essays in honour of Jean-Paul Fitoussi
Edited by K. Vela Velupillai

60 **The Struggle over Work**
The "end of work" and employment alternatives in post-industrial societies
Shaun Wilson

61 **The Political Economy of Global Sporting Organisations**
John Forster and Nigel Pope

62 **The Flawed Foundations of General Equilibrium Theory**
Critical essays on economic theory
Frank Ackerman and Alejandro Nadal

63 **Uncertainty in Economic Theory**
Essays in honor of David Schmeidler's 65th birthday
Edited by Itzhak Gilboa

64 **The New Institutional Economics of Corruption**
Edited by Johann Graf Lambsdorff, Markus Taube and Matthias Schramm

65 **The Price Index and its Extension**
A chapter in economic measurement
S.N. Afriat

66 **Reduction, Rationality and Game Theory in Marxian Economics**
Bruce Philp

67 **Culture and Politics in Economic Development**
Volker Bornschier

68 **Modern Applications of Austrian Thought**
Edited by Jürgen G. Backhaus

69 **Ordinary Choices**
Individuals, incommensurability, and democracy
Robert Urquhart

70 **Labour Theory of Value**
Peter C. Dooley

71 **Capitalism**
Victor D. Lippit

72 **Macroeconomic Foundations of Macroeconomics**
Alvaro Cencini

73 **Marx for the 21st Century**
Edited by Hiroshi Uchida

74 **Growth and Development in the Global Political Economy**
Social structures of accumulation and modes of regulation
Phillip Anthony O'Hara

75 **The New Economy and Macroeconomic Stability**
A neo-modern perspective drawing on the complexity approach and Keynesian economics
Teodoro Dario Togati

76 **The Future of Social Security Policy**
Women, work and a citizens' basic income
Ailsa McKay

77 **Clinton and Blair**
The political economy of the third way
Flavio Romano

78 **Marxian Reproduction Schema**
Money and aggregate demand in a capitalist economy
A.B. Trigg

79 **The Core Theory in Economics**
Problems and solutions
Lester G. Telser

80 **Economics, Ethics and the Market**
Introduction and applications
Johan J. Graafland

81 **Social Costs and Public Action in Modern Capitalism**
Essays inspired by Karl William Kapp's theory of social costs
Edited by Wolfram Elsner, Pietro Frigato and Paolo Ramazzotti

82 **Globalization and the Myths of Free Trade**
History, theory and empirical evidence
Edited by Anwar Shaikh

83 **Equilibrium in Economics**
Scope and limits
Edited by Valeria Mosini

84 **Globalization**
State of the art and perspectives
Edited by Stefan A. Schirm

85 **Neoliberalism**
National and regional experiments with global ideas
Edited by Ravi K. Roy, Arthur T. Denzau and Thomas D. Willett

86 **Post-Keynesian Macroeconomics**
Essays in honour of Ingrid Rima
Edited by Mathew Forstater, Gary Mongiovi and Steven Pressman

87 **Consumer Capitalism**
Anastasios S. Korkotsides

88 **Remapping Gender in the New Global Order**
Edited by Marjorie Griffin Cohen and Janine Brodie

89 **Hayek and Natural Law**
Eric Angner

90 **Race and Economic Opportunity in the Twenty-First Century**
Edited by Marlene Kim

91 **Renaissance in Behavioural Economics**
Harvey Leibenstein's impact on contemporary economic analysis
Edited by Roger Frantz

92 **Human Ecology Economics**
A new framework for global sustainability
Edited by Roy E. Allen

93 **Imagining Economics Otherwise**
Encounters with identity/difference
Nitasha Kaul

94 **Reigniting the Labor Movement**
Restoring means to ends in a democratic labor movement
Gerald Friedman

95 **The Spatial Model of Politics**
Norman Schofield

96 **The Economics of American Judaism**
Carmel Ullman Chiswick

97 **Critical Political Economy**
Christian Arnsperger

98 **Culture and Economic Explanation**
Economics in the US and Japan
Donald W. Katzner

99 **Feminism, Economics and Utopia**
Time travelling through paradigms
Karin Schönpflug

100 **Risk in International Finance**
Vikash Yadav

101 **Economic Policy and Performance in Industrial Democracies**
Party governments, central banks and the fiscal–monetary policy mix
Takayuki Sakamoto

102 **Advances on Income Inequality and Concentration Measures**
Edited by Gianni Betti and Achille Lemmi

103 **Economic Representations**
Academic and everyday
Edited by David F. Ruccio

104 **Mathematical Economics and the Dynamics of Capitalism**
Goodwin's legacy continued
Edited by Peter Flaschel and Michael Landesmann

105 **The Keynesian Multiplier**
Edited by Claude Gnos and Louis-Philippe Rochon

106 **Money, Enterprise and Income Distribution**
Towards a macroeconomic theory of capitalism
John Smithin

107 **Fiscal Decentralization and Local Public Finance in Japan**
Nobuki Mochida

108 **The 'Uncertain' Foundations of Post-Keynesian Economics**
Essays in exploration
Stephen P. Dunn

109 **Karl Marx's *Grundrisse***
Foundations of the critique of political economy 150 years later
Edited by Marcello Musto

110 **Economics and the Price Index**
S.N. Afriat and Carlo Milana

111 **Sublime Economy**
On the intersection of art and economics
Edited by Jack Amariglio, Joseph W. Childers and Stephen E. Cullenberg

112 **Popper, Hayek and the Open Society**
Calvin Hayes

113 **The Political Economy of Work**
David Spencer

114 **Institutional Economics**
Bernard Chavance

115 **Religion, Economics and Demography**
The effects of religion on education, work, and the family
Evelyn L. Lehrer

116 **Economics, Rational Choice and Normative Philosophy**
Edited by Thomas A. Boylan and Ruvin Gekker

117 **Economics Versus Human Rights**
Manuel Couret Branco

118 **Hayek Versus Marx and Today's Challenges**
Eric Aarons

119 **Work Time Regulation as Sustainable Full Employment Policy**
Robert LaJeunesse

120 **Equilibrium, Welfare and Uncertainty**
Mukul Majumdar

121 **Capitalism, Institutions and Economic Development**
Michael Heller

122 **Economic Pluralism**
Robert Garnett, Erik Olsen and Martha Starr

123 **Dialectics of Class Struggle in the Global Economy**
Clark Everling

124 **Political Economy and Globalization**
Richard Westra

125 **Full-Spectrum Economics**
Toward an inclusive and emancipatory social science
Christian Arnsperger

126 **Computable, Constructive and Behavioural Economic Dynamics**
Essays in honour of Kumaraswamy (Vela) Velupillai
Stefano Zambelli

127 **Monetary Macrodynamics**
Toichiro Asada, Carl Chiarella, Peter Flaschel and Reiner Franke

128 **Rationality and Explanation in Economics**
Maurice Lagueux

129 **The Market, Happiness, and Solidarity**
A Christian perspective
Johan J. Graafland

130 **Economic Complexity and Equilibrium Illusion**
Essays on market instability and macro vitality
Ping Chen

131 **Economic Theory and Social Change**
Problems and revisions
Hasse Ekstedt and Angelo Fusari

132 **The Practices of Happiness**
Political economy, religion and wellbeing
Edited by John Atherton, Elaine Graham and Ian Steedman

133 **The Measurement of Individual Well-Being and Group Inequalities**
Essays in memory of Z. M. Berrebi
Edited by Joseph Deutsch and Jacques Silber

134 **Wage Policy, Income Distribution, and Democratic Theory**
Oren M. Levin-Waldman

135 **The Political Economy of Bureaucracy**
Steven O. Richardson

136 **The Moral Rhetoric of Political Economy**
Justice and modern economic thought
Paul Turpin

137 **Macroeconomic Regimes in Western Industrial Countries**
Hansjörg Herr and Milka Kazandziska

138 **The Political Economy of the Environment**
Edited by Simon Dietz, Jonathan Michie and Christine Oughton

139 **Business Ethics and the Austrian Tradition in Economics**
Hardy Bouillon

140 **Inequality and Power**
The economics of class
Eric A. Schutz

141 Capital as a Social Kind
Definitions and transformations in the critique of political economy
Howard Engelskirchen

142 Happiness, Ethics and Economics
Johannes Hirata

143 Capital, Exploitation and Economic Crisis
John Weeks

144 The Global Economic Crisis
New perspectives on the critique of economic theory and policy
Edited by Emiliano Brancaccio and Giuseppe Fontana

145 Economics and Diversity
Carlo D'Ippoliti

146 Political Economy of Human Rights
Rights, realities and realization
Bas de Gaay Fortman

147 Robinson Crusoe's Economic Man
A construction and deconstruction
Edited by Ulla Grapard and Gillian Hewitson

148 Freedom and Happiness in Economic Thought and Philosophy
From clash to reconciliation
Edited by Ragip Ege and Herrade Igersheim

149 Political Economy after Economics
David Laibman

150 Reconstructing Keynesian Macroeconomics Volume 1
Partial perspectives
Carl Chiarella, Peter Flaschel and Willi Semmler

151 Institutional Economics and National Competitiveness
Edited by Young Back Choi

152 Capitalist Diversity and Diversity within Capitalism
Edited by Geoffrey T. Wood and Christel Lane

153 The Consumer, Credit and Neoliberalism
Governing the modern economy
Christopher Payne

154 Order and Control in American Socio-Economic Thought
U.S. social scientists and progressive-era reform
Charles McCann

155 The Irreconcilable Inconsistencies of Neoclassical Macroeconomics
A false paradigm
John Weeks

156 The Political Economy of Putin's Russia
Pekka Sutela

157 Facts, Values and Objectivity in Economics
José Castro Caldas and Vítor Neves

158 Economic Growth and the High Wage Economy
Choices, constraints and opportunities in the market economy
Morris Altman

159 Social Costs Today
Institutional analyses of the present crises
Edited by Wolfram Elsner, Pietro Frigato and Paolo Ramazzotti

160 Economics, Sustainability and Democracy
Economics in the era of climate change
Christopher Nobbs

161 **Organizations, Individualism and Economic Theory**
Maria Brouwer

162 **Economic Models for Policy Making**
Principles and designs revisited
S. I. Cohen

163 **Reconstructing Keynesian Macroeconomics Volume 2**
Integrated approaches
Carl Chiarella, Peter Flaschel and Willi Semmler

164 **Architectures of Economic Subjectivity**
The philosophical foundations of the subject in the history of economic thought
Sonya Marie Scott

165 **Support-Bargaining, Economics and Society**
A social species
Patrick Spread

166 **Inherited Wealth, Justice and Equality**
Edited by Guido Erreygers and John Cunliffe

167 **The Charismatic Principle in Social Life**
Edited by Luigino Bruni and Barbara Sena

168 **Ownership Economics**
On the foundations of interest, money, markets, business cycles and economic development
Gunnar Heinsohn and Otto Steiger; translated and edited with comments and additions by Frank Decker

169 **Urban and Regional Development Trajectories in Contemporary Capitalism**
Edited by Flavia Martinelli, Frank Moulaert and Andreas Novy

170 **Social Fairness and Economics**
Economic essays in the spirit of Duncan Foley
Edited by Lance Taylor, Armon Rezai and Thomas Michl

171 **Financial Crisis, Labour Markets and Institutions**
Edited by Sebastiano Fadda and Pasquale Tridico

172 **Marx and Living Labour**
Laurent Baronian

173 **A Political Economy of Contemporary Capitalism and its Crisis**
Demystifying finance
Dimitris P. Sotiropoulos, John G. Milios and Spyros Lapatsioras

174 **Against Utility-Based Economics**
On a life-based approach
Anastasios Korkotsides

175 **Economic Indeterminacy**
The dance of the meta-axioms
Yanis Varoufakis

176 **Freedom, Responsibility and Economics of the Person**
Jérôme Ballet, Damien Bazin, Jean-Luc Dubois and François-Régis Mahieu

177 **Reality and Accounting**
Ontological explorations in the economic and social sciences
Richard Matterssich

178 **Profitability and the Great Recession**
The role of accumulation trends in the financial crisis
Ascension Mejorado and Manuel Roman

179 Institutions and Development after the Financial Crisis
Edited by Sebastiano Fadda and Pasquale Tridico

180 The Political Economy of Gunnar Myrdal
A reassessment in the post-2008 world
Örjan Appelqvist

181 Gender Perspectives and Gender Impacts of the Global Economic Crisis
Edited by Rania Antonopoulos

182 Hegel, Institutions, and Economics
Performing the social
Carsten Herrmann-Pillath and Ivan A. Boldyrev

183 Producer Cooperatives as a New Mode of Production
Bruno Jossa

184 Economic Policy and the Financial Crisis
Edited by Łukasz Mamica and Pasquale Tridico

185 Information Technology and Socialist Construction
The end of capital and the transition to socialism
Daniel E. Saros

186 Beyond Mainstream Explanations of the Financial Crisis
Parasitic finance capital
Ismael Hossein-zadeh

Beyond Mainstream Explanations of the Financial Crisis

Parasitic finance capital

Ismael Hossein-zadeh

Routledge
Taylor & Francis Group
LONDON AND NEW YORK

First published 2014
by Routledge
2 Park Square, Milton Park, Abingdon, Oxon OX14 4RN

and by Routledge
711 Third Avenue, New York, NY 10017

Routledge is an imprint of the Taylor & Francis Group, an informa business

British Library Cataloguing in Publication Data
A catalogue record for this book is available from the British Library

Library of Congress Cataloging in Publication Data
Hossein-zadeh, Ismael, 1946–
Beyond mainstream explanations of the financial crisis : parasitic finance capital / Ismael Hossein-zadeh.
pages cm.
Includes bibliographical references and index.
1. Global Financial Crisis, 2008–2009. 2. Financial crises.
3. Neoclassical school of economics. I. Title.
HB37172008.H67 2014
330.9′0511–dc23

2013044402

ISBN: 978-0-415-63806-7 (hbk)
ISBN: 978-0-203-08419-9 (ebk)

Typeset in Times New Roman
by Wearset Ltd, Boldon, Tyne and Wear

MIX
Paper from responsible sources
FSC www.fsc.org FSC® C013056

Printed and bound in Great Britain by
TJ International Ltd, Padstow, Cornwall

Contents

Introduction 1

1 Neoliberal explanations of the financial crisis 8

2 Keynesian explanations of the financial crisis 27

3 Specious theories of mainstream economics 44

4 Evolution and characteristics of finance capital—a new phase, not just another cycle 63

5 Marxian views of financial crises 84

6 Debt cancelation—learning from biblical jubilee 110

7 The case for public banking 128

8 Beyond regulation and public banking 143

Index 170

Introduction

Taking advantage of the 2008 financial crash, the financial oligarchy and their proxies in the governments of the core capitalist countries have been carrying out a systematic economic *coup d'état* against the people the ravages of which include the following:

- Transfer of tens of trillions of dollars from the public to the financial oligarchy—brought about through fraudulent creation of debt money, exchanged for real money when it is chalked up as public debt to be paid through brutal austerity cuts;
- Extensive privatization of public assets and services, including irreplaceable historical monuments, priceless cultural landmarks, and vital social services such as water supply;
- Substitution of corporate/banking welfare policies for people's welfare programs;
- Allocation of the lion's share of government's monetary largesse (and of credit creation in general) to speculative investment instead of real investment;
- Systematic undermining of the retirement security of millions of workers and civil servants such as firefighters, teachers, school employees, and other public servants;
- Ever more blatant control of economic and/or financial policies by the representatives of the financial oligarchy.

Despite the truly historical and paradigm-shifting importance of these ominous developments, their discussion continues to remain outside the purview of the mainstream economics. Focusing on superficial descriptions or symptomatic and instrumental factors such as deregulation, subprime mortgage lending, securitization, greed, and the like, mainstream economics does not begin to touch upon, let alone explain, these crucially important issues. It has not even explained why the financial collapse took place in the first place; except for the supposedly "irrational behavior of economic agents" and "invasive government policies" (neoliberal explanation), or deregulation and "neoliberal ideology" (Keynesian explanation).

While blaming policies of deregulation, securitization, and other financial innovations as factors that facilitated the financial bubble and its implosion is not false, it masks the fact that these factors are essentially instruments or vehicles of the accumulation of fictitious finance capital. No matter how subtle or complex, they are basically clever tools or strategies for transferring surplus value generated elsewhere, or for creating fictitious value (through speculation) out of thin air.

The prevailing accounts thus tend to leave out of consideration the systemic dynamics of the accumulation of finance capital (as a parasitic or self-expanding growth process that can turn money into more money while bypassing the messiness of producing anything of real value), the inherent limits to that accumulation, production and division of surplus value, class relations, and the balance of social forces. Indeed, most of these accounts tend to shy away from even using words and expressions such as exploitation, surplus value or class struggle. They also tend to view the state as a disinterested entity above economic or class interests; a perception that fails to acknowledge the fact that the economic policy-making apparatus in most of the core capitalist economies is dominated largely by kleptocratic elites that are guided by the imperatives of big capital, especially finance capital.

Not only mainstream theories but also most of the contemporary Marxian theories of capitalist crisis have failed to offer a satisfactory explanation of the financial collapse and the ensuing Great Recession. Although the current domination of major capitalist economies by finance capital seems new, it is in fact a throwback to the capitalism of the late nineteenth and early twentieth centuries, that is, the capitalism of monopolistic big business and gigantic financial institutions. The rising economic and political influence of powerful financial interests at the time led a number of Marxist and other political economists such as John Hobson, Rudolf Hilferding and Vladimir Lenin to develop profound theories of the rise of finance capital and its destabilizing impact on advanced market economies, as well as on international relations.

However, as the Great Depression and the subsequent New Deal and Social-Democratic reforms significantly curtailed the size and the influence of big finance, they also led to an unfortunate fading of the rich Marxist tradition of a keen interest in the historical evolution of finance capital—as if the reforms and the post-WW II expansion of capitalism had permanently done away with the destabilizing properties of finance capital. Accordingly, the ensuing Marxist theories of crisis either disregarded or discounted the destabilizing role of the financial sector. Instead, they focused most of their attention on other (non-finance) theories of crisis: the underconsumption theory, the disproportionality theory, and the theory of "the tendency of the rate of profit to fall." With few exceptions, this neglect of the role of finance capital has created a regrettable void in the contemporary Marxian theories of capitalist crisis.

This book intends to fill the theoretical void of a satisfactory explanation of the 2008 financial collapse and the ensuing long recession that continues to this day. Instead of simply blaming the "irrational behavior of economic agents," as neoliberal economists do, or "right-wing" policy-makers and "neoliberal capitalism," as many left/liberal economists do, the study will focus on the core dynamics of capitalism, or the "laws of motion of capitalist development" (as Karl Marx put it), that not only created the huge financial bubble, but also subverted public policy in the face of such an obviously unsustainable bubble. The book will further argue that while the prevailing views of financialization as an instrumental culprit in the collapse of the market is not false, it fails to point out that financialization is basically an indication of an advanced stage of capitalism—the stage of the dominance of finance capital. The more fundamental issues to be addressed and explained are the submerged forces behind financialization, the material grounds that fostered the "irrational behavior" of market players, or precipitated the extensive deregulation of financial markets.

The first chapter of this book focuses on the conservative tradition of neoclassical economics, which has come to be known in recent decades as neoliberal economics. The discussion presented in this chapter shows why the neoliberal model of full employment general equilibrium lacks a theoretical foundation to explain either the 2008 financial crash or the ensuing long recession. Indeed, the model denies the existence of a crisis of the magnitude of the crash or of the subsequent recession; it explains away financial turbulences and economic crises by blaming them on external factors such as "irrational behavior" of market players, natural disasters, "supply shocks," or government intervention. Barring such "exogenous" factors, the "self-adjusting" power of the market mechanism is said to be capable of fending off major financial or economic crises. Accordingly, unregulated "efficient capital markets," where "rationally behaving agents know all the information about securities pricing," are supposed to price securities or financial assets "correctly," that is, according to the risks and rewards to the underlying real values—thereby ruling out the incidence or existence of a financial crash, or economic crisis.

Critics have rightly pointed out that characterizing mainstream economics as a scientific discipline is false. This chapter argues that not only is mainstream economics not scientific, it in fact borders on superstition and metaphysics. Prior to scientific findings of the geological origins or causes of earthquakes, many believed that they were expressions of the gods giving vent to their anger. Others believed that they were caused by a dragon that lived beneath earth; whenever it became angry and shook its tail and moved its colossal body it shook the earth as well. Neoliberal economists' explanation of periodic financial implosions (and of economic crises in general) by factors "external" to capitalist system tends to border on similarly unsavory explanations. It can also be argued that blaming capitalism's systemic failures on the "irrational behavior of economic agents" is akin to some simplistic interpretations of religion that attribute the misfortunes or miseries of humanity to their deviations from God's ways: had they not been misled by satanic temptations and strayed away from the Lord's path, they would not have been afflicted by misery.

This chapter's critique of the neoliberal paradigm will go beyond simply describing the neoliberals' view of the financial crisis, or merely exposing how unrealistic it is to assume, as the proponents of this view do, that unregulated capital markets will "correctly" price securities or financial assets. More importantly, it will show why or how despite all of its faults and flaws the paradigm has come to dominate the economic/finance discipline; and why or how despite its disgraceful record (in terms of either explaining or offering solutions) of recent years it continues to remain the official economic shibboleth of governments and policy makers, as well as of the overwhelming majority of academic textbooks on economics and finance. It also explains why so many intelligent and technically competent economists are so firmly devoted to such an abstract or esoteric model that, while interesting, does not explain much.

The second chapter provides a critique of the Keynesian explanations of the 2008 financial collapse and the ensuing Great Recession. Most Keynesian economists blame the financial implosion and the subsequent recession on neoliberal ideology, on Reagan's and/or Thatcher's economic doctrine, or on economists at the University of Chicago. The argument presented in this chapter demonstrates that the transition from Keynesian to neoliberal economics stemmed from much deeper roots than pure ideology; that the change started long before Reagan and Thatcher were elected; that neoliberal austerity policies are class based, not "bad," policies; and that the Keynesian reliance on the ability of the government to re-regulate and revive the economy rests on an optimistic perception that the state can control capitalism. The chapter argues that, contrary to such hopeful perceptions of the role of the state in economic affairs, public policy is more than simply an administrative or technical matter of choice; more importantly, it is a deeply socio-political matter that is organically intertwined with the class nature of the state and the policy making apparatus.

The chapter further argues that the Keynesian stimulus prescription which relies almost exclusively on strong demand, or high employment and high wages, is one-sided; because growth under capitalism is not just a function of strong demand but also of low costs, which often means low employment and low wages. In other words, economic growth under capitalism can be just as wage/demand driven (as was the case in the immediate post-WW II period), as cost/supply driven, as was the case in the 1980s and 1990s.

The chapter also highlights why or how the initial (mid-1930s–late 1960s) success of the Keynesian economics had more to do with the vigorous class struggles and pressures from the people at the time than the genius of Keynes; and why in the absence of another overwhelming pressure from the grassroots the Keynesian economic reforms could remain a fondly-remembered, one-time experience in the history of economic reforms.

The third chapter provides a critical analysis of neoclassical economics as a whole, that is, of a number of major shortcomings that are shared by both conservative-neoliberal and liberal-Keynesian traditions of neoclassicism. A major flaw of the neoclassical paradigm is its concept of credit and/or money supply, and therefore of the financial sector. Contrary to the neoclassical "circular flow" model, rooted in their faith in the (barter-like) Walrasian general equilibrium model, in the era of highly "financialized" capitalism, demand for credit is not limited to industrial or commercial credit, that is, to debt financing of real investments and sales. Perhaps more importantly, a large part of credit is nowadays created for speculative investment. In the age of big finance, parasitic finance capital, systematically transferring economic surplus from the real to the financial sector, has effectively undermined the neat neoclassical "circular flow" mechanism—where people's savings and producers' (retained) earnings are supposed to be recycled through financial intermediaries into productive investment. Sucking financial resources from the rest of the economy, as well as generating fictitious capital out of thin air through speculation/gambling, parasitic finance capital feeds on itself—just like a real parasite.

Neoclassical economists have not, so far, been able to reconcile the independent, parasitic growth of the financial sector with their "circular flow" and/or general equilibrium model. Sadly, instead of trying to incorporate the autonomously expanding financial sector into their real sector model, they have chosen to ignore it—lest it should disturb their shipshape, convenient model. Not surprisingly, they cannot explain, for example, the growing gap between corporate profitability and real investment—a divergence indicating that, in recent years, significant portions of corporate profits are not reinvested for capacity building; it is diverted, instead, to financial investment in pursuit of higher returns to shareholders' capital (Harding 2013). Nor can they explain the fact that while bank lending to the financial sector as a share of GDP has quadrupled since the 1950s, the similar ratio for bank lending to the real sector has remained almost unchanged (Hudson and Bezemer 2012).

To explain why the neoclassical economic paradigm is so shallow—nearly irrelevant to real world developments—this chapter also briefly looks back at the origins of the paradigm, and demonstrates that its superficiality is not altogether fortuitous; it is because the paradigm was developed primarily as an ideologically-driven theoretical construct to be counter-posed to the classical economic paradigm—not as an evolution, extension, or elaboration of that earlier paradigm (which in a holistic fashion studied economics in conjunction with politics, sociology and history) but as a counterfeit and mystifying substitute for it.

Chapter 4 is devoted to another major flaw in the neoclassical (both liberal and conservative) school of economic thought: a grave absence of a historical perspective. The crucially important void of a historical outlook explains why (with some exceptions) the overwhelming majority of mainstream economists failed to see that the financial meltdown of 2008 and the subsequent economic contraction represent more than just another recessionary cycle. More importantly, they represent a structural change, a new phase in the development of capitalism, the age of "finance capital," as the late German economist Rudolph Hilferding (1981) put it. The salient characteristics of the new stage include economic and political dominance of finance capital; debt/credit/money creation primarily for speculation and asset price inflation and only secondarily for productive investment; creation of new bubbles to remedy past bubbles; redistribution and transfer of national resources through fraudulent debt creation—to be paid through austerity cuts.

Chapter 5 is devoted to the evaluation of the Marxist views (both classical and contemporary) of the role of finance capital in market fluctuations and economic crises. While paying homage to Marx for his profound understanding of "the laws of motion of the capitalist mode of production," most left/liberal economists argue that, nonetheless, his analysis cannot be of much service to the study of contemporary banking and finance, as these are post-Marx developments. I will argue in this chapter that, in fact, a careful reading of his work on "fictitious capital" reveals keen insights into a better understanding of today's financial developments. I will further argue that the flawed treatment of finance capital by many of today's Marxist scholars represents not only a regrettable departure from earlier views of Marxists like Lenin and Hilferding but also from Marx's own treatment of finance capital.

Chapter 6 provides a brief overview of the history of debt cancelation. Using empirical evidence from both distant and recent pasts, the chapter demonstrates that, contrary to today's official views that debt cancelation may lead to economic disorder, as epitomized by the slogan "too big to fail," it is often economic recovery, not collapse, which results from canceling or writing down the oppressive debt burdens.

Historical records show that debt relief in the Bronze Age Mesopotamia, designed to restore economic revival and social harmony, took place on a fairly regular basis from 2400 to 1400 BC. Ancient documents also indicate that the Bronze Age tradition of debt cancelation may have served as the model for the biblical pronouncements of periodic debt relief, called Jubilee. Numerous passages in the Old Testament dealing with issues of economic equity and social justice call for periodic rebalancing of socioeconomic arrangements that would include debt cancelation and land restitution. Both logic and empirical evidence indicate, however, that the rationale behind the idea of debt cancelation/modification goes beyond moral issues of compassion and justice. Perhaps more importantly, it is grounded on broader and longer-term considerations of socioeconomic revival and sustainability. The chapter highlights a number of instances of economic renewal through successful policies and practices of debt relief—practices that were sometimes branded as creating a "clean slate," or a debt-free fresh start.

Chapter 7 points out that, as the late German Marxist economist Rudolf Hilferding argued, private banking system represents a fraudulent kind of socialism, modified to suit the needs of capitalism. It socializes other people's money for the benefits of the few. Evidence shows that between 35 and 40 percent of all consumer spending in the United States is appropriated by the financial sector—a hidden tribute or rent that systematically transfers economic resources from Main Street to Wall Street, thereby steadily exasperating inequality, draining people's economy and depressing their lives. The chapter delivers a convincing case that, contrary to popular perceptions in the core capitalist countries, there are indeed compelling reasons not only for higher degrees of reliability but also higher levels of efficiency of public-sector banking and credit system when compared with private banking—both on conceptual and empirical grounds.

Chapter 8 makes a strong case that while nationalization of commercial banks could mitigate or do away with market turbulences that are due to financial bubbles and bursts, it will not preclude other systemic crises of capitalism. These include profitability crises that result from high levels of capitalization, from insufficient demand and/or underconsumption, from overcapacity and/or overproduction, or from disproportionality between various sectors of a market economy.

The chapter further argues that regulations of financial intermediaries would not be an effective or long-term solution either because, for one thing, due to the political influence of powerful financial interests, their implementation is highly unlikely; for another, even if regulations are somehow implemented, they would provide only a temporary relief. For, as long as there is no democratic control, regulations would be undermined by the influential financial elites that elect and control both policy-makers and, therefore, policy. The dramatic reversal of the extensive regulations of the 1930s and 1940s, which were put in place in response to the Great Depression and World War II, to today's equally dramatic deregulations serve as a robust validation of this judgment. To do away with the recurring crises of capitalist system, therefore, requires more than nationalization or regulation of the financial institutions; it requires changing the system itself.

This book is distinctive on a number of grounds. For one thing, it is highly interdisciplinary, both in style and scope, organically combining economics, politics, sociology and history. For another, it is unique for its historical and/or Marxian approach or method of analysis, not only in terms of the historical evolution of finance capital but also of the class character of the state and institutions that nurture that evolution. In addition, the book is written in a way that, both in terms of content and style, will be of interest (as well as accessible) not only to a range of disciplines in academe but also to "non-expert" lay readers who are concerned with the recurring instability of financial markets or, more generally, with the woes and vagaries of the capitalist economic system.

References

Harding, R. (2013). Corporate investment: A mysterious divergence. *Financial Times*, July 24. Retrieved from www.ft.com/intl/cms/s/0/8177af34-eb21-11e2-bfdb-00144feabdc0.html#axzz2dN45MG7r (accessed August 29, 2013).

Hilferding, R. (1981 [1910]). *Finance capital: A study of the latest phase of capitalist development*. Tom Bottomore (Ed.). London: Routledge & Kegan Paul.

Hudson, M. and Bezemer, D. (2012). Incorporating the rentier sectors into a financial model. *World Economic Review*, *1*(1). Retrieved from http://wer.worldeconomicsassociation.org/article/view/36 (accessed April 05, 2013).

1 Neoliberal explanations of the financial crisis

Mainstream economics, also called neoclassical economics, consists of two major paradigms: the conservative paradigm, which has come to be known in recent decades as neoliberal economics, and the liberal paradigm, which is called Keynesian economics. The central difference between these two versions of neoclassical economics is rather well-known: whereas neoliberal economists tend to promote faith in the self-correcting power of the market mechanism, Keynesian economists view such a strong trust in the inherent ability of the market system to self-correct unwarranted. Accordingly, the Keynesians argue that the market's "invisible hand" may occasionally need the "visible" hand of the state in order to temper the potentially fatal gyrations of the market system, thereby helping to "protect capitalism from itself," as Keynes purportedly put it.

While Keynesians disagree with neoliberals on the self-adjusting power of the market mechanism to maintain or restore full employment equilibrium, they share with them almost all other principles of neoclassical economics. These include (a) the utilitarian ideology of economics, according to which the value or morality of economic activities are determined by their consequences, that is, the end justifies the means; (b) the marginal productivity theory of income distribution, according to which each factor of production receives a fair share of what is produced, which is equal to its contribution to production (at the margin); and (c) the theory of general equilibrium, which postulates that supply and demand interactions in competitive markets tend to establish a set of prices that will result in an overall equilibrium.

Caught by surprise

The neoliberal model of full employment general equilibrium, where the "balance" between supply and demand in all and every market guarantees the establishment of "rational" prices and "efficient" allocation of resources, is based on an abstract, ideal world of "perfect" competition in which equally- or similarly-positioned numerous economic agents compete with each other without anyone having any significant influence over the market supply, demand or price. The notion of "efficient" allocation of resources, of "just" distribution of income and of "automatic" market adjustments makes sense only in such an ideal (but unrealistic) world. Not surprisingly, in the face of the 2008 market crash neoliberal economists' optimistic projections that the 2002–2007 financial expansion could continue indefinitely left them "with ample egg on their studious faces," as Chris Giles of the *Financial Times* put it (November 26, 2008). Nor is it any surprise that their depiction of these abstract postulations as actual developments of real world markets has generated such a widespread distaste for their theories.

There is, of course, nothing wrong with building ideal models for analytical purposes. Indeed, creation of such imaginary constructs is often essential to a better understanding of actual developments. The problem arises, however, when model-builders tend to forget that their ideal models are fictional creations, and begin to gradually take them for real world situations. Mainstream economists' infatuation with their perfect model of market mechanism, and their tendency to confuse such an abstract construct with actual market developments, conjures up the story of Dr Frankenstein. Whether the disproportionate focus on economic models (at the expense of real world economics) is due to ideological/political proclivities, or mathematical elegance and technical appeals of model building, the fact remains that mainstream economists' commitment to their elegant models has played havoc not only with the credibility of their discipline, but also with major macroeconomic policies that are inspired or justified by such models. In an apropos reference to Karl Marx regarding the uses (and abuses) of models, David Graeber, author of *Debt: The First 5000 Years*, provides a concise and instructive commentary on the dangers of taking abstract models for reality:

> Karl Marx, who knew quite a bit about the human tendency to fall down and worship our own creations, wrote *Das Capital* in an attempt to demonstrate that, even if we do start from the economists' utopian vision, so long as we also allow some people to control productive capital, and, again, leave others with nothing to sell but their brains and bodies, the results will be in many ways barely distinguishable from slavery, and the whole system will eventually destroy itself.
>
> (2011: 353–354)

Critics of the mainstream economic paradigm have frequently pointed to a number of its unrealistic assumptions: "perfectly" competitive firms/markets, "rational" prices, "efficient" allocation of resources, "just" distribution of income, and "automatic" adjustment of any disequilibrium. A major deficiency of the model that is often overlooked, however, is the fact that it gravely trivializes the role of credit and/or finance—its parasitically independent expansion, its systematic draining of the real sector, and its destabilizing and depressive impact on the economy. Money supply and/or credit creation, and therefore the magnitude of investible funds, is treated in this model as confined or limited by the production capacity of the real sector: production or output determines national income, national income determines national savings, national savings determine (through the banking system and other financial intermediaries) the funding or financial resources for investment, investment determines production,... and so on. This circular relationship is illustrated in the model by what is called the "circular flow" diagram, which is taught in every economics department in the U.S. and beyond.

It is obvious, then, that the financial sector in this model plays essentially an intermediary or subsidiary role: it consolidates the numerous nationwide individual savings and funnels them toward the industrialists or manufacturers for productive investment. In other words, the financial sector is essentially a service sector for the real sector. This means that the growth or expansion of the financial sector in this framework is ultimately limited by that of the real sector, and that there is no room or reason for the rise of financial bubbles and instabilities, since finance capital tends to basically shadow the industrial capital.

While this may have been true in the earlier stages of capitalist development, when banks played an essentially intermediary role between savers and investors, it is certainly not the case in the era of big finance where "finance mostly finances finance," as Professor Jan Toporowski (2010) of the University of London put it. The fact that in advanced market economies a significant portion of credit creation is driven by speculative investment that is geared to profit making through the buying and selling of assets or ownership titles, instead of manufacturing production, is altogether absent in the neoclassical economists' neat general equilibrium or "circular flow" model. Accordingly, the destabilizing tendencies of financial expansions, as well as the depressive effects of their implosions, are altogether ignored in this model (Hudson and Bezemer 2012; Keen 2011).

Not surprisingly, in the face of the 2008 financial meltdown many of these economists, who were cheerfully projecting indefinite expansion of the financial bubble all the way up to the moment it actually imploded, have been dumbfounded. Lacking a scientific theory, a historical vision or a systemic knowledge of the dynamics of capitalist development, mainstream economists are basically deprived of the fundamental tools that are essential to an understanding and/or tackling of an economic ailment. Their sunny projections of the housing bubble and of the financial expansion that started in the early 2000s were so far off the mark that even the usually reserved British royalty could not contain its frustration at economic forecasters: "Why did no one see it coming?" Queen Elizabeth of Britain asked during a visit to the London School of Economics in the fall of 2008.

Soon after the meltdown of financial markets in September2008, Giulio Tremonti, Italy's finance minister, likewise expressed disappointment at professional economic predictors when he pointed out that Pope Benedict XVI had shown more acumen than mainstream economic experts in predicting financial crises. A church paper, titled "Church and Economy in Dialogue" and presented in a 1985 symposium in Rome, showed, according to Mr. Tremonti, "the prediction that an undisciplined economy would collapse by its own rules" (as cited in Giles 2008). The following are only a few examples of how mainstream economic big-wigs and their policy making cohorts were largely oblivious to the coming of the financial implosion.

In his Senate nomination hearing of 2005, Ben Bernanke, the Federal Reserve chairman, stated that, having gone through a number of cycles, the U.S. financial system had become nearly immune to major crises, as it had learned how to cope with financial fluctuations. He further argued that "The depths, the liquidity, the flexibility of the financial markets have increased greatly," thereby preventing them from developing into cataclysmic convulsions (ibid.).

Jean-Claude Trichet, president of the European Central Bank, likewise showed how ignorant he was of the impending market collapse: "Our base-line scenario is that we will have a trough in the profile of growth in the euro area in the second and third quarters of this year [2008] and, following this, a progressive return to ongoing moderate growth" (as quoted in Reuters 2008). Economists at the International Monetary Fund similarly displayed oblivion to the looming crash not long before it actually hit the U.S. and EU markets:

> Notwithstanding the recent bout of financial volatility, the world economy still looks well set for continued robust growth in 2007 and 2008. While the U.S. economy has slowed more than was expected earlier, spillovers have been limited, growth around the world looks well sustained.... Overall risks to the outlook seem less threatening than six months ago...
>
> (International Monetary Fund 2007: xv)

This small sample of statements made by major economic "experts" and policy-makers in the immediate days before the 2008 market crash shows that the putative brain-trusts of how capitalism operates were altogether oblivious to the imminent financial implosion until they were actually banged on the head by the crash. Belatedly acknowledging this intellectual vacuum, the IMF Chief Economist Oliver Blanchard recently admitted at a London forum (organized by the Bank of England) to "being completely blindsided by the eruption of the financial crisis in 2008, believing such things would no longer take place" (as cited by Beams 2013).

Just as economic policy makers and their bigwig advisors proved clueless in the face of the looming 2008 financial collapse, so they now seem equally helpless to prevent the expansion of another bubble, or to remedy the ongoing Great Recession that followed the 2008 crash—save for pumping massive amounts of money into the coffers of financial speculators, which seem to be largely helping inflate the new bubble. Their bewilderment was revealed at a gathering of top-level economists organized by the IMF after its spring 2013 meeting in Washington. Nobel Prize laureate George Akerlof "likened the economic crisis to a cat that had climbed a tree, did not know how to come down, and was now about to fall" (ibid.). Richard Fisher, a member of the Federal Open Market Committee, has likewise admitted that "nobody really knows what will work to get the economy back on course" and that no central bank "has the experience of successfully navigating a return home from the place where we now find ourselves" (ibid.).

Faith-based diagnosis of the crisis

> We must … see neoliberalism as practiced by Greenspan and his ilk as making capitalism a religion, the market a god and economics a form of theology.
>
> (Alex Andrews, *Guardian*)

One would imagine that the 2008 financial implosion, which showed how gravely mainstream economists had gone awry in their rosy predictions of the "indefinite" financial expansion, would have somewhat shaken the faith of these economists in the "self-correcting" ability of financial markets. Alas, the faith in market mechanism seems to be as strong as the faith in any otherworldly religion. Indeed, it is more like blind cultism than a reasonable faith of intelligent, thinking people. Whether as university professors or as advisors to policy makers, mainstream economists continue to teach the same materials and retell the same theories in the aftermath of the crash as they did before it—as if the crash and the ensuing Great Recession did not take place. In the aftermath of the market crash, the *New York Times* carried out a survey of major economics departments in an attempt to find out whether the crash had impacted the way the discipline is taught:

> Prominent economics professors say their academic discipline isn't shifting nearly as much as some people might think. Free market theory, mathematical models and hostility to government regulation still reign in most economics departments at colleges and universities around the country.… The belief that people make rational economic decisions and the market automatically adjusts to respond to them still prevails.
>
> (March 5, 2009)

In response to the *Times* survey, economist James K. Galbraith (of the Lyndon B. Johnson School of Public Affairs at the University of Texas) stated, "I don't detect any change at all." Economists are "like [an] ostrich with its head in the sand." Economics professor Robert J. Shiller of Yale University likewise responded, "I fear that there will not be much change in basic paradigms.… The rational expectations models will be tweaked to account for the current crisis. The basic curriculum will not change" (ibid.).

It may be argued that the time period between the market crash (September 2008) and the *Times*' survey (March 2009) was too short to expect curriculum changes. But the survey also pointed out that economics professors at Berkeley, University of Texas, University of Chicago, Harvard, Yale, and Stanford "say they are unaware of any plans to reassess their curriculums and reading lists, or to rethink the way introductory courses are organized."

True, there are a handful of departments that teach alternative schools of economic thought. These include the New School for Social Research, University of Massachusetts (Amherst and Boston), the University of Utah, and the University of

Missouri, Kansas City. However, neither the views of prominent economists from these departments are sought for policy purposes, nor are their scholarly writings included in curriculum materials or reading lists of the mainstream departments.

With unshakable belief in their neat but fictional model of market mechanism, neoliberal economists blame external factors and/or human follies for the financial meltdown: "irrational" behavior, government intervention, contingent conduct or actions of market players, and the like. Ruling powers and their ideological pundits have almost always blamed external factors or foreign elements for the socio-economic convulsions created by capitalism. In the realm of geopolitics, for example, international conflicts are said to have been brought about by dictatorial behavior of some foreign rulers, by global terrorism, by rogue states, by Islamic radicalism, and the like. Financial turbulences and economic crises are, likewise, explained away by blaming them on external factors such as human nature, irrational behavior of market players, natural disasters, wars, revolutions, "supply shocks," or government intervention. Barring such "exogenous" factors, the "self-adjusting" power of the market mechanism is said to be capable of fending off major financial or economic crises. According to neoliberal economics, unregulated "efficient capital markets," where "rationally behaving agents know all the information about securities pricing," are supposed to price securities or financial assets "correctly," that is, according to the risks and rewards to the underlying real values. In other words, the sum total of fictitious capital in this model is not supposed to deviate much from the sum total of real asset values. This supposedly self-adjusting mechanism may not preclude "temporary," "short-term" or "small" fluctuations; but such fluctuations are easily contained or regulated around a fundamentally reliable pattern of economic growth (Shaikh 1978).

This, in a nutshell, is the essence of neoliberal economists' view of the financial markets, of the basis of their faith in the benevolence or invulnerability of those markets, and of market mechanism in general. Actual developments in real markets, no matter how at odds with these economists' clever postulations, will neither disturb the idealized projections of the financial markets nor, therefore, their faith in the security or reliability of those markets. The faith of some neoliberal economists in the market mechanism is so strong that they tend to deny altogether the actual incidents of failure or fraud in real markets. Thus, as economics and law professor William K. Black pointed out:

> Fraud is impossible because securities markets are "efficient" and act as if they were guided by an "invisible hand." Markets cannot be efficient if there is accounting control fraud, so we know (on the basis of circular reasoning) that securities fraud cannot exist. Indeed, when mainstream economists try to explain why the securities markets automatically exclude frauds their faith-based logic becomes even more humorous.
>
> (As quoted in *Global Research* 2012)

When Alan Greenspan, the former head of the Federal Reserve Bank, confessed in the immediate aftermath of the 2008 market crash that his belief in the security or invulnerability of financial markets had been unwarranted, many viewed the admission for what it was: a crisis of faith—the faith that the unchecked market would always behave benevolently. It exposed what many critics had been saying for some time:

> [T]hat the character of neoliberal economics is essentially religious. This is counter-intuitive. Surely the policy of Greenspan and others is based on an understanding of the science of economics, particularly in the mainstream neoclassical form that is most often taught in universities around the world. It is certainly the case that neoclassical economics appears scientific. This is because it deploys huge quantities of complex mathematics, giving it the veneer of being what it has long hoped to be, a kind of social physics.
>
> (Andrews 2009)

The less-than salutary theoretical foundations of mainstream economics is often embellished with a scientific façade of elaborate mathematics and elegant but highly abstract models. Arguing that "modern economics is sick," the renowned economics professor Mark Blaug writes:

> Economics has increasingly become an intellectual game played for its own sake and not for its practical consequences. Economists have gradually converted the subject into a sort of social mathematics in which analytical rigor as understood in math departments is everything and empirical relevance (as understood in physics departments) is nothing. If a topic cannot be tackled by formal modeling, it is simply consigned to the intellectual underworld. To pick up a copy of *American Economic Review* or *Economic Journal*, not to mention *Econometrica* or *Review of Economic Studies*, these days is to wonder whether one has landed on a strange planet in which tedium is the deliberate objective of professional publication. Economics was condemned a century ago as "the dismal science," but the dismal science of yesterday was a lot less dismal than the soporific scholasticism of today. To paraphrase the title of a popular British musical: "No Reality, Please. We're Economists."
>
> (2002)

It would not be a far-fetched analogy to argue that mainstream economists' explanation of periodic financial implosions (and of economic crises in general) by factors "external" to capitalist system tends to border on superstition. As indicated in the Introduction to this volume, prior to scientific findings of the geological origins or causes of earthquakes, many believed that they were expressions of the gods' giving vent to their anger. Others believed that they were caused by a dragon that lived beneath earth; whenever it became angry and shook its tail and moved its colossal body it shook the earth as well.

It can also be argued that blaming capitalism's systemic failures on the "irrational" behavior of economic agents," both consumers and investors, is akin to some simplistic interpretations of religion that attribute the misfortunes or miseries of humans to their deviations from God's ways: had they not been misled by satanic temptations and strayed away from the Lord's path, they would not have been afflicted by misery. Metaphysics has always served as a convenient shortcut when scientific empirical inquiry is deemed too cumbersome or politically unpalatable. In the same way that the sinful deeds of humanity are said to condemn them to a wretched Otherworld, economic agents' deviations from market rules are believed to lead to economic turbulence which would doom them to financial misery in this world.

It must be pointed out, however, that market religion has a major disadvantage compared to traditional or celestial religions: it promotes greed, self-centeredness and material fetishism while lacking the humanitarian or compassionate ethos of godly religions. Its response to unemployment, indebtedness and economic hardship is epitomized in the unfeeling and insensitive philosophy of "trickledown" economics of neoliberalism, which was so skillfuly popularized (among others) by President Ronald Reagan (see Nelson 2002, for example).

Market religion creates its own prophets, in the persons of Alan Greenspan, Ben Bernanke, Milton Friedman, and the like. By elevating such people to all-knowing, larger than life individuals, the corporate–financial oligarchy can then use them to justify their economic policies—predatory policies that are systematically and methodically syphoning off national resources from the bottom up, from the grassroots to the elites, thereby causing further inequality, poverty and economic hardship for the overwhelming majority of the people.

> When critics of free markets point to instances of severe poverty, market supporters promise that eventually, since a rising tide floats all boats, the poor will be lifted up, that what is now apparently problematic is ultimately for the "greater good" in a way we cannot discern. It is clear that this is a market theodicy, justifying the ways of the market to men. When neoliberal politicians warn against governments interfering in the market, lest the irrational and temporary will of the electorate interfere with the "spontaneous order" of markets, this now seems like a dire warning that we must not "play God" and attempt to control the mysteries of the market that in our finitude, our "bounded rationality," we cannot properly fathom.
>
> (Andrews 2009; see also Goodchild 2002)

Deification of individual "experts" who are placed at helm of central banks or treasury departments, as well as mystification of economic know-how, can be better understood in this context, in light of capitalism's need for market prophets.

Creating new bubbles to patch up the burst ones

> Greenspan always contended that monetary policymakers can … clean up the after-effects of the bust—which meant reflating a new bubble, he argued.
>
> (Forsyth 2009)

It is now an open secret that U.S. monetary policymakers of late are no longer averse to creating financial bubbles, as such bubbles are viewed or portrayed as stimulating the economy. Instead of regulating or containing the disruptive speculative activities of the financial sector, the Federal Reserve Bank under both Ben Bernanke and his predecessor Alan Greenspan has been actively promoting asset price and/or financial bubbles. While this is marketed as a stimulus policy, the main beneficiaries have been the major players in the financial sector. Champions of this policy do not seem to be bothered by the destabilizing effects of the bubbles they help create, as they tend to believe (or hope) that the likely disturbances and losses from the potential bursting of one bubble could be offset by creating another bubble. In other words, they seem to believe that they have discovered an insurance policy for bubbles that burst by blowing new ones. Professor Peter Gowan of London Metropolitan University describes this misguided strategy in the following words:

> Both the Washington regulators and Wall Street evidently believed that together they could manage bursts. This meant that there was no need to prevent such bubbles from occurring: on the contrary, it is patently obvious that both regulators and operators actively generated them, no doubt believing that one of the ways of managing bursts was to blow another dynamic bubble in another sector: after dot-com, the housing bubble; after that, an energy-price or emerging market bubble, and so on.
>
> (2010: 52)

It is obvious that this policy of effectively insuring financial bubbles would make financial speculation a win-win proposition, a proposition that is aptly called "moral hazard," as it encourages risk-takings at the expense of others. Randal Forsyth of *Barron's* (2009) pointed out that knowing "the Fed would bail out the markets after any bust, they went from one excess to another". "So, the Long-Term Capital Management collapse in 1998 begat the easy credit that led to the dot-com bubble and bust, which in turn led to the extreme ease and the housing bubble" (ibid.).

It is also obvious that the neoliberal financial architects of recent years have eschewed not only the New Deal-Keynesian policies of demand management but also the free-market policies of non-intervention, as advocated, for example, by the Austrian school of economics. They tend to be interventionists when the corporate-financial oligarchy needs help, but champions of laissez-faire economics when the working class and other grassroots need help. Prior to the rise of big finance and its control of policy, bubble implosions were let to run their course: reckless speculation and mal-investments would go bankrupt; the real economy would be cleansed of the deadweight of the unsustainable debt; and (after a painful but relatively short period of time) the market would reallocate the real capital to productive uses. In the era of big finance and powerful financiers, however, that process of creating a "clean slate" is blocked because the financial entities that play a critical role in the creation of bubbles and bursts also control policy.

Despite their dubious and, indeed, destructive outcomes, champions of neoliberal economics continue to defend the claim of "efficient capital markets" in support of further market deregulations. Destabilizing financial strategies such as speculative securitization and fraudulent derivatives, especially the highly dubious credit default swaps, are euphemistically called financial innovations and promoted as strategies to reduce or eliminate asset price instability. Wall Street's power in bringing forth ever craftier financial innovations, which were supposed to indefinitely inoculate the market against economic crises, seemed to have made only the sky the limit to financial expansion. The infectiousness of this mentality went beyond Wall Street operators and other financial speculators. As pointed out previously, it also included top policy makers at the heads of the Treasury Department and Federal Reserve Bank, who miserably failed to envision the risks of crash in their policies of aggressive financial expansion. "While he [Greenspan] disavows again the responsibility for the boom and bust ... monetary policy played a key role in creating successive bubbles and busts during his tenure from 1987 to 2006" (ibid.). There is evidence that Greenspan was, in fact, quite proud of his policy of easy money and subprime lending, as this would supposedly bring the dream of homeownership within the reach of low-income citizens. For example, at the Federal Reserve System's Fourth Annual Community Affairs Research Conference in Washington, D.C. (April 8, 2005), he stated:

> Especially in the past decade, technological advances have resulted in increased efficiency and scale within the financial services industry. Innovation has brought about a multitude of new products, such as subprime loans and niche credit programs for immigrants.... With these advances in technology, lenders have taken advantage of credit-scoring models and other techniques for efficiently extending credit to a broader spectrum of consumers.... Where once more-marginal applicants would simply have been denied credit, lenders are now able to quite efficiently judge the risk posed by individual applicants and to price that risk appropriately. These improvements have led to rapid growth in subprime mortgage lending; indeed, today subprime mortgages account for roughly 10 percent of the number of all mortgages outstanding, up from just 1 or 2 percent in the early 1990s.

Top economic policy makers, major market operators and government regulators thus actively promoted risky and unscrupulous loan pushing that, for a while, led to high asset prices, high demand and high home-ownership. The overall homeownership rate rose from 64 percent in 1994 to an all-time high of 69.2 percent in 2004—an unprecedented (and, of course, misleading) development that led President George W. Bush to call the United States the "ownership society." Before long it became clear, however, that the majority of the new homeowners were actually debt-owners, as their homes actually belonged to mortgage holders. As the thus accumulated debts reached their unsustainable limits, dreams of homeownership turned to nightmares of homelessness.

Before the financial oligarchy came to dominate economic policy, traditional Keynesian monetary and fiscal policies targeted the real sector of the economy: they were used for the purposes of employment and/or demand management. Under the sway of big finance, however, such policies are now increasingly used in the service of the financial sector. Monetary policy is frequently used to facilitate the flow of cheap and massive amounts of money capital into major financial institutions on the grounds that the injection of more money into the financial sector would prompt enhanced lending to the real sector, thereby encouraging expansion, employment and growth. In reality, however, the huge amounts of cheap money thus injected into the financial sector have only marginally, if ever, leaked to the real sector. Instead of lending to the manufacturers for productive investment, banks and other beneficiaries of monetary policy use the nearly interest-free money for speculative investment in the financial sector, for buying and selling assets and commodities.

This type of parasitic investment was severely limited by the relatively strict regulation of the financial institutions following the Great Depression and World War II. But as the banks grew steadily in economic and, therefore, political power, they succeeded in systematically chipping away at those regulations, including the dismantling of the landmark regulatory Glass-Steagall Act of 1933, which strictly stipulated the types and quantities of investments that banks and other financial intermediaries could undertake. As the regulatory constraints have been gradually removed in the past several decades, financial bubbles and bursts have become a recurring pattern.

Thus, when the so-called Third World debt bubble burst in the 1980s, big finance abandoned the debt-burdened nations in South-Central America, thereby creating a severe credit crunch and a costly economic recession in those countries, and moved to new markets (in Russia, Turkey, Indonesia, Thailand, South Korea and others in South-East Asia) in search of fresh speculative ventures. After blowing a series of financial bubbles in these new markets, which were followed by bursts and economic crises in the second half of the 1990s, international financial speculators, once again, packed and hurriedly left the scene of their crimes, so to speak, in the hunt for newer fields of speculation. The technology sector was considered a favorable candidate for this purpose. Following the implosion of the tech- or dot-com bubble in the early 2000s, speculative finance moved to yet another market, the housing/real estate market. And following the 2007–2008 collapse of the housing bubble, Wall Street and its bagmen in the Treasury and the Federal Reserve Bank have been working feverishly to replenish the coffers of the speculators that caused the crash in the first place, to reflate their asset prices and to create new bubbles.

In this they seem to have succeeded, thanks, in large part, to the scandalously generous transfer of trillions of dollars to the Wall Street heavy-weights. Government aid to money-center banks has included not only the openly-discussed $700 billion TARP money but, more importantly, the little-known $16 trillion that have been bestowed upon Wall Street financial giants in a number of mysterious ways (see, for example, *Forbes* 2011). It has also included the injection of additional trillions of dollars into Wall Street through three rounds of the so-called "Quantitative Easing" policy of the Federal Reserve Bank, the third round of which has evolved as an ongoing, indefinite injection of $85 billion per month.

Perhaps an analogy with the hunting instinct of carnivores could be illuminating here: in the same fashion that a pack of hungry wolves seeks out, targets, stalks and, at the "right" moment, pounces on its prey, so too the handful of giant financial speculators of Wall Street routinely target lucrative markets, one after another, in pursuit of maximum profits in minimum time periods, sucking their economic blood, and leaving them in a shambles before seeking newer markets.

A new field of speculation (following the bursting of the housing bubble in 2008) targeted by international financial giants has been the commodities market, especially the energy and food markets. The following excerpt from Frederick Kaufman's illuminating *Foreign Policy* article, "How Goldman Sachs Created the Food Crisis," clarifies this point:

> The money tells the story. Since the bursting of the tech bubble in 2000, there has been a 50-fold increase in dollars invested in commodity index funds. To put the phenomenon in real terms: In 2003, the commodities futures market still totaled a sleepy $13 billion. But when the global financial crisis sent investors running scared in early 2008, and as dollars, pounds, and euros evaded investor confidence, commodities—including food—seemed like the last, best place for hedge, pension, and sovereign wealth funds to park their cash. "You had people who had no clue what commodities were all about suddenly buying commodities," an analyst from the United States Department of Agriculture told me. In the first 55 days of 2008, speculators poured $55 billion into commodity markets, and by July, $318 billion was roiling the markets. Food inflation has remained steady since.
>
> The money flowed, and the bankers were ready with a sparkling new casino of food derivatives. Spearheaded by oil and gas prices (the dominant commodities of the index funds) the new investment products ignited the markets of all the other indexed commodities, which led to a problem familiar to those versed in the history of tulips, dot-coms, and cheap real estate: a food bubble. Hard red spring wheat, which usually trades in the $4 to $6 dollar range per 60-pound bushel, broke all previous records as the futures contract climbed into the teens and kept on going until it topped $25. And so, from 2005 to 2008, the worldwide price of food rose 80 percent—and has kept rising.
>
> (2011)

This is indicative of the fact that Wall Street players' gambling on the basic sources of people's sustenance, their food, greatly contributes to the malnutrition of hundreds of millions of families around the world.

The argument that elaborate or complex "financial innovations" are useful tools in the hands of financial managers to eliminate or reduce the risks of asset-price instability is bogus on yet another ground: those "innovations" do not reduce or eliminate risk per se; they simply shift/transfer them from the financially savvy to others. This means that the macro or overall outcome of such innovations is, at best, a zero-sum game and, at worst, dangerous gambling behavior that can lead to general bankruptcy.[1]

Neoliberal economists' model of "perfect competition," where many equally- or similarly-positioned small players compete on a level playing field, seems to have blinded them to the reality of financial markets, which are dominated by a handful of giant players such as Goldman Sacks, JP Morgan Chase, Merrill Lynch, and Morgan Stanley. Evidence shows that, prior to the 2008 financial implosion, the five largest Wall Street investment banks held over $4 trillion of assets, and were able "to call upon or move literally trillions more dollars from the institutions behind them, such as the commercial banks, the money market funds, pension funds, and so on" (Gowan 2010: 52).

As these giant operators controlled the lion's share of the financial markets, they were able to expand their activities beyond investment banking. They also acted, for example, as both lenders and traders, a practice that is known as the lender-trader model. In this way they acquired an enormous power to gain access to or control investment and/or trading information.

> It sounds obvious now, but what the average investor didn't know at the time was that the banks had changed the rules of the game ... setting up what was in reality a two-tiered investment system—one for bankers and insiders who knew the real numbers, and another for the lay investor, who was invited to chase soaring prices the banks themselves knew were irrational.
>
> (Taibbi 2010: 214; see also Augar 2006)

This reality of Wall Street, where financial moguls blatantly manipulate both government authority and financial markets in pursuit of parasitic absorption of financial resources through fraudulent asset price inflation, is a far cry from the neoclassical economists' portrayal of a decentralized market place, where equally informed numerous players are no more than slavish price-takers.

A never-dating prescription

According to the neoliberal theory, the solution to economic imbalances lies with the "self-correcting" mechanism of the market's "invisible hand"—no government intervention or macro policy manipulation is needed. The nearly rapturous praise for the "self-adjusting" power of the market mechanism is especially prevalent during periods of calm or good economic times. In the face of market convulsions that tend to threaten the capitalist system, however, business and government leaders dispel all pretensions of deferring the fate of the market to Adam Smith's "invisible hand," and urgently rush to the rescue of the system with all kinds of restructuring schemes and crisis-management policies. These include not only domestic policies of economic, legal, political and institutional restructuring, but also external factors and foreign policy measures that are designed to capture new markets and enhance profitability on a global level. Whether such measures are called supply-side economics, austerity economics or "structural adjustment programs," they are, in fact, legal, political, institutional and, at times, military instruments of class struggle that are employed by business and government leaders in an effort to redistribute national resources from the bottom up in order to restore the "needed" levels of profitability to the system.

The neoliberal restructuring or austerity prescription for an ailing economy has no date on it—it never expires. Regardless of the cause or severity of the crisis, the prescription remains the same: austerity—always. Tragically, this dogged insistence on austerity as a perennial panacea to economic crises is often tantamount to trying to cure a poisoned patient with more of the same toxin: as economic surplus is siphoned off to the largely unproductive oligarchy in the financial sector and the real sector is deprived of (monetarily) effective demand, further cuts in social spending could aggravate the crisis in the manner of a vicious cycle. The perverse nature of this generic policy prescription can be attributed to the fact that neoliberal economics is designed to neither expose the real fault-lines of the capitalist system, nor to find solutions to market maladies that would be beneficial to the public. To the extent that it can be considered a discipline, or paradigm, it consists largely of a positive description of the actual economic developments, or ex-post justification of those developments. "The arguments of economists legitimate social and economic arrangements by providing these arrangements with quasi-religious justification. Economists are thus doing theology while for the most part unaware of that fact."[2]

There are striking parallels between theoretical debates and policy responses to the Great Depression of the 1930s, on the one hand, and Great Recession that followed the 2008 financial crash, on the other. Two major views emerged in response to the Great Depression: one associated with the British economist John M. Keynes, the other with the American economist Irving Fisher. While Keynes focused on behavioral or psychological factors to explain the Depression, Fisher pointed to monetary factors and over-indebtedness as the main culprits.

Keynes argued that the crash of the 1929 was precipitated by something akin to an emotional stampede on the part of consumers, followed by producers: a sudden loss of confidence triggered a widespread reduction in consumer spending, which then prompted producers to curtail investment spending in the face (or anticipation) of reduced demand. The vicious circle of lowered consumption spending, lowered investment spending, lowered employment, and further curtailment in consumption spending … is what led (or transformed) the Great Crash of late October 1929 to the multi-year Great Depression that followed it. Accordingly, Keynes sought to encourage the government to step in to fill the demand gap in the hope that this may then trigger production and employment expansion—hence the use of the term "demand management" as an explanatory expression for Keynesian economics (Keynes 2010). (As discussed in Chapter Two, Keynes does not really provide an explanation for the Great Crash, because "loss of confidence," or "consumer stampede," was essentially a reaction to the Crash, not an explanation or a cause of it. Loss of confidence and spending crunch may have led the Great Crash to become the Great Depression, but it did not cause the Crash.)

Fisher argued, by contrast, that the market crash was precipitated by an excessively heavy and unsustainable debt burden that drained disproportionately large amounts of corporate earnings, thereby condemning them to collapse. He further argued that what led the Crash to become the Depression was "debt deflation." In his widely read article "The Debt Deflation Theory of Great Depressions," Fisher explained that in the same manner that a cycle of debt and/or asset price inflation precipitates a strong demand and an expanding cycle in the real sector of the economy, so does a cycle of debt and/or asset price deflation (when people tend to shed debt and liquidate assets), lead to a declining cycle of the real economy—a vicious circle process which led the Great Crash to become the Great Depression. In other words, a credit cycle can lead to a real, non-financial cycle; just as a real cycle can bring about a financial cycle. Accordingly, Fisher called for "reflation" as solution to the crisis of "debt deflation":

> Unless some counteracting cause comes along to prevent the fall in the price level, such a depression as that of 1929–33 (namely when the more the debtors pay the more they owe) tends to continue, going deeper, in a vicious spiral, for many years. There is then no tendency of the boat to stop tipping until it has capsized. Ultimately, of course, but only after almost universal bankruptcy, the indebtedness must cease to grow greater and begin to grow less. Then comes recovery and a tendency for a new boom-depression sequence. This is the so-called "natural" way out of a depression, via needless and cruel bankruptcy, unemployment, and starvation.... On the other hand, if the foregoing analysis is correct, it is always economically possible to stop or prevent such a depression simply by reflating the price level up to the average level at which outstanding debts were contracted by existing debtors and assumed by existing creditors, and then maintaining that level unchanged.
>
> (1933: 346)

Although Fisher's "debt deflation" views were largely ignored in favor of Keynes' ideas of "demand management," they have enjoyed a revival of interest in recent years, especially in the context of the current financial crisis. The renewed interest in Fisher's theory of "debt deflation" can be seen not only among circles of heterodox economists such as Post-Keynesians, but also among many mainstream economists and policy makers. Generous expansion of money supply by central banks in the United States, the European Union, Japan and a number of other countries is seen by many as examples of Fisher's "reflation" prescription to counter or contain debt deflation. "Fisher's solution is simply reflation. If this sounds a lot like the playbook that Bernanke and the Fed are using, that's because it is" (Griffin 2008).

Sadly, though, today's (monetary) reflation pursued by central banks in the core capitalist countries, especially in the U.S., is considerably different to what Fisher had in mind. Implicit in Fisher's idea of countering debt deflation through monetary reflation was that asset prices would move in tandem with the prices of goods and services. In other words, he did not foresee a scenario, similar to that prevalent in today's U.S. economy, where monetary injections would lead (through the influence of powerful financial interests) largely to the financial sector and, therefore, to asset-price reflation without significantly affecting the real sector, or the prices of goods and services.

Contrary to impressions that Bernanke's generous supply of cheap money is a liberal stimulus measure, the primary purpose of his easy monetary policy has, in fact, been to reflate asset prices, to make toxic assets whole and to patch up the bubble that was burst in 2008 by creating another asset-price bubble. Through a combination of massive bailout of the "too-big-to-fail" financial institutions and colossal infusion of near-free money into the parasitic financial sector, Mr. Bernanke and his collaborators in the government and Wall Street seem to have, indeed, succeeded in achieving this goal, as evinced by the soaring asset prices of recent years. According to World Bank's biannual Global Economic Prospects report (January 2013), while real economic growth has stalled or turned negative in much of the world since the bank released its previous report in June 2012, stock prices have soared. Over the past six months, stock markets in the more-developed economies of North America, Europe and Japan have risen by 10.7 percent and in the so-called "developing countries" by 12.6 percent. The MSCI (Morgan Stanley Capital International) All-Country World Index has jumped by 17 percent since the end of 2011.

As discussed earlier in this chapter, in the aftermath of the collapse of the real estate bubble, giant financial speculators stampeded out of that sector and flocked to the commodities market, especially food and energy markets. Financial moguls such as Goldman Sachs, Morgan Stanley and Barclays are heavily involved in relentlessly betting on the price of food through complex derivative procedures that have gravely contributed to the escalating price of foodstuff in recent years. "Goldman Sachs made up to an estimated £251 million (US$400 million) in 2012 from speculating on food including wheat, maize and soy, prompting campaigners to accuse the bank of contributing to a growing global food crisis" (Ross 2013). There is overwhelming evidence that the derivatives bubble in the food market has been a major contributing factor in the rise of the price of foodstuff:

> Rampant speculation on food prices by the big banks has dramatically increased the global price of food and has caused the suffering of hundreds of millions of poor families around the planet to become much worse. At this point, global food prices are more than twice as high as they were back in 2003. Approximately 2 billion people on the planet spend at least half of their incomes on food, and close to a billion people regularly do not have

> enough food to eat.... Goldman Sachs and other big banks are treating the global food supply as if it was some kind of a casino game.
>
> (Snyder 2013)

Pointing out how the Fed and/or government policies have helped reflate asset prices and create new bubbles in the stock market, commodities market, bond market and derivatives market, financial commentators at *Washington's Blog* argue, "If you really think about it, the largest bubble in history is *fraud*, because it includes all of the above [bubbles].... Specifically, the housing crisis was caused by fraud. The government encouraged fraud, and helped cover it up." Likewise, "Huge swaths of the derivatives market are manipulated by fraud.... But instead of cracking down on the fraud, the government is *backing* it. And the bubble in bonds was caused by super-low interest rates," in turn, "caused by the government's zero interest rate policy and quantitative easing." And the fraud bubble continues to expand: the people are told that the zero interest policy, the policy of giving virtually free money to Wall Street banksters, is necessary to stimulate the economy and create jobs. In essence, however, "zero interest rate policy is just another stealth bailout for the big banks. And quantitative easing only helps the super-elite ... and hurts the economy and the little guy." This means that "the government's low interest rate policies were based upon a fundamental misrepresentation as to their purpose and probable effect" (2013).

While the stock market has expanded to the level of a new bubble that is waiting to burst, stagnation in the real sector continues unabated. The latest (January 2013) World Bank's biannual report on Global Economic Prospects significantly downgraded its previous (June 2012) projections of global economic growth. Six months earlier the agency had projected that the world economy would grow at an annual rate of 3.0 percent in 2013; but it now projects a rate of only 2.4 percent. The report shows that nearly five years after the September 2008 financial collapse on Wall Street, the real sector of the economy continues to be mired in doldrums, especially in Europe and Japan. It indicates as well, how the austerity policies pursued by governments, the IMF and central banks in countries plagued by the Great Recession have benefited the financial elites at the expense of the public (Gray 2013).

Notes

1 For an informative discussion of this issue see, for example, Toporowski 2010, Chapter 3.

2 This quotation is from Paul Heyne's review of Robert Nelson's book, *Economics as Religion.* Retrieved from www.psupress.org/books/titles/0–271–02095–4.html.

References

Andrews, A. (2009). Praying for a revolution in economics. *Guardian*, July 11. Retrieved from www.guardian.co.uk/commentisfree/belief/2009/jul/11/economics-greenspan-neoclassical (accessed July 23, 2013).

Augar, P. (2006). *The great merchants: How the investment banks played the free market game*. London: Penguin.

Beams, N. (2013). The failure of capitalism. *World Socialist Web Site*, May 3. Retrieved from www.wsws.org/en/articles/2013/05/03/pers-m03.html (accessed July 26, 2013).

Black, William K. (2012). Mainstream economics is a cult. *Global Research*, June 30. Retrieved from www.globalresearch.ca/mainstream-economics-is-a-cult/31696.

Blaug, M. (2002). Disturbing currents in modern economics. *Challenge*, May. Retrieved from www.autisme-economie.org/article26.html (accessed December 14, 2012).

Fisher, I. (1933). The debt-deflation theory of Great Depressions. *Econometrica, 1* (4): 337–357.

Forbes (2011). The Fed's $16 trillion bailouts under-reported. September 20. Retrieved from www.forbes.com/sites/traceygreenstein/2011/09/20/the-feds-16-trillion-bailouts-under-reported/ (accessed October 7, 2013).

Forsyth, R. (2009). Ignoring the Austrians got us in this mess. *Barron's*, March 12. Retrieved from http://online.barrons.com/article/SB123680667244600275.html (accessed October 18, 2013).

Giles, C. (2008). The vision thing. *Financial Times*, November 26. Retrieved from www.ft.com/intl/cms/s/0/1c1d5a9e-bb29–11dd-bc6c-0000779fd18c.html (accessed August 01,2013).

Goodchild, P. (2002). *Capitalism and religion: The price of piety*. London: Routledge.

Gowan, P. (2010). The crisis in the heartland. In M. Konings (Ed.), *The great credit crash*. London and New York: Verso.

Graeber, D. (2011). *Debt: The First 5000 years*. Brooklyn, NY: Melville House.

Gray, B. (2013). Worldwide recession: Forecast for global economic growth. The failures of monetary policy. *Global Research*, January 24. Retrieved from www.globalresearch.ca/worldwide-recession-forecast-for-global-economic-growth-the-failures-of-monetary-policy/5319355 (accessed September28, 2013).

Greenspan, A. (2008). We will never have a perfect model of risk. *Financial Times*, March 17.

Griffin, B. (2008). Irving Fisher on debt, deflation, and depression. *Seeking Alpha*, November 5. Retrieved from http://seekingalpha.com/article/104135-irving-fisher-on-debt-deflation-and-depression (accessed December 22, 2012).

Hudson, M. and Bezemer, D. (2012). Incorporating the rentier sectors into a financial model. *World Economic Review, 1* (1). Retrieved from http://wer.worldeconomicsassociation.org/article/view/36 (accessed April 05, 2013).

International Monetary Fund (2007). *World economic outlook: Spillovers and cycles in the global economy*. April, Washington, DC: IMF. Retrieved from www.imf.org/external/pubs/ft/weo/2007/01/ (accessed September 26, 2013).

Kaufman, F. (2011). How Goldman Sachs created the food crisis. *Foreign Policy*, April 27. Retrieved from www.foreignpolicy.com/articles/2011/04/27/how_goldman_sachs_created_the_food_crisis?page=0,0 (accessed September 27, 2013).

Keen, S. (2011). *Debunking economics: The naked emperor dethroned?* London: Zed Books.

Keynes, J. M. (2010). *The general theory of employment, interest, and money*. Whitefish, MT: Kessinger Publishing, LLC.

Nelson, R. (2002). *Economics as religion: From Samuelson to Chicago and beyond*. Philadelphia, PA: Pennsylvania State University Publications.

New York Times (2009). Ivory tower unswayed by crashing economy. March 5. www.nytimes.com/2009/03/05/books/05deba.html?pagewanted=all&_r=0.

Reuters (2008). Trichet says euro zone growth to hit trough in Q2, Q3. July 18. Retrieved from www.reuters.com/article/2008/07/18/us-ecb-trichet-growth-idUSSP65948 20080718 (accessed October &, 2013).

Ross, M. (2013). Goldman Sachs made up to £250 million betting on food prices in 2012. World Development Movement. Retrieved from www.wdm.org.uk/food-and-hunger/goldman-sachs-made-%C2%A3251-million-betting-food-prices-2012 (accessed June 29, 2013).

Shaikh, A. (1978). An Introduction to the History of Crisis Theories. In Economics Education Project, *U.S. capitalism in crisis*. New York: Union for Radical Political Economics (URPE).

Snyder, M. (2013). The derivative bubble: Speculating on food prices, banking on famine. *Global Research*, January 24. Retrieved from www.globalresearch.ca/the-derivative-bubble-speculating-on-food-prices-banking-on-famine/5320379 (accessed February 17, 2013).

Taibbi, M. (2010). *Griftopia: Bubble machines, vampire squids, and the long con that is breaking America*. New York: Spiegel & Grau.

Toporowski, J. (2010). *Why the world economy needs a financial crash and other critical essays on finance and financial economics*. London: Anthem Press.

Washington's Blog (2013). The biggest bubble in history: Fraud. January 24. Retrieved from www.washingtonsblog.com/2013/01/the-biggest-bubble-in-history-fraud.html (accessed September 28, 2013).

World Bank (2013). Global economic prospects: Assuring growth over the medium term. January, Washington, D.C.

2 Keynesian explanations of the financial crisis

This chapter focuses primarily on the dominant (or traditional) paradigm of Keynesian economics, which is also called "liberal" neoclassical economics, and which is widely taught in economics departments in the United States and beyond. There are also Left and/or Post-Keynesian economists, whose discussion is beyond the purview of this study.

Contrary to neoliberal economists who view major financial instabilities as abnormal or exceptional occurrences, Keynesians view them as integral parts of relatively advanced market economies. Whereas neoliberals perceive financial instability as a manifestation of the "irrational" behavior of the market players, Keynesians see such financial volatilities as indicators of rational agents' inventiveness in taking advantage of moneymaking opportunities to maximize their profits, or optimize their bets. There is nothing unusual, irrational, or abnormal in the dynamics of this market-driven behavior—and its logical outcome: financial instability.

Accordingly, Keynesian economists argue that instead of blaming market players' "irrational" behavior for financial instability, as neoliberals do, such behavior must be monitored, disciplined or guided through "appropriate" public policy. Financial instability is, therefore, to be blamed more on insufficient or inappropriate public policy than on the market or economic agents' behavior. Properly managed or regulated, wild financial gyrations can be tempered into no more than small or controllable fluctuations (Shaikh 1978).

Predictably, Keynesian economists and policy makers view the unbridled market deregulation of the past several decades as the main culprit behind both the financial inflation that started in 2002 and its ultimate implosion in 2007–2008. Reinstitution of the regulatory safeguards that were put in place in response to the (1929–1933) Great Depression is, therefore, seen as a major step in the direction of tempering the "financialization" trend of the economy and the ongoing financial turbulence. While re-regulation, especially reinstatement of the 1933 Glass–Steagall Act of limiting the destabilizing tendencies of commercial banks, may curtail the speculative behavior of major Wall Street players, it would not automatically lead to economic revival. To bring this about, Keynesian economists advocate the use of the public sector as the lender of the last resort to rekindle the dormant economy. So, utilization of government authority to carry out the twin strategies of regulation and demand management/stimulation is a policy package that is promoted or supported by almost all Keynesian economists and policy makers.

While blaming deregulation and the resulting crafty financial "innovations" as factors that contributed to the market crash is not false, it masks the fact that such factors are inherent to the essential dynamics or strategies of the accumulation of finance capital. In a real sense, blaming deregulation and/or financialization as primary factors behind the market collapse begs the question. The more fundamental questions are: Why deregulation in the first place? What changed or undermined the regulatory safeguards that were established in response to the Great Depression?

Keynesian and other liberal economists' responses to these questions are woefully deficient. They tend to blame the abandonment of the Keynesian, New Deal, or Social-Democratic economics largely on neoliberal ideology, on Ronald Reagan's supply-side economics, or on economists at the University of Chicago. Indeed, they tend to characterize the 2008 financial collapse and the ensuing Great Recession as a crisis of "bad" policies of "neoliberal capitalism," not of capitalism per se (Kotz 2009).

I would argue in this chapter that the transition from Keynesian to neoliberal economics stemmed from much deeper roots or dynamics than pure ideology; that the transition started long before Reagan arrived in the White House; that neoliberal austerity policies are class based, not "bad," policies; and that the Keynesian reliance on the willingness and ability of the government to re-regulate and revive the economy through demand management is based on their wishful thinking or illusion that perceives the state as a disinterested entity that can manage and/or control capitalism. I would further argue that the Keynesian stimulus prescription that relies largely on strong demand, or high employment and high wages, is one-sided; because growth under capitalism is not just a function of strong demand but also of low costs, which often means low employment and low wages. In other words, economic growth under capitalism can be just as wage/demand driven (as was the case in the immediate post-WW II period), as cost/supply driven, as was the case in the 1980s and 1990s.

Deeper than "neoliberal ideology"

The questioning and the gradual abandonment of the Keynesian demand management strategies took place not simply because of purely ideological proclivities of "right-wing" Republicans or the personal preferences of Ronald Reagan, as many liberal and radical economists argue, but because of actual structural changes in economic or market conditions, both nationally and internationally. New Deal-Keynesian-Social Democratic policies were pursued in the aftermath of the Great Depression and WW II as long as socio-political forces and economic conditions of the time rendered such policies effective. Those favorable conditions included the need to invest in and rebuild the devastated post-war economies around the world, the nearly unlimited demand for U.S. manufactures, both at home and abroad, and the lack of competition for both U.S. capital and labor. These propitious circumstances allowed U.S. workers to demand respectable wages and benefits while at the same time enjoying higher rates of employment. The high wages and the strong demand then served as a delightful stimulus that precipitated the long expansionary cycle of the immediate post-war period in the manner of a virtuous circle.

By the late 1960s and early 1970s, however, both U.S. capital and labor were no longer unrivaled in global markets. Furthermore, during the long cycle of the immediate post-war expansion U.S. manufacturers had invested so much in fixed capital, or capacity building, that by the late 1960s their profit rates had begun to decline as the capital–labor ratio of their operations had become too high. In other words, the enormous amounts of the so-called "sunk costs," mainly in the form of fixed capital, or plant and equipment, had significantly eroded their profit rates (Shaikh 1987).

More than anything else, it was these important changes in the actual conditions of production, and the concomitant realignment of global markets, which occasioned the gradual reservations and the ultimate abandonment of the New Deal-Keynesian economics. Contrary to the repeated claims of the liberal/Keynesian partisans, it was not Ronald Reagan's ideas or schemes that lay behind the plans of dismantling the New Deal reforms—indeed, as shown in the next section of this chapter, steps to hammer away at those reforms had been taken long before Reagan arrived in the White House. Rather, it was the globalization, first, of capital and, then, of labor that rendered Keynesian or New Deal-type economic policies no longer attractive to capitalist profitability, and brought forth Ronald Reagan and neoliberal austerity economics (see Shutt 1998, for example).

Professor Jan Toporowski of the University of London (among others) shows that Keynesianism was abandoned not by evil neoliberals but because de-facto or spontaneous growth of unregulated internationalization of financial/credit markets made Keynesian-type regulations, which were put in place in the immediate aftermath of the Great Depression and WW II, literally unenforceable.

> It should be emphasized that Keynesian stabilization policies were not abandoned for purely ideological reasons; i.e., because, as many critics of neoliberalism argue, a laissez-faire animus spread from Chicago, infecting politicians of all parties and persuading them of the benefits of free markets. In fact, Keynesianism never worked very well and, in particular, Keynesian systems of financial regulation (capital controls and managed exchange rates) could not withstand the growing pools of unregulated international credit, the Euromarkets, which came to dominate international finance.
>
> (2010: 18)

When financial regulations, capital controls and a new international monetary system were established at the Bretton Woods (NH, New England) Conference in the immediate aftermath of WW II, international financial or credit markets were effectively non-existent. The U.S. dollar (and to lesser extent gold) was, by and large, the only means of international trade and credit. Under those circumstances, international credit took place largely through the International Monetary Fund (IMF) and the central banks of the lending/borrowing countries—hence, the enforceability of controls.

This picture of international credit/financial markets, however, gradually changed; and by the late 1960 and early1970s, those markets had grown to the tune of hundreds of billion of dollars, thereby allowing international credit transactions outside of the IMF-central banks channels. The two major factors that significantly contributed to drastic inflation of international financial markets were (a) the computer-generated international credit, and (b) the immense proliferation of Euro-dollars—Euro-dollars are U.S. dollars deposited in overseas banks, especially European banks.

The Bretton Woods' granting the U.S. dollar the status of the main international reserve currency—on a par with gold—was tantamount to opening up an unlimited gold mine to the United States. It effectively granted the United States the unique privilege of *seigniorage*: its citizens and/or importers could shop and pay for their imports from anywhere in the world just as they would at home. While this certainly had (and still has) its advantages, it also led to a significant outflow of dollars from the United States, which provided for the escalating growth of Euro-dollars. Another major source of the accumulation of Euro-dollars was the enormous U.S. military spending overseas. The recycling of the so-called petrodollars in the 1970s and 1980s by major transnational banks further expanded the means of international credit. In a literally mushrooming fashion, the footloose-and-fancy-free global finance/credit has grown so big during the past several decades that it has made domestic or national controls and regulations virtually ineffectual:

> Critics of international finance have made various proposals to stabilize the system and make it more appropriate to the purposes of economic and social development. The most common suggestion has been a return to the cross-border capital controls that existed during the 1940s and the 1950s. Such controls, in many cases, were not eliminated until the 1990s. However, international bank deposits and financial assets held abroad are now so large that it would be difficult to enforce such controls. Indeed, the main reason for getting rid of such regulations was precisely because they could not be enforced.
>
> (Toporowski 2010: 25)

It is obvious, then, that the weakening or undermining of control and/or regulatory safeguards was brought about not so much by purely ideological tendencies of certain politicians or policy makers as it was by the actual developments in international financial markets. (This is, of course, not to discount or trivialize the role of political ideology, economic interests or policy biases; it is rather to set the record straight.) As demonstrated below, it is equally obvious that the initial steps in the direction of eroding the New Deal-Keynesian economics and related regulatory precautions began long before Ronald Reagan was sent to the White House.

It started long before Reagan arrived in the White House

As mentioned above, most liberal economists and politicians trace the origins of neoliberal policies, and the abandonment of the New Deal-Keynesian economics, to President Reagan: his election in 1980 and the subsequent rise of neoliberalism brought forth an economic doctrine that has gradually led to the reversal of the Keynesian demand-management strategies of economic stimulation. So, for the majority of these economists and politicians, Reagan is the pivotal figure and 1980 is the watershed year:

> Before 1980, economic policy was designed to achieve full employment, and the economy was characterized by a system in which wages grew with productivity. This configuration created a virtuous circle of growth. Rising wages meant robust aggregate demand, which contributed to full employment. Full employment in turn provided an incentive to invest, which raised productivity, thereby supporting higher wages.
>
> After 1980, with the advent of the new [neoliberal] growth model, the commitment to full employment was abandoned as inflationary, with the result that the link between productivity growth and wages was severed. In place of wage growth as the engine of demand growth, the new model substituted borrowing and asset price inflation. Adherents of the neoliberal orthodoxy made controlling inflation their primary policy concern, and set about attacking unions, the minimum wage, and other worker protections.
>
> (Palley 2009)

The claim that the abandonment of Keynesian policies in favor of neoliberal ones began with the 1980 arrival of Ronald Reagan in the White House is, however, factually false. Indisputable evidence shows that the date on the Keynesian prescriptions of economic stimulation expired at least a dozen years earlier. Keynesian policies of economic expansion through demand management had run out of steam (i.e., reached their systemic limits) by the late 1960s and early 1970s; they did not come to a sudden, screeching halt the moment Reagan sat at the helm. "The foundations of neoliberalism were established in economic theory by liberal Democrats at the Brookings Institution, and in political practice by the Carter administration" (Nasser 2009).

Indeed, baby-steps backward to pre-Keynesian neoclassicism were taken as early as during the presidency of John F. Kennedy. For example, in 1962 President Kennedy argued that while "most of us are conditioned for many years to have a political viewpoint—Republican or Democrat, liberal, conservative or moderate," in reality the most pressing government concerns were "technical problems, administrative problems" that "do not lend themselves to the great sort of passionate movements which have stirred this country so often in the past" (as quoted in Nasser 2009).

It is a well-established historical record that the institution of the New Deal economic policies would not have been possible without the compelling grassroots pressure in response to the economic hardship of the Great Depression. Yet, it is obvious (from this statement) that President Kennedy is here trying to reduce economic policies to purely "technical, administrative problems" that "do not lend themselves to … passionate movements"—in effect, trying to depreciate the importance of the politics of class struggle.

Arguments that "policies of economic equity represented costly trade-offs in terms of efficiency" were made by economic advisors of the Democratic administrations long before Reaganomics solemnized such arguments. Arthur Okun and Charles Schultze had each served as chair of the Council of Economic Advisors to Democratic presidents. In his *Equality and Efficiency: The Big Tradeoff*, Okun (1975) argued that "the interventionist goal of greater equality had inefficiency costs that injured the private economy." Schultze (1977) likewise claimed that "politically neutral evidence proved that government policies which impact markets in the name of fairness and equality are necessarily inefficient." He further argued that "promotion of social goods as the direct object of government policy was bound to disadvantage the very people policymakers intended to protect, and to destabilize the private economy in the process" (as quoted in Nasser 2009). It is worth noting that both Okun's and Schultze's books were published by the ostensibly liberal Brookings Institution.

As attorney Jerome Kalur points out, "Chamber of Commerce and Business Roundtable efforts to gain control of government regulatory decision-making were initiated at least nine years before" the election of Ronald Reagan to presidency—"when corporate attorney Lewis Powell submitted to the Chamber his now well-known memorandum 'Attack of American Free Enterprise System' " (2013). In concert with Powell's legal offensive against labor and regulatory standards, big business moved swiftly to "impede union organizing" and "to eliminate regulatory controls via streams of think-tank propaganda from the likes of The American Enterprise Institute (1972), The Heritage Foundation (1973), and the Cato Institute (1977)" (ibid.). Kalur continues:

> When Powell handed his memorandum to the Chamber, American business had 175 registered lobbyist firms at its service. By 1982, the number of K Street corporate financed arm-twisters had grown to 2,500. Corporate supported PACs numbered 400 in the early 70s and 1,200 by 1980. In short, big business was already causing a decline in union memberships, strongly influencing federal agencies and laws, and mastering the SEC long before the advent of the Reagan presidency. With Powell elevated to the Supreme Court corporate America was by 1978 advancing toward its goal of unrestricted campaign contributions through clandestine vehicles.
>
> (Ibid.)

While theoretical turnaround from New Deal-Keynesian economics by the luminaries of the Democratic Party pre-dated President Carter, policy implementation of such theories took place under the Carter administration. It must be acknowledged that, along with the curtailment or slowing down of social spending, President Carter also managed to slightly slow down the growth of military spending—though only during the first half of his term in office. His policy of restraining public spending was in line with economic policies of the so-called Trilateral Commission (of which he was a leading member) whose agenda of improving U.S. competitiveness in global markets included "fiscal discipline" on the part of the government. Reagan picked up the Democrat's copy of gradual agenda of neoliberalism and ran with it, replacing the rhetoric of capitalism-with-a-human-face with the imperious, self-righteous rhetoric of rugged individualism that greed and self-interest are virtues to be nurtured.

President Clinton did not ease the supply-side economic policies of the Reagan years, and President Obama is also not hesitating to carry out such policies. In collaboration with the financial oligarchy and the Federal Reserve Bank, his administration has made available trillions of dollars in cash infusions, loans and guarantees to the parasitic financial sector, but for state governments that are facing massive budget deficits and bankruptcy, it has refused to provide assistance. The White House is sitting by while states and other local governments across the country lay off workers and slash spending on education, health care, pension plans and other essential social programs.

The left/liberal supporters of President Obama who bemoan his "predicament in the face of brutal Republican challenges" should look past his liberal/populist posturing. Evidence shows that, contrary to Barack Obama's claims, his presidential campaigns were heavily financed by the Wall Street financial titans and their influential lobbyists. Large Wall Street contributions began pouring into his campaign only after he was thoroughly vetted (in 2007) by the powerful Wall Street interests and was deemed the most useful—indeed, ideal—candidate for presidency (Martens 2008).

The role of the state—hopes, myths and illusions

The Keynesian view that the government can fine-tune the economy through "appropriate" fiscal and monetary policies to maintain continuous growth (at or near full employment) is based on the idea that capitalism can be controlled or manipulated by the state and managed by professional economists from government departments; that is, capitalism run by "experts" in the interest of all. Economic policy making, according to this view, is largely a matter of technical expertise or economic know-how, that is, a matter of choice. The effectiveness of the Keynesian model is, therefore, based largely on a hope, or illusion; since in reality the power relation between the state and the market/capitalism is usually the other way around. Economic policy making is more than simply an administrative or technical matter of choice; more importantly, it is a deeply socio-political matter that is organically intertwined with the class nature of the state and the policy making apparatus. The Keynesian illusion has been nurtured or masked by two major myths.

The first myth stems from the perception that attributes the implementation of the New Deal and Social Democratic economic reforms that followed the Great Depression and WW II to the genius of Keynes. This is a myth because those reforms were more a product of the fierce class struggles and overwhelming pressures from the grassroots than the brains of experts like Keynes. The harrowing socioeconomic turbulence of the 1930s generated momentous social upheavals and extensive working class struggles. The ensuing "threat of revolution," as Franklin D. Roosevelt (FDR) put it, and the "menacing" pressure from below prompted reform from above. Indeed, beyond narrow academic circles, Keynes was not even heard of in the United States when most of the New Deal reforms were put in place.

As an articulate economist and a steadfast champion of the preservation of capitalism, however, Keynes provided the theoretical or intellectual rationale for the badly-needed reforms in order to save capitalism by fending off revolution. The auspicious coincidence of the publication of his famous book, *The General Theory of Employment, Interest and Money* (1936), with the implementation of the New Deal-Social Democratic economic reforms in the U.S. and Western Europe provided Keynes with much more credit for those reforms and the subsequent economic recovery than he deserved.

The second myth stems from the perception that attributes the long economic expansion of the 1948–1968 period in the U.S. to the efficacy or success of Keynesian policies of economic management. While it is certainly true that expansive government policies of the time played a big role in the fantastic economic developments of that period, additional favorable conditions or factors also contributed to the success of that expansion. These included the need to invest and rebuild the devastated post-war economies around the world, the need to supply the vast post-war global demand for consumer as well as capital goods, lack of competition for U.S. products and capital in global markets—in short, the fact that there was enormous room for growth and expansion in the immediate post-war period.

Harboring these myths and illusions, many Keynesian economists envisioned a silver-lining in the 2008 financial meltdown and the ensuing Great Recession. Since they viewed the financial turbulence and the ensuing recession as the "crisis of neoliberal economics," not of capitalism as such, they saw an opportunity for a new dawn of Keynesian economics, or the coming of a "second New Deal." Well-known Keynesians (and Post-Keynesians) such as Paul Krugman, Joseph Stiglitz and Dean Baker wrote passionately on the need to revive Keynesian policies, to implement extensive stimulus packages, and to reinstate the Glass Steagall Act and other regulatory measures that were put in place in response to the Great Depression. The excitement on the part of many Keynesians about the prospects of what they perceived as an almost automatic switching of policy gears from neoliberal to Keynesian economics led George Melloan of the *Wall Street Journal* to write (perhaps sarcastically) "We're all Keynesian's Again."

Nearly six years later, it is abundantly clear that Keynesian policy prescriptions are falling on deaf ears, as neoliberalism continues to keep Keynesianism at bay. Not only has President Obama, the purported champion of "change" in the United States, but also the nominally socialist and Social-Democratic governments of Europe have adopted the unbridled austerity policies of neoliberalism.

Shunned, Keynesian hopes and illusions have turned into disappointment and anger. For example, using his column in the *New York Times*, Professor Paul Krugman frequently lashes out at the Obama administration for ignoring the Keynesian policies of economic expansion and job creation and, instead, following policies that are not different from those of neoliberal Republicans:

> The truth is that creating jobs in a depressed economy is something government could and should be doing.... Think about it: Where are the big public works projects? Where are the armies of government workers? There are actually half a million fewer government employees now than there were when Mr. Obama took office.
>
> (Krugman 2011)

This is a good example of Keynesian illusions: the belief in the ability of government to control and/or manage capitalism; the perception that government "could and should" invest in job creation but, somehow, does not do it. In theory, or ideally, a government could and should invest in job creation; but that would be a different government, a disinterested government independent of special interests, not a government that is beholden to big money and powerful financial interests. True, a capitalist government may, under certain circumstance, invest in economic growth and job creation, as the core capitalist governments did in response to the Great Depression of the 1930s. But, as indicated previously, those reforms were not carried out voluntarily; they were implemented largely under duress, pressure from the masses, and the threat of revolution.

Keynesian economists' frustration with the neoliberal policies of the Obama administration is misplaced: expecting milk from a he-goat can indeed be exasperating. At the heart of their disappointment is the unrealistic perception that economic strategies and policies are largely intellectual products, and that policy making is primarily a matter of technical expertise and personal preferences: economists or policy makers who are far-sighted, good-hearted or better equipped with "smart" ideas would opt for "good" or Keynesian-type capitalism; while those lacking such admirable qualities would foolishly, misguidedly or heartlessly choose "bad" or neoliberal policies.

So, strong economic revival is only one step away if policymakers can find the intellectual clarity and political will to end the sluggish economy (Krugman 2013; Palley 2009; Kotz 2009). What Keynesian (as well as many left/progressive) economists overlook is the fact that it is neither a matter of choice nor, therefore, of "bad" vs. "good" policy; it is a matter of class policy. These economists are angry because they tend to be oblivious or shy away from the politics of class, that is, the politics of policy making. Instead, they seem to think that economic policy making results mainly from a battle of ideas and theories, and they are disappointed because they are losing that battle.

Professor Krugman passionately writes, "Where are the big public works projects? Where are the armies of government workers?" What he fails to mention is that those "armies of government workers" were put to work not courtesy of FDR, or because of Keynes' brilliant ideas (in fact, as mentioned earlier, when the FDR administration initially embarked on the implementation of the extensive public works projects it did not even know Keynes was alive), but because much larger armies of workers and other grassroots threatened the capitalist system by persistently marching in the streets and demanding jobs. It is interesting that many Keynesian economists admirably fight (of course, in the realm of ideas) for the rights of workers but shy away from calling on them to rise up to demand their rights.

It is not enough to have a good heart or a compassionate soul; it is equally important not to lose sight of how public policy is made under capitalism. It is not enough to repeatedly bash Ronald Reagan as a wicked king and praise FDR as a wise king. The more important task is to explain why the ruling class ousted the wise king and ushered in the wicked one. Government policy makers are certainly not stupid. Why, then, did they switch from the policies of Keynes and New Deal economics to those of Reagan and neoliberal economics? As Professor Peter Gowan of London Metropolitan University puts it, "Keynesians make an essentially false argument in favor of re-regulation when they fail to see the oneness of the State and the Wall Street" (2010).

Growth and employment: supply-side vs. demand-side arguments

Not only is the liberal economists' account of the actual developments that led to the demise of Keynesianism and the rise of neoliberalism inaccurate, so is their explanation of the ongoing problems of unemployment and economic stagnation. By blaming the persistently high rates of unemployment on "neoliberal capitalism" instead of capitalism per se, proponents of Keynesian economics tend to lose sight of the structural or systemic causes of unemployment: the secular and/or systemic tendency of capitalist production to constantly replace labor with machine, and to thereby create a sizeable pool of the unemployed, or a "reserve army of labor," as Karl Marx put it. This means, of course, the higher the degree of industrialization and automation, the higher the potential of the reserve army of labor to expand. Marx described this tendency of capitalism to constantly create high levels of unemployment as an essential condition for profitable capitalist production in the following words:

> The greater the social wealth, the functioning capital, the extent and energy of its growth, and, therefore, also the absolute mass of the proletariat and the productiveness of its labour, the greater is the industrial reserve army.

> The same causes which develop the expansive power of capital, develop also the labour power at its disposal. The relative mass of the industrial reserve army increases therefore with the potential energy of wealth. But the greater this reserve army in proportion to the active labour army, the greater is the mass of a consolidated surplus population, whose misery is in inverse ratio to its torment of labour. The more extensive, finally, the lazarus layers of the working class, and the industrial reserve army, the greater is official pauperism. *This is the absolute general law of capitalist accumulation.* Like all other laws it is modified in its working by many circumstances, the analysis of which does not concern us here.
>
> (1967: 644)

Marx argued that the fundamental laws of demand and supply of labor under capitalism are therefore heavily influenced, by the market's ability to regularly produce a reserve army of labor, or a "surplus population." The reserve army of labor, whose size is determined largely by the imperatives of capitalist profitability, is therefore as important to capitalist production as is the active (or actually employed) army of labor. Just as a regular and timely adjustment of the level of a body of water behind an irrigation dam is crucial to a smooth or stable use of water, so is an "appropriate" size of a pool of the unemployed critical to the profitability of capitalist production:

> The industrial reserve army, during the periods of stagnation and average prosperity, weighs down the active labour-army; during the periods of overproduction and paroxysm, it holds its pretensions in check. Relative surplus population is therefore the pivot upon which the law of demand and supply of labour works. It confines the field of action of this law within the limits absolutely convenient to the activity of exploitation and to the domination of capital.
>
> (1967: 639)

It is clear that the Marxian theory of the reserve army of labor, which shows how unemployment arises under capitalism and why it is essential to its profitability, provides a much deeper understanding of the current plague of unemployment than the Keynesian view, which blames it on "neoliberal" capitalism—and which is essentially tantamount to explaining something by itself.

In the era of globalization of production and employment, the reserve army of labor has drastically expanded beyond national borders. According to a recent report by the International Labor Organization (ILO), between 1980 and 2007 the global labor force rose from 1.9 billion to 3.1 billion, a growth rate of 63 percent. Historical transition to capitalism in many less-developed parts of the world, which has led to the so-called de-peasantization, or proletarianization and urbanization, especially in countries such as China and India, is obviously a major source of the enlargement of the worldwide labor force, and its availability to global capital. The ILO report further shows that, worldwide, the ratio of the active (or employed) to reserve (or unemployed) army of labor is less than 50 percent, that is, more than half of the global labor force is unemployed.[1]

It is this vast and readily available pool of the unemployed, along with the ease of production anywhere in the world—not some "evil intentions of right-wing Republicans or wicked neoliberals," as many Keynesians argue—that has forced the working class, especially in the U.S. and other advanced capitalist countries, into submission: going along with the brutal austerity schemes of wage and benefit cuts, of layoffs and union busting, of part-time and contingency employment, and the like. Ruthless neoliberal policies of the past several decades, by both Republican and Democratic parties, are more a product of the structural changes in the global capitalist production than their cause. This is not to say that economic policies do not matter; but that such policies should not be attributed simply to capricious decisions, malicious intentions or ideological schemes.

It might be argued:

> who cares what caused the unemployment? The fact is that it is a suffocating problem for millions; and why not simply replicate the Keynesian-type stimulus policies that were adopted in the immediate aftermath of the Great Depression and World War II?

This is indeed the view of most of the liberal economists and policy makers.

While prima facie this sounds like a reasonable suggestion, it suffers from the problem of issuing careless prescriptions based on inaccurate or flawed diagnoses. Not surprisingly, repeated Keynesian calls of the recent years for embarking on Keynesian-type stimulus packages in order to help end the recession and alleviate unemployment continue to sound hollow. Under the changed conditions of production from national to global level, and in the absence of overwhelming political pressure from workers and other grassroots, there are simply no refills for Dr. Keynes's prescriptions, which were issued under radically different socioeconomic conditions, under national circumstances or frameworks, not international or global ones.

Theoretically, the Keynesian strategy of a "virtuous circle" of high employment, high wages, strong demand, and high growth is both simple and reasonable: massive government spending in the face of a serious economic downturn would raise employment and wages, inject a strong purchasing power into the economy, which would, in turn, spur producers to expand and hire, thereby further raising employment, wages, demand, supply.... Many well-known Keynesians (Krugman 2013; Baker 2010; Palley 2013; Reich 2010, for example) have in recent years repeatedly put forth this strategy of economic stimulation—only to see them fall on deaf ears. Why?

While in theory the Keynesian "virtuous circle" proposition is a relatively simple and fairly reasonable strategy, it suffers from a number of problems. To begin with, it seems to assume that employers and government policy makers are genuinely interested in bringing about full employment, but somehow do not know how to achieve this goal. Full employment production, however, may not necessarily be the ideal, or profit-maximizing, level of production; which means it may not be a real objective of business and/or government decision makers. As explained earlier, a sizeable pool of the unemployed is as essential to capitalist profitability as is the number of workers "needed" to be actually employed. In its drive to keep the labor cost as low as possible, by keeping the working class as docile as possible, capitalism tends to often prefer high unemployment and low wages to low unemployment and high wages. This explains why, for example, the stock market often tends to rise when there is a report of rising unemployment, and vice versa. It also explains why in reaction to the ongoing high levels of unemployment in the United States, the Obama administration has been making a lot of hollow, echoing noise about "jobs programs" without seriously embarking on a genuine plan of job creation a la FDR. Instead, taking advantage of the crisis situation, the ruling business–government policy makers have embarked on an unprecedented austerity program of spending cuts whose main objective is to reduce the U.S. labor cost to the levels of its international competitors in China, India and the like.

It is surprising that despite the obviousness of this strategy, and the almost elementary business/capitalist rationale behind it, many liberal/Keynesian economists seem incapable of seeing or grasping it. Trained in the Keynesian "demand-side" economics (the notion that "sufficiently" strong demand is the only engine of growth), these economists refuse to accept the view, or the empirical evidence, that "supply-side" or austerity economics too can lead to growth—by lowering labor cost and enhancing investor confidence. For example, the economics Nobel Laureate Paul Krugman finds it "strange" that the Obama administration and the European governments are cutting spending during a period of sluggish demand and high unemployment. Apparently unable to find economic reasons for the austerity cuts, he attributes them to "the underlying political and psychological reasons."[2]

Second, the Keynesian argument that a "virtuous circle" of high employment, high wages, strong demand, and high growth is relatively easily achievable only if it were not due to the opposition of employers, or "bad" policies of neoliberalism, is based on the assumption that employers/producers are somehow oblivious to their own self-interest. In other words, the argument presumes that it is not in the interests of employers to drive the wages too low as this would be tantamount to undermining consumer demand for what they produce. If only they were mindful of the benefits of the proverbial "Ford wages" to their sales, the argument goes, could they help both themselves and their workers, and bring about economic growth and prosperity for all. The well-known liberal professor (and former Labor Secretary under President Clinton) Robert Reich's view on this issue is typical of the Keynesian argument:

> For most of the last century, the basic bargain at the heart of the American economy was that employers paid their workers enough to buy what American employers were selling.... That basic bargain created a virtuous cycle

> of higher living standards, more jobs, and better wages.... The basic bargain is over.... Corporate profits are up right now largely because pay is down and companies aren't hiring. But this is a losing game even for corporations over the long term. Without enough American consumers, their profitable days are numbered. After all, there's a limit to how much profit they can get out of cutting American payrolls...
>
> (2011)

There are two major problems with this (typically Keynesian) argument. The first problem is that it assumes (implicitly) that U.S. producers depend on domestic workers not only for employment but also for sale of their products—as if it were a closed economy. In reality, however, U.S. producers are increasingly becoming less and less dependent on domestic labor for either employment or sales as they steadily expand their production and sales markets abroad. Transnational capital's consumer and labor markets are now spread across the globe. As Professor Alan Nasser of Evergreen State College (Olympia) recently pointed out, "On both the supply [employment] side and the demand side, the U.S. worker/consumer is perceived as incrementally inessential" (2011).

President Obama and his top economic advisors have been especially keen, indeed aggressive, on expanding U.S. export markets to make up for the loss of domestic purchasing power. For example, in a speech (on his National Export Initiative) to the annual conference of the Import-Export Bank (March 11, 2010) the president pointed out: "The world's fastest-growing markets are outside our borders. We need to compete for those customers because other nations are competing for them" (Nasser 2011). Mr. Obama's chairman of the Council on Jobs and Competitiveness, Jeffrey Immelt, likewise states: "Today we go to Brazil, we go to China, we go to India, because that's where the customers are" (ibid.).

The second problem with Professor Reich's (and many of his like-minded Keynesians') argument of "high wages as the engine of virtuous cycles" of growth and employment is that wages and benefits are micro- or enterprise-level categories that are decided on by individual employers and corporate managers, not by some macro or national level planners of aggregate demand (as in a centrally-planned economy). In other words, individual producers (large or small) view wages and benefits first, and foremost, as a major cost of production that needs to be minimized as much as possible; and only secondarily, if ever, as part of the national aggregate demand that may (in roundabout ways) contribute to the sale of their products. This is another example of how Marx's theory of capitalist exploitation and wage-determination—as a subsistence-based historical category—is superior to the Keynesian view that wishfully hopes that producers would be wise and generous enough to pay "sufficient" wages in order to sell their products.

It follows from this brief discussion that, as pointed out above, not only may growth and expansion not be precipitated or accompanied by high wages, as Keynesian economists claim, but (on the contrary) by low wages, or low cost of labor. More often than not, capitalism flourishes on the poverty and, therefore, compliance and low cost of labor. Marx characterized capitalism's ability to create a big pool of the unemployed (in order to create a largely poor and meek working class) as "immiseration" and submission of labor force—a built-in mechanism that is essential to the "general law" of capitalist accumulation:

> It follows therefore that in proportion as capital accumulates, the lot of the labourer, be his payment high or low, must grow worse. The law, finally, that always equilibrates the relative surplus population, or industrial reserve army, to the extent and energy of accumulation, this law rivets the labourer to capital more firmly than the wedges of Vulcan did Prometheus to the rock. It establishes an accumulation of misery, corresponding with accumulation of capital. Accumulation of wealth at one pole is, therefore, at the same time accumulation of misery, agony of toil slavery, ignorance, brutality, mental degradation, at the opposite pole, *i.e.*, on the side of the class that produces its own product in the form of capital.
>
> (1967: 645)

Perhaps the major flaw of the Keynesian reform or restructuring package, in a nutshell, is that it consists of a set of populist proposals that are devoid of politics, that is, of political mechanisms that would be necessary to carry them out. It rests largely on the hope that, as discussed earlier, in an independent or disinterested fashion, the state can control and manage capitalism in the interest of all. This is, however, no more than wishful thinking, since in reality it is the powerful capitalist interests that elect and control the government, not the other way around.

In response to criticisms of this kind, Keynesians are quick to invoke the experience of the "golden" years (1948–1968) of the U.S. economy in support of their arguments. It is true that during that long cycle of expansion high employment, high wages, high demand and high growth reinforced each other in the fashion of a virtuous cycle. As pointed out earlier, however, the constellation or convergence of a set of propitious socioeconomic conditions—unlimited demand for U.S. goods and services both at home and abroad, unrivaled U.S. capital in global markets and, perhaps most importantly, political pressure from workers and other grassroots for radical reform—that precipitated and nurtured that long cycle of expansion were unique historical circumstances of the time. Keynesians tend to portray that unique historical experience, the wonderful "golden" years of the U.S. economy in the immediate post-war period, as a general or universal characteristic of capitalist development. It goes without saying, however, that empirical observations or conjunctural developments under certain or specific circumstances ought not to be facilely extrapolated, generalized and elevated to the level of a general theory, or a universal and timeless pattern of actual developments. Such an intellectual exercise would be tantamount to empiricism—not scientific or objective inquiry into a theoretical understanding of the actual socioeconomic developments of the day.

To sum up, the Marxian theory of unemployment, based on his theory of the reserve army of labor, provides a much more robust explanation of the protracted high levels of unemployment than the Keynesian view that attributes the plague of unemployment to the "misguided" or "bad" policies of neoliberalism. Likewise, the Marxian theory of subsistence or near-poverty wages, also based on his theory of the reserve army of labor, provides a more cogent account of how or why such poverty levels of wages, as well as a generalized or nationwide predominance of misery, can go hand-in-hand with high levels of corporate profits and/or stock markets than the Keynesian perceptions, which view a high level of wages as a necessary condition for an expansionary economic cycle.

Perhaps more importantly, the Marxian view that meaningful, lasting economic safety-net programs can be carried out only through overwhelming pressure from the masses—and only on a coordinated global scale—provides a more logical and promising solution to the problem of economic hardship for the overwhelming majority of the world population than the neat, purely intellectual, and nearly apolitical Keynesian stimulus packages on a national level. No matter how long or loud or passionately our good-hearted Keynesians beg for jobs and other New Deal-type reform programs, their pleas for the implementation of such programs are bound to be ignored by governments that are elected and controlled by powerful moneyed interests. Only by mobilizing the masses of workers and other grassroots and fighting, instead of begging, for an equitable share of what is truly the product of their labor, the wealth of nations, can the working majority achieve economic security and human dignity.

Notes

1 International Labour Organization (ILO), *The global employment challenge*, Geneva, 2008; as cited in John Bellamy Foster, Robert W. McChesney and R. Jamil Jonna, The global reserve army of labor and the New Imperialism. *Global Research*, November 6, 2011. Retrieved from www.globalresearch.ca/index.php?context=va&aid=27549).

2 How the case for austerity has crumbled. *New York Review of Books*, June 6, 2013. Retrieved from www.nybooks.com/articles/archives/2013/jun/06/how-case-austerity-has-crumbled/?pagination=false.

References

Baker, D. (2010). *False profits: Recovering from the bubble economy*. San Francisco, CA: Berrett-Koehler Publishers.

Gowan, P. (2010). The Crisis in the Heartland. In M. Konings (Ed.) *The Great Credit Crash*. London and New York: Verso.

Kalur, J. S. (2013). Review of Andrew Kliman's *The failure of capitalist production*. amazon.com. March 14. Retrieved from www.amazon.com/gp/cdp/member-reviews/A1WTYY0ETLH4VQ/ref=cm_pdp_rev_more?ie=UTF8&sort_by=MostRecentReview#R2ZKCGGBY64VF3 (accessed August 28, 2013).

Keynes, J. M. (2010). *The general theory of employment, interest, and money*. Whitefish, MT: Kessinger Publishing, LLC.

Kotz, D. M. (2009). The financial and economic crisis of 2008: A systemic crisis of neoliberal capitalism. *Review of Radical Political Economics*, *41*(3): 305–317.

Krugman, P. (2013). *End this depression now!* New York: W. W. Norton and Company.

Krugman, P. (2011). No, we can't? Or won't? *New York Times*, July 10. Retrieved from www.nytimes.com/2011/07/11/opinion/11krugman.html?_r=0.

Martens, P. (2008). The Obama Bubble Agenda. *CounterPunch*, May 6. Retrieved from www.counterpunch.org/martens05062008.html.

Marx, K. (1967). *Capital*. (Vol. 1). New York: International Publishers.

Melloan, G. (2009). We're all Keynesians again: Nobody can accuse the Fed of inaction. *Wall Street Journal*, January 13 (p A17).

Nasser A. (2011). The political economy of redistribution: Outsourcing jobs, offshoring markets. *CounterPunch*, December 2–4. Retrieved from www.counterpunch.org/2011/12/02/outsourcing-jobs-offshoring-markets/ (accessed March 19, 2013).

Nasser, A. (2009). New deal liberalism writes its obituary. *CounterPunch*, September 21. Retrieved from www.counterpunch.com/nasser09212009.html (accessed March 16, 2012).

Okun, A. (1975). *Equality and efficiency: The big tradeoff*. Washington, DC: Brookings Institution Press.

Palley, T. (2013). *From financial crisis to stagnation*. Cambridge: Cambridge University Press.

Palley, T. (2009). America's exhausted paradigm: Macroeconomic causes of the financial crisis and Great Recession. New American Contract, Washington, DC. Retrieved from http://newamerica.net/files/Thomas_Palley_America%27s_Exhausted_Paradigm.pdf (accessed March 11, 2012).

Reich, R. (2011). Restore the basic bargain (personal blog), November 28. Retrieved from http://robertreich.org/post/13469691304 (accessed September 29, 2013).

Reich, R. (2010). *Aftershock: The next economy and America's future*. New York: Alfred A. Knopf.

Schultze C. (1977). *The public use of private interest*. Washington, DC: Brookings Institution Press.

Shaikh, A. (1987). The falling rate of profit and the economic crisis in the U.S. In Robert C. *et al.* (Eds.) *The imperiled economy*, Book I. New York: *Union for Radical Political Economy*.

Shaikh, A. (1978). An introduction to the history of crisis theories. In Economics Education Project, *U.S. Capitalism in Crisis*. New York: Union for Radical Political Economics (URPE).

Shutt, H. (1998). *The trouble with capitalism: An enquiry into the causes of global economic failure*. London: Zed Books.

Stiglitz, J. (2010). *Freefall: America, free markets, and the sinking of the world economy*. New York: Norton and Company.

Toporowski, J. (2010). *Why the world economy needs a financial crash and other critical essays on finance and financial economics*. London: Anthem Press.

Wray, R. (2008). Financial markets meltdown: What can we learn from Minsky? Public Policy Brief no. 94, The Levy Economic Institute of Bard College, Annandale-on-Hudson, NY.

3 Specious theories of mainstream economics

As discussed in the previous two chapters, both Keynesian and neoliberal explanations of the 2008 financial implosion and the ensuing Great Recession are woefully deficient. They failed to either predict the coming of the crisis, or provide a reasonable explanation when it actually arrived. Nor do they provide an effective solution to the high rates of unemployment and the harrowing living conditions of the overwhelming majority of the people. In fact, the neo-classical economists, working within the straitjacket of the "general equilibrium" model, where there is an "efficient" balance between supply and demand at "rational" price levels in each and all markets, ruled out the incidence of a crisis of the length and magnitude of the one that followed the 2008 market crash. Although their theory allows for occasional disequilibrium, they maintain that such "temporary" or "short-term" imbalances would soon be corrected either by "automatic market adjustments" (the neoliberal paradigm), or by timely government "fine-tuning" of the market (the Keynesian paradigm). As Professor Michel Chossudovsky and his co-author Andrew Marshall (among others) point out:

> By failing to examine the interplay of powerful economic actors in the "real world" economy, the processes of market rigging, financial manipulation and fraud are overlooked. The concentration and centralization of economic decision-making, the role of the financial elites, the economic think tanks, the corporate boardroom: none of these issues are examined in the universities' economics programs. The theoretical construct is dysfunctional; it cannot be used to provide an understanding of the economic crisis.
>
> (2010: xviii)

It is altogether reasonable to argue that neoclassical economics (both conservative and liberal) have created more confusion than clarification, more obfuscation than elucidation. "Economic science" has, indeed, become "an ideological construct which serves to camouflage and justify the New World Order" (ibid.).

Chapter 1 of this book provided a critique of the conservative (or neoliberal) tradition of the neoclassical economics while Chapter 2 provided an evaluation of its liberal (or Keynesian) tradition. In this chapter I shall provide a critical analysis of the neoclassical economics as a whole, that is, of a number of major shortcomings that are shared by both traditions. (As pointed out in the introductory remarks to Chapter 1, the two traditions have much more in common than what differentiates them.) In the first part of the chapter I will evaluate the neoclassical theory of money supply, credit and/or finance capital. In the second part I will focus on the origins of the neoclassical paradigm, and on how it was developed primarily as an ideologically-driven theoretical construct to be counter-posed to the classical economic paradigm—not as an evolution, extension, or elaboration of that earlier paradigm but as a bogus and mystifying substitute for it.

Flawed theory of credit/money supply—and of finance capital

A major reason for mainstream economists' bewilderment in the face of rising financial bubbles and bursts is that, according to their theoretical framework, expansion of finance capital on a macro or national level is not supposed to deviate much from that of industrial capital, as the magnitude of the former is essentially determined or limited by the requirements of the real sector of the economy. The theory maintains that there is an auspicious synergy between the financial and real sectors of an economy: finance capital tends to shadow industrial capital as if its main function is to grease the wheels of the real sector, that is, of manufacturing and commercial undertakings—just as it was more or less the case in the early stages of capitalism, when there was not yet a large, independent financial sector.

This theoretical mindset of neoclassical economists, both neoliberal and Keynesian, follows from their faith in the (barter-like) Walrasian general equilibrium model in which there exists a continuous balance between supply and demand, or between income (as the monetary equivalent of supply, or output) and expenditures (or the "monetarily effective" demand). Production is the starting point in this model: as manufacturers employ labor and means of production to produce goods and services, they also generate income in the form of cost of production, that is, in the form of wages/salaries, interest income, and rental income, etc. As the recipients of incomes thus generated turn around and purchase what they have produced, or helped to be produced, they thereby also establish equilibrium between income and expenditures, or between supply and demand. The income–expenditure balance here is altogether tautological: what is cost of production to employers is (at the same time) income for factors of production. This (continuous or repetitive) relationship is illustrated in mainstream macroeconomic textbooks by a simple diagram called the "circular flow" diagram, or mechanism.

The circular flow mechanism does allow for temporary discrepancies between income/supply and expenditures/demand, as when, for example, a portion of people's incomes, especially of high incomes, is saved, not spent. But this would not seriously disturb the balance between aggregate incomes and expenditures because the savings would be borrowed (through financial intermediaries and institutions such as banks) and invested by manufacturers, thereby closing the temporary gap between income and spending. In a simple macroeconomic model, as long as aggregate national savings (S) are equal to aggregate national investment expenditures (I), that is, as long as "temporary leakages" from the circular flow are offset by injections, equilibrium between supply and demand would prevail.

In the neoliberal view the balance between S and I and, therefore, between income and spending, or demand and supply, is guaranteed by market mechanism: an excess of S over I would be only short-lived as this (temporary) oversupply of loanable funds would soon lead to lower rates of interest, or lower cost of borrowing, which would then encourage businesses and manufacturers to borrow and invest more. This process of borrowing and investing the cheapened or undervalued S would continue until the excess S is used up and equality between S and I is restored.

In the Keynesian view, however, such a spontaneous or automatic restoration of balance between S and I is not guaranteed, which means that a situation of S>I, or insufficient investment spending, may persist for a long time. Under conditions of relative uncertainty, even low interest rates would not induce manufacturers to borrow and invest, or expand. Nor would the owners of savings be willing to part with their savings when interest rates are too low; preferring, instead, to stay liquid in the hope of garnering higher returns when rates go up in the future—the often cited Keynesian term "liquidity trap" or "liquidity preference" was coined in this context. Under such conditions the government can step in, borrow the "idle" savings and spend them ("in behalf of their wealthy owners," as Keynes put it), thereby closing the savings–investment (or income–expenditures) gap.

It is obvious from this brief picture that, according to mainstream economics, the supply of credit and/or the volume of finance capital is determined or limited by the magnitude of aggregate supply, or national output; specifically, by the volume of national savings, which in turn is determined by the magnitude of national output. Although the central bank's policy of "fractional reserve banking" can somewhat stretch the volume of credit beyond the volume of savings, loanable finance capital, according to these economists, is ultimately constrained by the total amount of national savings.

While this may have been true in the early stages of capitalism (when banks as financial intermediaries between savers and investors recycled "idle" savings into money capital for productive investment), it is not the case in the era of advanced capitalist economies where well-established financial markets have become not only independent of but, in fact, dominant over the real or non-financial sector of the economy. The credit system in mature market economies of today is no longer confined by domestic savings or central bank regulation of money supply. The institutional structure of the monetary/financial system which gives the commercial banks the power of creating money many times the amount of their reserves—by virtue of the so-called fractional reserve system—makes the supply of money much more flexible than the domestic savings or formal central bank regulations permit. Commercial banks and other financial institutions are quite resourceful in expanding their lending capacity beyond their legal limits. The apparent idea behind these limits is that, based on the amount of their loanable deposits (as determined by reserve requirements), the commercial banks first determine their lending capacity and then go looking for customers. But the realities are quite the other way around. Half of all new business loans are made to big corporations under credit lines the companies have negotiated with their bankers, legally entitling them to borrow agreed-upon amounts. As one officer of the New York Federal Reserve has put it, "In the real world, banks extend credit ... and look for reserves later. In one way or another, the Federal Reserve will accommodate them" (Heilbroner and Galbraith 1990: 383).

There are a number of ways through which financial intermediaries find reserves beyond their formal or legal lending capacity—ways that have come to be known as "liability management." One way is the use of unutilized reserves (i.e., unutilized lending capacity) of other financial intermediaries. Within the well-developed financial markets of today, funds can easily be moved from financial intermediaries with excess reserves to those with shortages. Another way of expanding their lending capacity is for the financial intermediaries to convince depositors to hold their financial assets in higher yielding forms of deposit which carry lower reserve requirements. Financial intermediaries can also draw upon foreign sources in order to expand their lending capacity, either their own offshore branches or other institutions. The increasing use of this practice has in fact been a major impetus for the explosive growth of the Eurodollar market since the mid-1960s, and it has become a major source of the United States' loanable funds. With so much resourcefulness of commercial banks in augmenting their lending capacity and creating money (debt money, to be sure), their drive for speculative loan-pushing is easily understandable.

Contrary to the neoclassical "circular flow" model, in the era of highly "financialized" capitalism, or the stage of "finance capital," as the late German economist Rudolph Hilferding (1981) put it, demand for credit is not limited to industrial or commercial credit, that is, to debt financing of real investments and sales. In the age of well-developed stock markets, futures markets, real estate markets, commodities markets, derivatives markets, and similar markets for speculation, a large part of credit is demanded for speculative debt financing, or speculative investment—investment in buying and selling of existing assets with the expectation of capital gain. Under these circumstances, parasitic finance capital, feeding on itself by sucking out economic surplus/profits from the real sector, has effectively undermined the neat neoclassical "circular flow" mechanism—where people's savings and industrialists' (retained) earnings are supposed to be recycled through financial intermediaries into productive investment. In the era of the dominance of finance capital, substantial amounts of the real sector's profits-cum-savings that "leak out" of the circular flow into the financial sector never come back to be reinvested productively, as mainstream economic theory postulates. Instead, those savings are systematically syphoned off the real economy and invested in the unproductive, parasitic financial sector.

> One can understand why the financial sector has had so little interest in tracing the effect of rising money and credit on diverting income from the circular flow between producers and consumers, diverting business revenue from new capital formation, and stripping industrial assets and natural resources. Most model builders isolate these long-term structural, environmental and demographic feedbacks as "externalities." But they are part and parcel of reality. So one is tempted to say that the financial element of economic models is too important to be left to bankers and the think tanks they sponsor.
>
> (Hudson and Bezemer 2012)

Many economists have argued that the escalating financialization of the past several decades has been prompted by the "lackluster" growth and/or "low" rates of return in the real sector of the economy (Kliman 2011; Brenner 2009; Bellamy Foster and Magdoff 2010). Evidence shows, however, that capital flight from the real to the financial sector has continued even when profitability has been robust in the real sector. For example, real-sector profit rates were, or have been, quite healthy during all four periods of 1983–1987, 1993–2000, 2003–2007 and 2009–2013. Nonetheless, financialization continued, or has continued, unabated even during these periods of healthy profits; indicating that the lure of speculative profits, greatly facilitated by the extensive deregulation of the financial sector, is strong enough to induce money capital to abandon manufacturing in pursuit of higher returns in the financial sector.

Capital flight from the real to the financial sector, and the divergence between corporate profitability and real investment were highlighted in an article by Robin Harding published in the *Financial Times* (July 24, 2013). Headlined "Corporate Investment: A Mysterious Divergence," the article revealed that, in the past three decades or so, a "disconnect" has developed between corporate profitability and real investment; indicating that, contrary to previous times, a significant portion of corporate profits is not reinvested for capacity building. It is diverted, instead, to financial investment in pursuit of higher returns to shareholders' capital. Prior to 1980s, the two moved in tandem—both about 9 percent of GDP. Since then, and especially in the very recent years, whereas real investment has declined to about 4 percent of GDP, corporate profits have increased to about 12 percent of GDP.

> Profits in the US are at an all-time high but, perversely, investment is stagnant.... According to GMO, the asset manager, profits and overall net investment in the U.S. tracked each other closely until the late 1980s, with both about 9 per cent of gross domestic product. Then the relationship began to break down. After the recession, from 2009, it went haywire. Pre-tax corporate profits are now at record highs—more than 12 per cent of GDP—while net investment is barely 4 per cent of output.
>
> (Ibid.)

The systematic funneling of savings and profits away from the real to the financial sector has, indeed, been encouraged in recent years by the regulators. The *Financial Times* reported that: "In the past two decades most regulators have encouraged banks to shift assets off their balance sheets into SIVs [Special Investment Vehicles] and conduits" (February 5, 2008). Special Investment Vehicles and conduits, like Private Equity Groups, are part of a vast network of shadow (trading) banks that specialize in buying and selling of companies, in managing/supervising with hedge, and in interacting and dealing with a whole host of other "financial engineering" services. Not surprisingly, the financial sector has been growing much faster in recent decades than the real sector of the economy, as it is increasingly absorbing larger and larger shares of national resources:

> In the real world most credit today is spent to buy assets already in place, not to create new productive capacity. Some 80 percent of bank loans in the English-speaking world are real estate mortgages, and much of the balance is lent against stocks and bonds already issued. Banks lend to buyers of real estate, corporate raiders, ambitious financial empire-builders, and to management for debt-leveraged buyouts.
>
> (Ibid.)

Professor Michael Hudson (of the University of Missouri, Kansas City) and a number of other financial experts have labeled the rapidly expanding financial sector as the FIRE sector—standing for finance, insurance and real estate. Designation of the term FIRE conveys (understandably) a negative connotation as the excessive expansion of this sector tends to re-allocate resources from productive to unproductive activities, to undermine the potential for real socioeconomic growth and to further aggravate the already lopsided distribution of income and resources against the overwhelming majority of the people. Figure 3.1 clearly shows this ominous trend: it shows that while bank lending to the FIRE sector as a share of GDP has quadrupled since the 1950s, the similar ratio for bank lending to the real sector has remained nearly unchanged.

The following are a few additional examples of the astronomical growth of the FIRE sector during the past three decades or so: Between 1980 and 2005, profits in the financial sector increased by 800 percent, more than three times the growth in non-financial sectors. In the early 1990s there existed only a couple of hedge funds; by 2007, their number had grown to 10,000. The number of mortgage brokers, replacing old-style Savings & Loans and regional banks, has likewise mushroomed in recent years/decades: 50,000 of them, employing nearly 400,000 brokers, more than the whole U.S. textile industry (Fraser 2012). As the unusually candid manager of the hedge fund Raymond Dalio of Bridgewater Associates bluntly put it:

> The money that's made from manufacturing stuff is a pittance in comparison to the amount of money made from shuffling money around. Forty-four

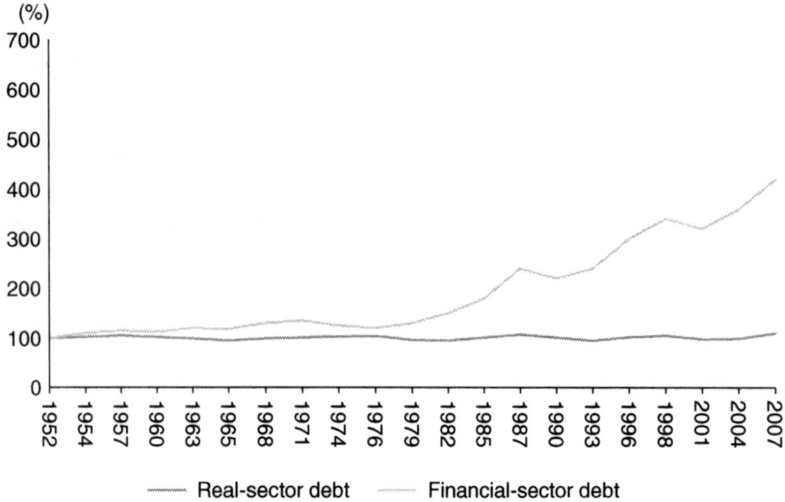

Figure 3.1 Total U.S. bank loans to real and financial sectors (% of GDP), 1952–2007 (source: Based on the Z Table in the U.S. flow of fund accounts, series FL794194005.Q; as cited (and graphed) in Bezemer 2012: 20, Graph 1).

> percent of all corporate profits in the U.S. come from the financial sector compared with only 10 percent from the manufacturing sector.
>
> (As quoted in Phillips 2009: 211)

As the market mechanism underlying the steady rise and expansion of parasitic finance capital has torpedoed the well-groomed neoclassical "circular flow" model, it has also greatly undermined the Keynesian notion of "liquidity preference." According to this idea, in the face of "overcapacity" and/or insufficient demand in the real sector, which would create an economic atmosphere of uncertainty and stagnation, manufacturers tend to retrench or abstain from further investment, or capacity building. Due to market uncertainty, they would instead prefer cash, as would banks and other entities in possession of money, or liquidity—hence the term "liquidity preference." While this concept may occasionally be the case (especially in the earlier stages of capitalism, or when Keynes put forth the hypothesis in the 1930s), in the era of widely financialized market structures it has lost validity. For, in light of the financial sector's "creative" financial innovations, owners of financial balances (savings) are much less likely to hold cash, as Keynes argued, than invest in all kinds of lucrative financial/speculative instruments. In the age of diverse and enticing financial investment opportunities, holding cash (or staying "liquid," as Keynes put it) is not the only or the best option to protect one's savings against low interest rates and uncertainty in the real sector; investment in financial assets seems to be a more attractive alternative.

It was this mechanism of independent development of fictitious finance capital that gradually removed most of the regulatory obstacles from its path of expansion; steadily outgrowing all proportions relative to the real economy, increasingly becoming unsustainable, and ultimately imploding in 2008. It was also this process of the independently expanding finance capital—with only fictional connection to the underlying real values in the economy as a whole—that caught mainstream economists, trapped in their neat "circular flow" model, by surprise. As noted earlier, the model is built on the basis of these economists' near-barter economic paradigm, an economy where money is implicitly treated as largely a means of exchange or circulation—not as an ideal or ultimate repository of the accumulated wealth. In this model, financial cycles neatly follow real cycles: they expand when real cycles expand, and contract when they contract. As such, there is hardly any possibility for financial bubbles to emerge and expand independent of the real sector of the economy—the financial sector is treated essentially as a service or subsidiary sector to the real sector.

The circular flow model can, of course, serve as a useful tool or concept for analytical purposes. The problem is that mainstream economists seem to have been stuck in the abstract model, in the earlier stages of capitalism, unable to see how in the era of giant banks and other colossal financial institutions finance capital can (and does) grow independent of industrial capital, thereby leading to financial inflations, followed by implosions.

It might be argued: who cares whether a financial bubble follows a real sector expansion or whether it is formed ab-ovo, i.e., in the absence of such an expansion. Such a distinction, however, is critically important to an understanding of how in the age of advanced financial markets finance capital has become largely independent of industrial capital, and how it has therefore undermined the neoclassical concepts of general equilibrium, of circular flow mechanism, and of national savings as the main source of supply of money and/or credit. Sucking financial resources from the rest of the economy, as well as generating fictitious capital out of thin air through speculation/gambling, parasitic finance capital feeds on itself—just like a real parasite. Neoclassical economists have not, so far, been able to reconcile the financial sector with their circular flow and/or general equilibrium model. Sadly, instead of trying to incorporate the financial sector into their real sector model, they have chosen to ignore it lest it should disturb their shipshape, convenient model (Hudson and Bezemer 2012).

Ideological foundations of the neoclassical economics

> In pointing out the consequences of a set of abstract assumptions, one need not be committed unduly as to the relation between reality and these assumptions.
>
> (Paul Samuelson, Nobel Laureate in Economics, 1966: 791)

The quotation in this prologue from the famed economist Paul Samuelson, maintaining that the internal consistency of a theory—in the sense that the findings or conclusions of the theory follow logically from its premises or assumptions—is more important than its relevance (or irrelevance) to the real world, is by no means an exception or a minority view among neoclassical economists. It is, indeed, typical of this school of economic thought. Here is another example from another Nobel Laureate economist:

> Economic theory proper, indeed, is nothing more than a system of logical relations between certain sets of assumptions and the conclusions derived from them.... The validity of a theory proper does not depend on the correspondence or lack of it between the assumptions of the theory or its conclusions and observations in the real world. A theory as an internally consistent system is valid if the conclusions follow logically from its premises, and the fact that neither the premises nor the conclusions correspond to reality may show that the theory is not very useful, but does not invalidate it. In any pure theory, all propositions are essentially tautological, in the sense that the results are implicit in the assumptions made.
>
> (Vickery 1964: 5)

In a critique of this blatant disregard for actual developments in the real world, Professor Michael Hudson (of the University of Missouri, Kansas City) writes:

> Such disdain for empirical verification is not found in the physical sciences. Its popularity in the social sciences is sponsored by vested interests. There is always self-interest behind methodological madness. That is because success requires heavy subsidies from special interests, who benefit from an erroneous, misleading or deceptive economic logic. Why promote unrealistic abstractions, after all, if not to distract attention from reforms aimed at creating rules that oblige people actually to earn their income rather than simply extracting it from the rest of the economy?
>
> (2009)

In a similar vein, a group of French graduate students in economics recently wrote an open letter, akin to a manifesto, critical of their academic education in economics as "autistic" and "pathologically distant from the problems of real markets and real people":

> We wish to escape from imaginary worlds! Most of us have chosen to study economics so as to acquire a deep understanding of the economic phenomena with which the citizens of today are confronted. But the teaching that is offered ... does not generally answer this expectation.... This gap in the teaching, this disregard for concrete realities, poses an enormous problem for those who would like to render themselves useful to economic and social actors.
>
> (As quoted in Bigelow 2005)

The word "autistic" may be offensive and politically incorrect; but it certainly provides an apt description of mainstream economics.

How or why did economics, as a crucially important subject of inquiry into an understanding of social structures, evolve in this fashion, that is, as an apparently rigorous and technically elaborate discipline without much usefulness in the way of understanding or solving economic problems? Why does the neoclassical/mainstream economic paradigm ignore actual developments in favor of elegant but abstract models and myths?

An attempt at answering these questions would not be very fruitful without looking into the origins of the neoclassical economics, and how it supplanted the classical economics that prevailed from the early stages of capitalism until the second half of the nineteenth century—supplanted not as an extension or elaboration of that earlier school of economic thought but as a deviation from or antithesis to it.

Well-known classical economists like Adam Smith, David Ricardo, John Stuart Mill and Karl Marx sought to understand capitalism, the relatively new mode of production that evolved from the demise of feudalism. They studied the essence of value, the determinants of price (beyond or prior to the interaction between supply and demand) and the foundations of growth and accumulation—in short, the sources of the "wealth of nations," as Smith put it, or "the laws of motion of capitalist production," as Marx put it. They also sought to understand the basis or logic of the distribution of economic resources under the new mode of production, the origins of the various types of income: wages/salaries, interest income, rental income, and profits. To this end, they distinguished two major types of work or economic activities: productive and unproductive—productive labor, productive investment and productive enterprise (manufacturing) versus unproductive labor, unproductive/financial investment and unproductive enterprises such as buying and selling, or speculation. Accordingly, they saw the capitalist social structure as consisting of different classes of conflicting or antagonistic interests with one another: capitalists, workers, landlords, tenants/renters, and the poor.

Not surprisingly, the study of these issues was called "political economy," as moral, philosophical and political questions underlying these issues were integrally intertwined with economic questions. Indeed, Karl Marx argued that politics was essentially a condensed expression of economics. Although Marx's keenly insightful analysis of capitalism, as reflected in his three volume opus-magnum *Capital*, was (and still is) largely censored as too radical, the works of Smith, Ricardo and Mill were widely read and discussed, by both scholars and policy makers. Two books in particular, Smith's *Wealth of Nations* (1776) and Ricardo's *Principles of Political Economy and Taxation* (1817), proved to be of profound and lasting impact. "These books offered explanations of how societies become wealthy and how they can stay that way. They made the accelerated pace of urban life and industrial workshops seem understandable as part of a program that modern history would follow" (Bigelow 2005).

These classical economists wrote in an era that could still be considered a time of transition: transition from feudalism to capitalism. Although feudalism, landed aristocracy and mercantilism were in decline in Western Europe, especially in Britain, the powerful interests vested in those older modes of social structure and economic activity still fiercely resisted the rising new mode of production, the modern industrial capitalism, and its champions, called the "bourgeoisie." In other words, the ruling elites were divided between those whose interests were vested in the declining old order and those who benefited from the rising order of industrial capitalism. In the second half of the eighteenth and first half of nineteenth centuries, the conflicting interests of these two factions of the ruling elites served as powerful economic grounds for a fierce political/ideological struggle between the partisans of the two sides. Whereas the (declining or endangered) elites of the old system viewed the rising bourgeoisie as undermining their traditional rights and privileges through industrialization and urbanization, the modern capitalist elites viewed the old establishment as hindering rapid industrialization and marketization by blocking or delaying, for example, the development of capitalist production in agriculture, and by extracting exorbitant fees and rents for the use of what they owned: land and natural resources.

In the ensuing ideological battle between the champions of the old and new orders, the writings of Smith, Ricardo, Mill and those who shared their ideas proved quite helpful to the proponents of the new order. As influential intellectuals who were concerned that the hindering influences and extractive businesses of the old establishment may hamper a clean break from the old modes of economic activity, they wrote passionately about what created real values and "wealth of nations," or conversely, what was wasteful and, therefore, stinted the pace of industrialization, "proletarianization"/"depeasantization" and national development.

> Classical political economists from the Physiocrats through Adam Smith, John Stuart Mill and their Progressive Era followers were reformers in the sense that they treated the rentier sectors as extracting transfer payments rather than earning a return for producing actual output ("services"). Their labor theory of value found its counterpart in the "economic rent theory of prices" to distinguish the necessary costs of production and doing business (reduced ultimately to the value of labor) from "unearned income" consisting mainly of land rent, monopoly rent, and financial interest and fees. The various categories of rentier income were depicted as the "hollow" element of prices.
>
> (Hudson and Bezemer 2012)

To this end, their writings included lengthy discussions of the labor theory of value—the theory that human labor constitutes the essence of value—and the related notions of productive and unproductive labor or activities. They characterized the propertied classes that reaped income, profit or rent by virtue of controlling the assets or properties that the economy needed in order to function as the "rentier," "unproductive" or "parasitic" classes. Rentier classes collect their unearned proceeds from ownership "without working, risking, or economizing", wrote John Stuart Mill of the landlords and money-lenders of his day, arguing that "they grow richer, as it were in their sleep." Mill also famously asked:

> What claim have they, on the general principle of social justice, to this accession of riches? In what would they have been wronged if society had, from the beginning, reserved the right of taxing the spontaneous increase of rent, to the highest amount required by financial exigencies?
>
> (As quoted in Hudson and Bezemer 2012)

The policy objective of the classical analysis is unmistakable: "to minimize the economy's cost structure by freeing industrial capitalism from these carry-overs from feudalism." Their guiding principle "was to minimize the role of rentier income (economic rent) by public investment, tax policy and regulation" (ibid.).

It is thus obvious that during the early stages of industrial revolution, when the old establishment still posed serious challenges to the relatively new and evolving capitalist mode of production, the view of human labor as the source of real values, expounded by the classical economists, provided a strong theoretical case or justification for industrial expansion and/or capitalist development.

> During this period, industrial capitalists were usually involved in directing, coordinating, and overseeing the actual processes of production. The central focus or objective of their endeavors had been rapid accumulation of industrial capital, and their main intellectual concern had been to understand the source of capital accumulation. The labor theory of value perspective had furnished the most serviceable insights into the process of capital accumulation, focusing on the distinction between productive and unproductive labor. It had shown how productive labor was the source of the surplus labor [or value] that made the expansion of capital possible. Thus, in its earliest formulations, the labor theory of value reflected the perspective of, and was serviceable in the fulfillment of the objective needs of, the industrial capitalist class.
>
> (Hunt 2002: 282)

Although the rising capitalist class found the labor theory of value (and its logical implications for class conflicts) potentially troubling, that concern was temporarily pushed to the backburner as the main threat at this stage of capitalist development came from the landowning/rentier classes, not the working class. Indeed, history shows that in nearly all the so-called "bourgeois-democratic" revolutions, signifying the historical transition from pre-capitalist to capitalist formations, the burgeoning working class, the newly proletarianized peasants, sided with the bourgeoisie against its pre-capitalist protagonists. Instances of such epochal transitions include the well-documented revolutions in England (1648), France (1789), Germany (1848) and the United States (1861–1865), better known as the Civil War.

By the mid-nineteenth century, however, this pattern of social structure and/or class alliances was drastically changed. Concentration of capital and the rise of corporation had by the last third of the nineteenth century gradually overshadowed the role of individual manufacturers as the drivers of the industrial development. "The accumulation became systematized, institutionalized, and regularized." In place of owners/managers, more and more "corporate managers were hired to direct and oversee industrial enterprises and to channel profits automatically as part of a perpetual accumulation process." Accordingly, the now-mature and confident bourgeoisie came gradually "to resemble, in social and economic functions, the landlord class. Increasingly, profits and interest came to be the result of passive ownership," similar to absentee landownership (Hunt 2002: 283).

Along with agricultural production on an increasingly capitalistic basis, these developments meant that the interests of the ruling circles were no longer as much in conflict with one another as they had been during the earlier, transitional periods to capitalism. Furthermore, the rise of corporation and continued concentration of capital was gradually leading to the concentration of greater and greater numbers of workers in large scale manufacturing sites; which gradually precipitated working class struggles against capitalists for better wages and working conditions. This obviously meant a radical reconfiguration of social and/or class alliances: the industrial bourgeoisie and the landowners were no longer adversaries, as they were all now capitalists and allies; and the working class, which had earlier supported the bourgeoisie against the landed aristocracy, was their class enemy. What added to the fears of the capitalist class of the growing and relatively militant working class was the spread of Marx's theory of "labor as the essence of value," and the corresponding theory of distribution, which were by the mid- to late-nineteenth century frequently discussed among the leading circles of industrial workers, especially in Britain and France.

These changes in actual social and economic developments, in turn, triggered changes in the ruling class's preferences regarding theories of capitalist production and/or market mechanism. Industrial capitalists who had earlier used the labor theory of value to their advantage in their struggle against the old, precapitalist establishment were now quite fearful of and hostile toward that theory. Instead, "the theoretical and ideological needs of the owners of industrial capital became identical with those of the landlords and merchant capitalists. They all needed a theory that sanctioned their ownership"; a theory that obfuscated, instead of clarifying, the origins of real values and the sources of wealth and/or income—hence, the shift from classical to neoclassical economics (ibid.).

The formal theoretical shift from classicism to neoclassicism was pioneered (in the last three decades of the nineteenth century) by three economists: William Stanley Jevons, Carl Menger and Leon Walras. A detailed discussion of these pioneers of neoclassical economics is beyond the purview of this study. Suffice it to say that all three categorically shunned the labor theory of value in favor of utility theory of value. Jevons, the forerunner of the three, confidently argued, for example, that "value depends entirely upon utility." Indeed, he was quite indignant of those who attributed value to labor:

> A student of economics has no hope of ever being clear and correct in his ideas of science if he thinks of value as at all a thing or an object, or even as anything which lies in a thing or object.... The word value, so far as it can be correctly used, merely expresses the circumstance of its exchanging in a certain ratio for some other substance.
>
> (As quoted in Hunt 2002: 251)

At the heart of the theoretical/philosophical shift was, therefore, the move from labor to utility as the source of value: a commodity's value no longer came from its labor content, as classical economists had argued, but from its utility to consumers. The new paradigm thus shifted the focus of economic inquiry from the factory and production to the market and circulation/exchange. By the same token as the new school of economic thought abandoned the classicals' labor theory of value in favor of the utility theory of value, it also discarded the concept of value, which comes from human labor, in favor of price, which is formed in the sphere of circulation, or market, by supply and demand interactions. Henceforth, there was no difference between value and price; the two have since been used interchangeably or synonymously in neoclassical economics.

The distinction between value and price categories was important to classical economists such as Smith, Ricardo and Marx. To understand the limits to the productive capacity of a market economy and, therefore, the conditions for production and/or reproduction of the capitalist system, these economists first abstracted from the price and the sphere of exchange altogether. Only after studying the process of production, the formation of the values of commodities and the conditions for the accumulation and "reproduction" of capital did they extend their study from abstract to concrete, from partial to total, and from production to circulation and/or the market. This systemic approach would allow, they believed, for a better understanding of the relationship between value or labor categories, on the one hand, and price or monetary categories, on the other. It would allow, for example, how a commodity's value, which is determined in the process of production by the amount of labor time embodied in it, is affected by the forces of supply and demand once it is moved from production to the market; that is, how or to what extent its price may deviate from its value, depending on the quantities supplied or demanded of that commodity. It would also show that not only profits but also interest and rental incomes ultimately come from surplus value. It followed that, therefore, for an economy to be viable, the (monetary) sum of these various categories of income or earnings should not exceed or deviate much from the underlying magnitude of surplus value (or net national income/output) generated in that economy. Implications of this method of inquiry, which keeps a close tab on the relationship between real and financial categories, and which was abandoned by neoclassical economists, for financial bubbles and, therefore, economic stability/instability are enormous.

These developments explain why from the middle of the nineteenth century onward the capitalist class found the neoclassical field of inquiry, which focused on the sphere of circulation or the market, a safer place than the classicals' focus on the factory or production, which clearly showed that their profits came from the surplus value created by labor, that higher wages meant lower profits (and vice versa), and that there existed an inherent conflict between their interests and those of the working class. Once the focus of inquiry was thus shifted from how commodities are produced to how they are bought and sold, the distinction between workers and capitalists, between producers and appropriators, became invisible. In the marketplace all people appear as essentially identical: they are all households, consumers or "economic agents" who derive utility from consuming commodities, and who pay for those commodities according to the amount of the utility/pleasure they derive from their consumption. They are also identical in the neoclassical sense that they are all "rational," "calculating," and utility "maximizing" market players. Neoclassical forefather Stanley Jevons wrote:

> To satisfy our wants to the utmost with the least effort—to procure the greatest amount of what is desirable at the expense of the least that is undesirable—in other words, to *maximize pleasure*, is the problem of economics.
>
> (As quoted in Hunt 2002: 252)

A major implication of this new perspective was that (in the marketplace and, therefore, in a market economy) social harmony and "brotherhood," not class conflict, was the prevailing mode of social structure. "The supposed conflict of labor with capital is a delusion," Jevons asserted, arguing that "We ought not look at such subjects from a class point of view," because "in economics at any rate [we] *should regard all men as brothers.*" Jevons further argued:

> He who pays a high price must either have a very great need of that which he buys, or very little need of that which he pays for it; on either supposition there is gain by exchange. In questions of this sort there is but one rule which can be safely laid down, namely that no one will buy a thing unless he expects advantage from the purchase; *and perfect freedom of exchange, therefore, tends to the maximizing of utility.*
>
> (As quoted in Hunt 2002: 254)

The view of a social structure as equally or similarly positioned individuals in the market domain is somewhat similar to a religious perspective of social composition: we are all Christians, Muslims, Jews, Buddhists, etc. It is also analogous to a nationalist or nationalistic perspective: we are all Americans, Chinese, Mexicans and the like; we all have common interests, and we all need to make sacrifices.

It should be pointed out (in passing) that the utility theory of value did not start with Jevons. The theory had already been spelled out in the late eighteenth and early nineteenth centuries by earlier economists such as Jeremy Bentham, Jean-Baptiste Say, Thomas Malthus and Claude Frédéric Bastiat. However, Jevons and his utilitarian contemporaries of the second half of the nineteenth century added a new concept to the received theory: the concept of marginal utility or, more specifically, diminishing marginal utility. According to this concept, the utility derived from the use or consumption of a commodity diminishes with every additional unit consumed. Furthermore, total utility can increase while marginal utility decreases as long as the latter is positive; meaning that the former would be maximum when the latter diminishes to zero. Additionally, it is the marginal, not total, utility that determines how much of each commodity "a rational," "calculating" and "optimizing" consumer should use/consume. That optimum level of consuming or purchasing a commodity will be reached when the marginal utility of that commodity, that is, the mental or subjective marginal price/worth of the commodity to the consumer, becomes equal to the market price.

Despite the fact that Jevons' addition of the concept of marginal utility to the received utility theory of value was conceptually very simple (indeed, the whole concept of utility and the so-called "law of diminishing marginal utility" are altogether truisms), it nonetheless proved to be instrumentally or technically a very important notion in the neoclassical economics. For, the term "marginal" was soon extended to other economic categories such as marginal cost, marginal revenue, and the like; thereby paving the way for the application of differential calculus to economics—hence, the dawn of "marginalism," or "marginal revolution." "By introducing the notion of marginalism into utilitarian economics, Jevons had found a way in which the utilitarian view of human beings as rational, calculating maximizers could be put into mathematical terms" (Hunt 2002: 252).

To maximize the total utility that a consumer derives from consuming a number of commodities x, y and z, a "rational" consumer, according to the neoclassical theory, would or should allocate his/her budget between the purchase of these items such that the utility derived from the last dollar spent on each and every item garners the same amount of utility. Using differential calculus, this perception of the "rational" behavior of an "ideal" consumer is shown as: $MU_x / P_x = MU_y / P_y = MU_z / P_z$, where MU stands for marginal utility and P stands for price. [Mathematical proof or illustration of these ratios and relations is beyond the purview of this discussion; nor is it germane to the discussion. Suffice it to point out that the equality between marginal utility–price ratios follows from the mathematical proposition that to maximize certain quantity (in this case total utility) that is a function of a number of variables (in this case x, y and z), subject to certain constraints (in this case budget and/or prices of x, y and z), the first derivative of the function with respect to each variable has to be (or be set) equal to zero. Readers interested in details of this discussion can readily find the respective mathematical calculations, which are incidentally quite simple, in any introductory microeconomics textbook].

Whereas the utilitarian views of the earlier economists had been firmly discredited in the late eighteenth and early nineteenth centuries by proponents of the labor theory of value as truisms that did not explain much of the real world economic developments, the math-coded utilitarianism of Jevons (and his fellow neoclassicals since then) has been shielded from such criticisms by a protective cover of mathematical veneer. Despite the fact that, aside from the mathematical mask, the new notion of utility represented no conceptual or theoretical advances over the earlier version, it was celebrated as a "revolution" in economic thought, the so-called "neoclassical revolution." Presenting a body of largely axiomatic principles, or religious-like normative guidelines (such as how "rational" consumers should behave), by means of elaborate and mesmerizing mathematics is like covering weeds with Astroturf, or masking a poor quality cake with ornamental icing.

In their drive to abstract from the complexities of real-world economics in order to make their discipline more amenable to mathematical modeling and, therefore, look scientific, not only do neoclassical economists tend to distort the reality of actual economic developments, they also misrepresent or abstract from real human behaviors and characteristics:

> In conceiving their discipline as a search for mathematical laws, economists have abstracted to their own ideal conditions, which for the most part consist of an utterly denuded vision of man himself. What they consider "friction" is the better part of what makes us human: our interactions with one another, our irrational desires. Today we often think of science and religion as standing in opposition, but the "scientific" turn made by Jevons and his fellows only served to enshrine the faith of their evangelical predecessors. The evangelicals believed that the market was a divine system, guided by spiritual laws. The "scientific" economists saw the market as a natural system, a principle of equilibrium produced in the balance of individual souls.
>
> (Bigelow 2005)

Despite its irrelevance, or uselessness, neoclassical economics is neither uninteresting nor illogical. Within its own premises and presuppositions it is interesting, logical and mathematically rigorous; which explains why it is packaged as a scientific discipline. But, again, it falls pitifully short of explaining how real world markets or economies work, or how economic crises, as inherent occurrences to a capitalist economy, take place; or what to do to counter such crises that would help not only the capitalist/financial elites but the society at large. Although most mainstream economists proudly characterize their discipline as scientific, adornment of the discipline by a façade of mathematics does not really make it scientific. In reality, the math superstructure simply masks the flawed or unreliable theoretical foundation of the discipline.

A major argument of this chapter (and of this study as a whole) has been that the inability or weakness of the neoclassical economics in providing an understanding of the 2008 financial collapse (and the ensuing Great Recession) is that it is heavily infected with a class-based ideological bias that renders it incapable of providing either an objective diagnosis of the crisis, or a humane prescription for its recovery. Accordingly, I have argued that, as pointed out earlier in this chapter, the neoclassical economics (both conservative and liberal) has created more confusion than clarification or understanding.

This does not mean that the many economists who teach their discipline or otherwise work as economic professionals are necessarily guilty of obfuscation, or deliberately promoting a faulty paradigm. Most economists sincerely believe in the integrity of their discipline as they carry out highly specialized research or produce scholarly publications. Economists' confidence or faith in their discipline, however, does not make it any less flawed. They simply teach or carry out elaborate scholarly research work within a faulty paradigm without questioning, or even detecting, some of the submerged defects that make the discipline dysfunctional. How is this possible? Why is it that most economists are unaware of the specious theoretical foundations of their discipline?

The answer, at least in part, is that the attraction to, or perhaps entrapment in, the economics field of study usually starts with the first economics class they take. It is rather well-known that most students are turned off by their first encounter with the discipline. But the small minority who like the subject tend to become quite enamored with it. These are usually students who either have an interest in or a good training in mathematics and quantitative methods of analysis or study. And since mainstream economics has increasingly become quantified, they get a kick out of applying their mathematical skills to the discipline. And as they delve deeper into the study of neoclassical economics at the graduate level, and apply their technical abilities to the discipline, they tend to become fascinated by the neatness of the models they build, by the impressive multivariate regressions they run and analyze, by the elegant graphs they draw, or by the impressive mathematical equations they construct. The fact that such mathematical or quantitative exercise often takes place in an abstract world of near-irrelevancy is either unimportant, or only of secondary importance to their mesmerizing findings. As economics professor Steve Keen notes:

> Neoclassical economics has become a religion. Because it has a mathematical veneer, and I emphasize the word veneer, they actually believe it's true. Once you believe something is true, you're locked into its way of thinking unless there's something that can break in from the outside and destroy that confidence.
>
> (cited in Campbell 2010)

It can be argued that even then, that is, even in the event of "something breaking in from the outside," most economists, deeply wedded to their profession—and dependent on it as the source of both intellectual and financial survival—would most likely be in denial, and would continue working within the only academic tradition or path they know how to navigate.

References

Bellamy Foster, J. and Magdoff, H. (2010). Financial implosion and economic stagnation. In M. Chossudovsky and A. G. Marshall (Eds.) *The Great Global Economic Crisis*. Montreal, Canada: Center for Research on Globalization.

Bezemer, D. J. (2012). Finance and growth: When credit helps, and when it hinders. University of Groningen (the Netherlands). Retrieved from http://ineteconomics.org/sites/inet.civicactions.net/files/bezemer-dirk-berlin-paper.pdf (accessed September 23, 2013).

Bigelow, G. (2005). Let there be markets: The evangelical roots of economics. *Harper's*, May. Retrieved from http://harpers.org/archive/2005/05/let-there-be-markets/ (accessed February 11, 2013).

Brenner, R. (2009). What is good for Goldman Sachs is good for America: The origins of the current crisis. Unpublished paper, Center for Social Theory and Comparative History, University of California (Los Angeles). Retrieved from www.sscnet.ucla.edu/issr/cstch/papers/BrennerCrisisTodayOctober2009.pdf (accessed November 10, 2012).

Campbell, D. (2010). Post-autistic economics. Retrieved from http://deborahcampbell.org/writing/politics/post-autistic-economics/ (accessed September 30, 2013).

Chossudovsky, M. and Marshall, G. A. (Eds.) (2010). *The great global economic crisis*. Montreal, Canada: Center for Research on Globalization.

Financial Times (2008). Spanish banks spared huge writedowns.

Fraser, S. (2012). The archeology of decline: Debtpocalypse and the hollowing out of America. *TomDispatch.com*, December 2. Retrieved from www.tomdispatch.com/blog/175623/ (accessed September 30, 2013).

Harding, R. (2013). Corporate investment: A mysterious divergence. *Financial Times*, July 24. Retrieved from www.ft.com/intl/cms/s/0/8177af34- eb21–11e2-bfdb-00144feabdc0.html#axzz2dN45MG7r (accessed August 29, 2013).

Heilbroner, R. and Galbraith, J. (1990). *Understanding macroeconomics*. Englewood Cliffs, NJ: Prentice Hall.

Hilferding, R. (1981 [1910]). *Finance capital: A study of the latest phase of capitalist development*. Tom Bottomore (Ed.). London: Routledge & Kegan Paul.

Hudson, M. (2009). Krugman's attack on my review of Samuelson. December 20. Retrieved from http://michael-hudson.com/2009/12/krugmans-attack-on-my-review-of-samuelson/.

Hudson, M. and Bezemer, D. (2012). Incorporating the rentier sectors into a financial model. *World Economic Review*, *1*(1). Retrieved from http://wer.worldeconomicsassociation.org/article/view/36 (accessed April 05, 2013).

Hunt, K. E. (2002). *History of economic thought: A critical perspective* (2nd ed.). New York and London: M. E. Sharpe.

Jevons, W. S. (1970). *The theory of political economy* (2nd ed.). R. D. Collison Black (Ed.). Baltimore, MD: Penguin.

Kliman, A. (2011). *The failure of capitalist production: Underlying causes of the Great Recession*. Retrieved from www.marxisthumanistinitiative.org/economic-crisis/new-book-the-failure-of-capitalist-production.html (accessed July 8, 2013).

Phillips, K. (2009). *Bad money: Reckless finance, failed politics, and the global crisis of American capitalism*. New York: Penguin.

Samuelson, P. A. (1966). *The collected scientific papers of Paul A. Samuelson* (Vol. 2). Cambridge, MA: MIT Press.

Vickery, W. (1964). *Microeconomics*. New York: Harcourt, Brace, and World.

4 Evolution and characteristics of finance capital—a new phase, not just another cycle

> It is well enough that people ... do not understand our banking and monetary system, for if they did, I believe there would be a revolution before tomorrow morning.
>
> Henry Ford, American automobile industrialist[1]

> Just as some great thinkers in the middle ages devoted themselves to alchemy, similarly in the realm of finance capital men and women devote themselves to the pursuit of the absurd, converting money into money without production. However these modern alchemists are revered as brilliant of mind, bold of spirit and are rewarded for their semi-criminal behaviour beyond dreams of avarice.
>
> John Weeks, Professor Emeritus of Economics

As pointed out in Chapter 2, many Keynesian economists envisioned an opportunity in the 2008 financial meltdown and the ensuing economic crisis: in the "crisis of neoliberal economics," they saw an opening for a new dawn of Keynesian economics, or the coming of a "second" New Deal. More than five years later, it is abundantly clear that such expectations amounted to no more than wishful thinking, as neoliberal economics continue to be dominant in both academic and policy circles while the much-hoped-for Keynesian prescriptions are completely ignored. The question is why? Why did the dreams of a Keynesian renewal turn into disappointment? Where or why did the Keynesians go wrong in their prognosis of the "dawn of another New Deal"?

A major reason for why Keynesian economists have gone awry in their optimistic expectations is a deplorable lack of class perspective in their analysis, which is grounded in the unrealistic premise that policy-making is a simple matter of technical expertise or economic know-how, that is, a matter of choice. A second (and related) major flaw in the these economists' perspective stems from their misconceptions about the social origin, the economic role and the political power of the state: an outlook that perceives the state power as above economic or class interests, and that it can, therefore, control the market, or capitalism, in the interests of all.

This chapter is devoted to another major flaw in the Keynesian (as well as the neoliberal) school of economic thought: the grave absence of a historical perspective. This crucially important void explains why most mainstream economists failed to see that the financial meltdown of 2008 and the subsequent economic contraction represented more than just another recessionary cycle. More importantly, they represented a structural change, a new phase in the development of capitalism, the age of "finance capital," as the late German economist Rudolph Hilferding (1981) put it. The gradual rise of finance capital to the present state of dominance began in the late 1960s and early 1970s; after its speculative behavior had been severely restricted following the imperatives of the Great Depression and the financial needs of WW II. Financial innovations of recent years/decades are internally-driven processes and strategies that are incidental to the dynamics of the expansion of capitalism in general, and of finance capital in particular. Contrary to Keynesian critics of deregulation and other neoliberal policies, such innovations are as much the effects of neoliberal policies of deregulation as they are the causes of those policies (Toporowski 2010; Kindleberger 2000).

Earlier instances of financial innovations

Although the current domination of advanced market economies by finance capital seems new, it is in fact a throwback, or retrogression, to the capitalism of the late nineteenth and early twentieth centuries, when monopolistic big businesses and giant financial institutions dominated advanced market economies of the time. In pre-capitalist economies as well as in the early stages of capitalism, credit for commercial or production purposes was usually granted against physical collaterals such as real estate. That kind of credit, however, proved insufficient for the financing of major infrastructural projects such as the construction of extensive railroad networks, or large-scale production enterprises that proliferated in the second half of the nineteenth century. Such large-scale industrial and engineering undertakings brought forth the institution of modern corporations and, along with it, a new category of financial innovation: company stocks and bonds. The passage of Companies Acts in the second half of the nineteenth century in a number of rapidly industrializing countries greatly facilitated the establishment of modern corporations that could secure credit by issuing stocks and bonds. These developments also brought forth a new form of wealth or property ownership: financial assets, against which credit could be secured in the same manner as against tangible assets.

Of course, bond trading has a much earlier history than the nineteenth century. Kings and other pre-capitalist rulers frequently issued bonds (and annuities too) to secure funds for the financing of wars or other needs of royal families. Even the issuance of company stocks as a financing tool started long before nineteenth century. A ground-breaking instance of such financial innovation was the notorious John Law's scheme, in the first decades of the eighteenth century, to secure bank credit to finance his French Mississippi Company, as well as the comparable scheme in the case of South Sea Company. Law also pioneered the share option, and the ventures themselves represented a prototype of the privatizations of state companies that became so common after the 1980s. The disastrous bankruptcy of Law's ventures, also known as the bursting of the Mississippi and South Sea bubbles, may well have set back the progress of credit innovation for a century and a half. They did, however, reveal "the part that financial innovation plays in cycles of boom and bust in financial markets" (Toporowski 2010: 29).

Occasional uses of stocks and bonds in those earlier times, however, were neither systematic nor really systemic. Furthermore, the collateral in those earlier times consisted largely of physical or palpable assets. It was only in the second half of the nineteenth century that credit innovations based on financial assets became a common and systematic practice. As this practice greatly enhanced the potential for credit extension and financial inflation, it also increased the risk of financial instability. Increased lending/borrowing against financial assets led to increased demand for those assets and, therefore, increased price of the assets. The rise in the value of the collateral (financial assets), in turn, made more lending/borrowing possible. In the manner of a vicious circle, this mutually-reinforcing process of high asset prices, high purchasing power/demand and high debt set in motion a spiral of asset price inflation and credit expansion, whose ultimate outcome could only be financial implosion—as evinced, for example, by the so-called Roaring Twenties and the subsequent 1929 Great Crash, followed by the Great Depression.

The need to insure or to lower the risk of financial cycles of boom and bust brought forth a new kind of financial innovation: financial futures and derivatives. These are essentially betting or contracts over the fluctuations in the price of financial assets. Two most common among a variety of derivatives are "difference contracts" and "call" or "put" contracts. A difference contract is a commitment to pay the difference between a price specified in the contract, called the "strike" price, and the market price at a given time in the future over a given period. A "call" or "put" contract is a commitment to buy or sell an asset at a fixed price in the future. Contracts of this nature had been noted as early as the time of John Law's South Sea Bubble. But those earlier derivatives contracts were limited to non-tradable private arrangements between individuals, or contracting parties. Derivatives became publicly-traded financial assets only in the second half of the nineteenth century. "Once markets in financial derivatives were established, those derivatives became financial assets, however ephemeral, in their own right" (Toporowski 2010: 43).

The widespread investment in derivatives market in the second half of the nineteenth century prompted a heated debate between the proponents and opponents of these new and fast growing types of financial assets. "Already during the 1890s there was a lively debate among economists, bankers and policy-makers as whether and how this last kind of financial innovation should be regulated" (ibid.). Proponents argued that derivatives contracts, functioning as insurance against asset price fluctuations, were beneficial to the goal of eliminating or reducing volatility in financial markets, thereby encouraging investors to more confidently invest not only in financial assets, but also in commercial and industrial enterprises. They further argued that the more the people took advantage of these new financial innovations (as a form of insurance), "the more financially stable their lives would be. Any losses sustained on such contracts arose because they were not managed properly. With the right advice from experts in the markets, derivatives were beneficial" (ibid.: 44).

Opponents, by contrast, viewed derivatives "as simply a more sophisticated form of gambling which could ruin the otherwise sound finances of individuals and firms. Like any other kind of gambling, they argued that it should be strictly controlled" (ibid.). Critics further argued that derivatives contracts could serve as insurance against price instability if such contracts between the initial signatories or parties remained non-tradable, or if they were strictly regulated. Otherwise, instead of stabilizing, they reasoned, derivatives could be more destabilizing; since large investors in derivatives contracts would try (and often succeed) to sway the market in the direction that would make their bets the winners. Furthermore, since in the absence of meaningful regulation there is no limit on how much derivatives investors can bet on in a contract, inflation of fictitious capital in derivatives markets can easily outgrow all reasonable proportions relative to the collateral that is supposed to sustain the inflated fictitious capital.[2] Despite the critics' powerful arguments, advocates of unrestrained use of derivative won:

> As in the 1970s, the advocates won. They had a major practical advantage: asset markets were and are unstable. Money could be made out of that instability using financial derivatives, and no one has yet invented a foolproof way to prevent people with money from using it to make even more money no matter how ruinous the consequences may be for society.
>
> (Toporowski 2010: 44)

The triumph of unregulated markets, including of financial derivatives, in the second half of the nineteenth century significantly accelerated the surging tide of concentration and centralization of capital in the late nineteenth and early twentieth centuries. The mushrooming of big business—all kinds of mergers, conglomerates, trusts and cartels—in this period also created anxiety, indeed alarm, among a faction of the U.S. ruling class regarding the dangers of the inordinate rise of the power of monopolies, and the equally drastic curtailment of competition in the marketplace. This reaction to the unprecedented growth of economic and political power of big business ushered in a number of anti-trust laws: The Interstate Commerce Act (1887), the Sherman Antitrust Act (1890), the Clayton Antitrust Act (1914), and the Federal Trade Commission Act (1914). These restrictions, however, focused primarily on the manufacturing/industrial sector; the rapidly rising financial sector continued to expand largely unrestricted. The success of the financial sector in escaping regulatory restrictions, however, turned out to be a pyrrhic victory; for the speculative activities and the unchecked growth of this sector was a major contributor to the stock market bubble of the 1920s, which culminated, first, in the 1929 Great Crash, followed by the ensuing Great Depression. The easy/unrestricted supply of money by the

Federal Reserve Bank, which experienced a 62 percent growth in the 1923–1929 period, also played an important role in facilitating the speculative financial inflation and its ultimate implosion.

The harrowing experience of the Great Depression, followed by the devastating years of World War II, generated momentous social upheaval and extensive working class struggles worldwide. The ensuing "threat of revolution," as FDR put it, and the "menacing" pressure from below prompted reform from above—hence, the New Deal reforms in the U.S. and socialist/Social-Democratic reforms in Europe. The passage of the Banking Act (better known as the Glass-Steagall Act) of 1933 in the United States severely restricted the destabilizing speculative behavior of commercial banks. The financing needs of the War, which funneled the major bulk of national savings into government debt/bonds, also required strict control of credit/financial markets. Combined, these historic developments, significantly curtailed the size, the speculative business and the influence of giant financial interests. Alas, not for long.

Post-WW II expansion of finance capital

> The financial sector, properly functioning, primarily recycles idle balances into additional capital formation. Years of financial deregulation fostered the creation of new instruments, ever more reliant on Ponzi-like methods of profit acquisition, by reversing this dynamic and sucking profits out of production to expand the financial sector at the expense of productive investment.... The relationship between the financial sector and the nonfinancial sector had effectively morphed from symbiotic to parasitic.
>
> (Barry Finger, editorial board member of *New Politics*, 2010)

As the New Deal and Social-Democratic reforms from above saved Western capitalism from more radical social change from below, they also provided grounds for its revival and expansion. By the late 1960s and early 1970s, finance capital, headed by major U.S. banks, had risen to its pre-Depression levels of concentration; and by the late 1970 and early 1980s, the renewed growth of the financial sector gained an accelerated tempo. Financial sector profits come from a number sources: from interest earnings, from asset price inflation and (perhaps most importantly, in recent years) from speculative trading in a number financial assets such as derivatives, hedge funds, credit swap defaults, and the like. The sector's profits as a share of total domestic profits grew from about 10 percent in the 1950–1960s to over 40 percent in the early 2000s. At the same time, the sector's financial assets "grew from about a third of total U.S. economy financial assets ... to 45 percent.... Their value was approximately equal to the U.S. GDP in the early 1950s, whereas now it amounts to 4.5 times of the U.S. GDP" (Epstein and Crotty 2011: 4).

A number of factors contributed to this fantastic rise of finance capital. Top among them was the tremendous overall economic growth in the United States in the immediate post-war period (1948–1968), which came to be known as the

Golden Age of the U.S. economy. That remarkable real economic growth also precipitated the growth of the financial sector and the escalation of financial intermediaries. Prophetically, Karl Marx had anticipated nearly a century earlier that,

> With the growth of material wealth the class of money-capitalists grows; on the one hand, the number and the wealth of retiring capitalists, rentiers, increases; and on the other hand, the development of the credit system is promoted, thereby increasing the number of bankers, money-lenders, financiers, etc.
>
> (1967: 510)

This escalating trend of the financial sector is clearly reflected, among other indicators in Table 4.1, which shows a steady rise in the share of the financial sector's income of total national income over the past 40-plus years, from 3.7 percent in 1960–1969 to 8 percent in 2007.

Another factor that has significantly contributed to the expansion of the financial sector has been the establishment of pension funds and retirement plans, commonly known as 401K plans. Although these plans were designed to expand the pool of national savings in order to funnel them into productive investment, in practice they have fallen short of the intended target. Instead, following the drastic shifts of these funds during the 1970s and 1980s from the real to the financial sector, the major bulk of this vast pool of "compulsory savings" ended up financing not productive industrial investment but parasitic speculative investment.

> The more or less compulsory subscription to the financial markets entailed by such schemes was supposed to increase the amount of savings available for business investment. In practice the promised industrial renaissance failed to materialize. It worked out that this was because the inflow of credit

Table 4.1 Income share of the financial sector of GDP, U.S. (1920–2007)

Year	*Financial sector's income share of GDP*
1920–1929	3.6
1930–1939	4.9
1940–1949	3.4
1950–1959	2.9
1960–1969	3.7
1970–1979	4.1
1980–1989	4.7
1990–1999	6.0
2000–2006	7.4
2007	8.0

Source: Based on (Weeks 2010: 144).

> into the financial markets, or financial inflation, made those markets themselves far more attractive and remunerative as vehicles for investment than the arduous business of making more lasting use-values. As I noted at the time, "in an era of finance, finance mostly finances finance."
>
> (Toporowski 2010: ix–x)

A third contributing factor to the post-war escalation of finance capital was the enormous growth of Euro-dollars: U.S. dollars deposited in overseas banks. As discussed in Chapter 2, the Bretton Woods Conference (1944) on international monetary matters made the U.S. dollar as good as gold—thanks to, in large part, to the extremely superior economic position of the United States at the time, including the possession of more than 70 percent of the worldwide gold supply. Also, as discussed in that chapter, a number of factors contributed to the rapid proliferation of Euro-dollars: U.S. underwriting of the vast Marshall Plan expenditures, war and post-war U.S. military spending abroad, and the disproportionate rise in U.S. imports relative to its exports. (This last incident was made possible by (a) the relative economic prosperity and the strong purchasing power of U.S. consumers, and (b) the fact that they could buy from other parts of the world just as they shopped at home, using the same currency—the dollar). Combined, these factors precipitated a massive outflow of U.S. dollars—hence, the inflation of Euro-dollars.

For nearly a quarter century (1945–1968) the U.S. dollar was even preferable to gold, because in addition to being the main international means of payment and the main repository of saving/wealth, as gold was, it could also grow when invested in the financial system. Euro-dollars had another major advantage over national currencies (including dollars within the U.S. borders): they were unregulated and, therefore, free of capital and foreign exchange controls that were relatively strict in the immediate post-War period. "The Euro-dollar markets spun off a variety of new financial instruments, from syndicated lending to Euro-currency bonds and securities" (Toporowski 2010: 31). Unsurprisingly, not only people from other countries held tight to U.S. dollars, but also U.S. financial investors preferred to offshore their dollars as this would allow them to engage in all kinds of unregulated speculative financial innovations (such as speculation in foreign exchange markets, or issuing and dealing in Euro-currency bonds) that were prohibited at home.

Another (fourth) contributing factor to the financial inflation since the 1970s has been the government policy of bailing out the unscrupulous, speculating financial institutions as they fall on the verge of bankruptcy, instead of letting them suffer the consequences of their adventurous investments. By thus periodically replenishing the capital base of financial institutions that go bankrupt, they are encouraged and/or enabled to go further in their reckless financial ventures and precipitate new financial bubbles—each bubble larger than the previous one, and each bailout costlier the one before it.

> As a general rule of thumb, each crisis from the international debt crisis in 1982 to the Russian crisis of 1998 cost twice as much to refinance as the

> previous one; so that the 1995 Mexican crisis cost twice as much as the 1982 debt crisis to resolve; the 1997 East Asian Crisis cost twice as much as the Mexican crisis to settle; and the Russian crisis cost twice as much as the East Asian Crisis.
>
> (Toporowski 2010: 23)

Evidence shows that the "too-big-to-fail" banks (such as Bank of America, Wells Fargo, City Group Inc. and JPMorgan Chase & Co.) that were rescued in response to the 2008 financial implosion have emerged from the crisis larger than they were in the immediate days preceding the collapse. "Bigger banks like JPMorgan Chase (JPM), Citigroup (C) and Wells Fargo (WFC) are actually larger than ever before…" (Reeves 2013). In light of the fact that many small, independent banks were let go under while the money-center giants were (and still are) showered with all sorts of financial assistance, courtesy of the public purse, this should come as no surprise.

Just as the rise of finance capital in the second half of the nineteenth century led to the 1890s debate over the rising power of big finance, so did the gradual inflation of finance capital in the post-war period—after being deflated by the Depression and the ensuing regulations—lead to the 1970s debate over the "proper" role of the financial sector. Specifically, the debate focused on whether the disproportionately rapid expansion of the financial sector, along with its persistent introduction of ever newer financial instruments, were destabilizing, as the critics argued, or tempering and stabilizing market fluctuations, as advocates maintained. In the ensuing tug of ideological war between the Monetarists/neoliberals on the one side and the liberal/Keynesians on the other, Nobel-Prize winner economist and archetype Monetarist Milton Friedman "played a significant role in urging financial liberalization and license for the trading of new [financial] instruments." Echoing "the 1890s argument that financial derivatives are a useful protection against financial instability," Friedman argued that unrestricted financial markets would bring about a "stable equilibrium" between the constantly fluctuating asset prices and the underlying real values (Toporowski 2010: 31–33). Also like the 1890s debate, the Monetarists won; which explains why since then the control and/or management of monetary instruments, that is, of money supply and/or interest rate, has become the name of the game in the official economic polity circles.

It is obvious from this brief historical overview that, as mentioned earlier, the rise of finance capital to economic and policy dominance came about largely as an endogenous development or evolution of advanced capitalist production. Contrary to the claims of liberal-Keynesian economists and policy makers, gradual processes of market deregulation and financialization started long before Ronald Reagan arrived in the White House. Nor were those developments simply the product of neoliberal "conspiracies." In subtle ways, Reagan's election represented the inauguration of the rise to dominance of Monetarism/neoliberalism and, by the same token, the memorialization of the Keynesian/New Deal economics.

Not surprisingly, his departure from the White House did not signify the end of his neoliberal economic policies; as those policies have been continued to this day under both Democratic and Republican administrations. Neoliberal ideology has evolved as much as a product of the dynamics of the actual developments of finance capital as it has as its cause. The link between neoliberal economic policies and the actual economic developments can be characterized by a symbiotic, mutually-reinforcing relationship: as the rise and expansion of finance capital brought forth neoliberal thinking, it also paved the way for increasingly daring and speculative conduct of the financial sector. In the meantime, powerful financial interests moved to methodically place their Wall Street "experts" at the helm of policy making positions at the Federal Reserve Bank, the Treasury Department and Regulatory agencies. The election of Ronald Reagan was, essentially, part of this systematic stacking of the key political and economic decision-making positions with the favorite operatives of monetarism, neoliberalism and austerity economics.

Dictatorship of finance capital

> Give me control over a nation's currency, and I care not who makes its laws.
>
> (Baron M. A. Rothschild[3])

> Like a desperate man, faced with bankruptcy, who begins to dismantle the house for firewood, capitalism seeks in the first instance to dismantle all competing demands on profits—to strip down the state and drastically curtail its activities—in order to reclaim surplus value for the accumulation process.
>
> (Barry Finger, editorial board member of *New Politics*, 2010)

A major hallmark of the age of finance capital is domination or control of economic policy by powerful financial interests. This can be clearly seen in the context of all the more developed and highly financialized capitalist economies of today. Extensive deregulations that led to the 2008 financial crisis, the scandalous bank bailouts in response to the crisis, the continued showering of the "too-big-to-fail" financial institutions with nearly-free money, the failure to impose effective restraints on these institutions after the crisis, and the brutal austerity policies that further exploit the already distressed poor and working people in order to pay for the gambling losses of the high finance can all be traced to the political and economic power of the financial oligarchy.

It was perhaps this kind of ominous prospect of policy controls by parasitic finance capital that prompted a number of early statesmen to warn against entrusting the profit-driven private banks with the critical task of money supply and credit creation:

> The [private] Central Bank is an institution of the most deadly hostility existing against the principles and form of our constitution.... If the

> American people allow private banks to control the issuance of their currency, first by inflation and then by deflation, the banks and corporations that will grow up around them will deprive the people of all their property until their children will wake up homeless on the continent their fathers conquered.
>
> (Thomas Jefferson, third U.S. President)

In 1836, Andrew Jackson abolished the Bank of the United States, arguing that it exerted undue and unhealthy influence over the course of the national economy. From then until 1913, the United States did not allow the formation of a private central bank. During that period of nearly three quarters of a century, monetary policies were carried out, more or less, according to the U.S. Constitution: Only the "Congress shall have power … to coin Money, regulate the Value thereof" (Article 1, Section 8, U.S. Constitution). Not long before the establishment of the Federal Reserve Bank in 1913, President William Taft (1909–1913) pledged to veto any legislation that included the formation of a private central bank.

Soon after Woodrow Wilson replaced William Taft as president, however, the Federal Reserve Bank was founded (December 23, 1913), thereby centralizing the power of U.S. banks into a privately owned entity that controlled interest rate, money supply, credit creation, inflation, and (in roundabout ways) employment. It could also lend money to the government and earn interest, or a fee—money that the government could create free of charge. This ushered in the beginning of the gradual rise of national debt, as the government henceforth relied more on borrowing from banks than self-financing, as it had done prior to its granting the power of money-creation to the private banking system. Three years after signing the Federal Reserve Act into law, however, Wilson is quoted as having stated:

> I am a most unhappy man. I have unwittingly ruined my country. A great industrial nation is controlled by its system of credit. Our system of credit is concentrated. The growth of the nation, therefore, and all our activities are in the hands of a few men. We have come to be one of the worst ruled, one of the most completely controlled and dominated governments in the civilized world. No longer a government by free opinion, no longer a government by conviction and the vote of the majority, but a government by the opinion and duress of a small group of dominant men.[4]

While many independent thinkers and policy makers of times past thus viewed the unchecked power of private central banks as a vice not to be permitted to interfere with a nation's monetary/economic policies, most mainstream economists of today view the independence of central banks (from the people and the elected bodies of government) to control or influence such policies as a virtue—always equating independence from government and citizens with independence in general. The implication is that a central bank that is independent from public opinion or authority is a purely technocratic, disinterested policy-making entity that is solely devoted to national economic interests, free of all political and economic influences. Nearly every macroeconomic textbook contains at least a chapter on money and banking a major segment of which is devoted to the "advantages" of the "independence" of private central banks from elected officials to determine the "proper" level of money supply, of inflation or of the volume of credit that an economy may need.

Proponents of central bank "independence" argue that such independence provides a central bank with the opportunity to set its own policy goals free from partisan considerations, or electoral exigencies of the contending political forces. This "independence" would further allow a central bank to define the "best" way of achieving those policy goals, including the kind and quantity of the monetary instruments to be employed (change in money supply or interest rate, for example), as well as the timing of the use of such instruments. It is argued that an independent central bank can thus fashion a more dependable policy by providing the market and/or market players with the confidence to respond only to signals from the central bank, instead of politically-driven government agencies or administrations.

Prima facie, or in theory, the soundness of this advocacy of central bank independence cannot be questioned or disputed. (Not surprisingly, during my nearly 30 years of teaching economics, I rarely encountered students who suspected this abstract notion of central bank independence.) In reality, however, central bank independence largely means independence from the people and the elected bodies of government.

> Independence has really come to mean a central bank that has been captured by Wall Street interests, very large banking interests. It might be independent of the politicians, but it doesn't mean it is a neutral arbiter. During the Great Depression and coming out of it, the Fed took its cues from Congress. Throughout the entire 1940s, the Federal Reserve as a practical matter was not independent. It took its marching orders from the White House and the Treasury—and it was the most successful decade in American economic history.
>
> (Brown 2013a)

Whereas the unbridled financial sector in the core capitalist countries of the United States, Europe and Japan, where central banks are relatively more independent from government, have condemned their economies to a chronic recession and uncertain future, less-financialized economies of countries such as Russia, China, Brazil, and India have weathered the crisis much better—although they too are bound to suffer from the financial contamination spreading from the core. The relative success of the latter group of countries to avoid deeper economic contraction of the magnitude of the crises in the "heartland" capitalist countries is attributed, at least in part, to the fact that their economies have benefit from public ownership of the credit and banking system. Contrary to the U.S., European and Japanese credit and/or monetary policies that drain their economies of resources in order to fill the deep pockets of the knights of finance, publicly-owned banks in China, Brazil, India and Russia have provided counter-cyclical, stimulating credit for real/productive investment in their economies, thereby averting the long and deepening recession that has afflicted the core capitalist economies (Brown 2012).[5]

How did the Federal Reserve and the Wall Street money-center banks gain so much power to control monetary and/or economic policies at a national level? More generally, why are national economic policies increasingly shifting out of public hands into those of powerful financial interests?

The simple and obvious answer is that *those who control a society's money control the society itself*, as has been occasionally stated ever since civilizations began dealing with money and private property. Acquiring, accumulating and controlling the major bulk of a nation's financial resources leads to policy control in a number of ways. A most common and obvious method in today's more-developed capitalist countries is financial contributions to the election of favorite policy makers; or lucrative deals between powerful financial interests and policy-making or regulatory agencies through aggressive lobbying—essentially bribing. According to the Center for Responsive Politics, cited by CNNMoney, in the 2012 election season alone Wall Street donations to the candidates supporting the financial sector amounted to $2.5 billion (Liberto 2012).

> High finance has corrupted regulatory agencies, falsified account-keeping by "mark to model" trickery, and financed the campaigns of its supporters to disable public oversight. The effect is to leave banks in control of how the economy allocates its credit and resources.
>
> (Hudson 2012b)

In an essay titled "The Rich Have Stolen the Economy," Paul Craig Roberts, Assistant Secretary of the Treasury in the Reagan administration, has forcefully argued that "The political system is unresponsive to the American people. It is monopolized by a few powerful interest groups that control campaign contributions." Roberts further writes: "Interest groups have exercised their power to monopolize the economy for the benefit of themselves, the American people be damned" (2009).

In a similar vein, but of course much earlier, Marx and Engels argued in *The Communist Manifesto* that under capitalism "the bourgeoisie has at last, since the establishment of modern industry and of the world market, conquered for itself, in the modern representative state, exclusive political sway"; and that "the executive of the modern state is but a committee for managing the common affairs of the whole bourgeoisie." Marx and Engels were often scoffed at by the capitalist ruling elites and their political pundits when they made this statement over 160 years ago. Critics tauntingly dismissed them as having overstated their case. Perhaps it is time to dust off and read old copies of *The Manifesto*, if only to better understand the incestuous political and business relationship between the state and the financial oligarchy of our time.

The central bank and its shareholders, which are the commercial banks, also control economic policy in more subtle ways than lobbying policy-makers and paying for their election. Additionally, they wield power because governments have come to depend on them for a variety of reasons; mainly because they are authorized to control a nation's money supply and its credit/monetary policy. They do this through creation of credit (or money), management of interest rate, administration of "open market operations" (buying and selling government securities), and targeting of the inflation level—which implicitly also means targeting of the employment/unemployment level. Perhaps more importantly, the banking system exerts economic and political influence because central banks are tasked with the monopolistic power of acting as lenders of last resort during periods of financial instability and economic crises; that is, when commercial banks abstain from lending to businesses, thereby creating what is called credit crunch.

Designation of central banks as lenders of last resort, however, is not in the public interest; it is designed to serve the interests of the banking system. There is absolutely no reason for a nation's treasury department not to serve as the lender of last resort, without the mediation of a private central bank. Not only would this be less costly to the borrowers, it would also enable the government to allocate credit to productive/real investments, instead of speculative/financial ones.

> Governments can create new credit electronically on their own computer keyboards as easily as commercial banks can. And unlike banks, their spending is expected to serve a broad social purpose, to be determined democratically. When commercial banks gain policy control over governments and central banks, they tend to support their own remunerative policy of creating asset-inflationary credit—leaving the clean-up costs to be solved by a post-bubble austerity. This makes the debt overhead even harder to pay—indeed, impossible.
>
> (Hudson 2012a)

Borrowing money (through the central bank) from commercial banks instead of public-money creation to finance budget deficits, or to stimulate stagnant and cash strapped economies, is an absurd monetary policy and a convoluted way of credit creation—at unnecessary interest charges or other types of fees. To put it more bluntly, it is a perverse and ironic policy: granting the power of money/credit creation to profit-driven banks and, as a result, becoming their economic slaves.

> Bankers are holding economies hostage, threatening a monetary crash if they do not get more bailouts and nearly free central bank credit, and more mortgage and other loan guarantees for their casino-like game. The resulting "too big to fail" policy means making governments too weak to fight back.
>
> (Ibid.)

Perhaps the most subtle and insidious strategy of the financial sector's control of economic policy is its successful inculcation of policy-making apparatus, as well as of economic think tanks and academic circles, with the ideology or political philosophy that there are no alternatives to neoliberal economic policies. Simultaneously, the public is infused with the anti-government perception that its intervention in national economic affairs would simply be bureaucratic distortion of otherwise "efficient," "rational" and "benevolent" free markets. Financial or Wall Street growth is portrayed as real growth; and policies of economic stimulation have, accordingly, come to mean stimulation of the financial sector.

> Sponsoring an ideological attack on government, they accuse public bureaucracies of "distorting" free markets (by which they mean markets free for predatory behavior). The financial sector is now making its move to concentrate planning in its own hands.... The popular media and even academic economic theorists have been mobilized to pose as experts in an attempt to convince the public that financial policy is best left to technocrats—of the banks' own choosing, as if there is no alternative policy but for governments to subsidize a financial free lunch and crown bankers as society's rulers.
>
> (Ibid.)

While inflation of financial markets is portrayed as improvement in the living conditions of all, in reality Wall Street prosperity has increasingly become synonymous with main street austerity and poverty. For, that prosperity is achieved largely at the expense of the public; specifically, it is achieved through (a) the multi-trillion dollar cheap, nearly-free money to the financial sector, and (b) lower taxes on unearned incomes of the rentier class. As this combination of curtailing government revenue and expanding its expenditures (in order to finance its vast Wall Street welfare programs) tends to add to national debt and deficit, it thereby paves the way for justifying all kinds of brutal austerity measures, including encroachment upon such hitherto sacred trust funds as Social Security and Medicare.

Austerity through *shock therapy*

> The commitment to privatize government property is one of the main components of the restructuring plans imposed by the "troika" of IMF, ECB (European Central Bank) and European Commission on euro-area countries when they avail themselves of aid from the euro rescue packages.
>
> (Deutsche Bank, 2011)

A major hallmark of the stage of finance capital is accelerated accumulation of fictitious capital through asset-price inflation; recently facilitated by increasingly easy and larger allocations of credit to the financial sector. Not only have the banks and other financial institutions come to lend/invest more in the more profitable (albeit riskier) financial sector, instead of the real sector, but also government-sponsored "stimulus" monies are funneled or recycled through the banking system within this sector. "Instead of financing tangible investment to expand production and innovation, most loans are made against collateral, with interest to be paid out of what borrowers can make elsewhere. Despite being unproductive in the classical sense, it was remunerative for [borrowers/investors] ... riding the wave of asset-price inflation" (Hudson 2012b).

The unsavory record of the Federal Reserve Bank indicates that, as Professor Tremblay recently put it, it has "a recurring and nagging tendency to create financial bubbles and economic booms and busts that end up—more often than not—benefiting large banks and their CEOs, at a huge cost to the real economy." The professor further notes, "The Fed is really an institution primarily designed to subsidize large banks with public money" (2013). Win–win gambling is, of course, an oxymoronic expression. Yet, that's exactly what Wall Street banks and other financial institutions are doing: they win as long as the financial bubbles they create continue expanding, but they also win when the bubbles burst; since they are then compensated for their losses with bail-out monies and all kinds of other shady rescue plans. Two such dubious plans that were, for example, used in response to the 2008 market crash to transfer trillions of dollars to the failed financial institutions were Term Asset Facility (TAF) and Term Asset-backed Securities Loan Facility (TALF).

For the financial elite to have pulled off such a successful financial coup has, therefore, a lot to do with the fact that market mechanism is subverted by monetary policy that protects the gambling behavior of the banking interests against losing outcomes of such behavior. "Just as the Greenspan Fed created the housing bubble and let the derivatives market explode, thus sowing the seeds of the 2007–2008 financial crisis," points out Professor Tremblay, "the Bernanke Fed, using faulty economic analysis, has embarked upon a policy of zero short-term interest rates for many years" (ibid.). Bernanke's open-ended quantitative easing (QE) is essentially tantamount to giving Wall Street banks good money in exchange for bad money, that is, in exchange for their toxic assets whose prices have artificially been kept at their inflated levels of pre-2008 market crash. Professor Tremblay further writes:

> It is becoming increasingly obvious that the Bernanke Fed's monetary policy of fixing short-term interest rates at close to zero percent ... was primarily designed not to help the U.S. economy but to shore up the super large American banks that were on the verge of bankruptcy when the investment bank Lehman Brothers failed on September 15, 2008. Indeed, with this policy, the Bernanke Fed has transferred hundreds of billions to these super banks at a huge cost to the rest of the economy and to international holders of U.S. dollars.
>
> (Ibid.)

Who pays for, or what happens to, the massive fictitious capital that implodes and becomes toxic when a financial bubble bursts? The answer is, of course, the people—through extensive measures of austerity cuts. Under liberal capitalism of the competitive industrial era, a long cycle of economic contraction would usually wipe out not only jobs and production, but also the debt burdens that were accumulated during the cycle of expansion that led to the cycle of contraction. In the age of finance capital, however, debt overhead is propped up through its monetization, or socialization, even during a most severe financial meltdown such as that which occurred in 2008. Indeed, due to the influence of powerful financial interests, national or taxpayers' debt burden is further exacerbated by the government's generous bailout plans of the bankrupt financial giants, that is, by simply transferring or converting private to public debt. In essence, this is a policy of redistributing national resources from the bottom up. Not surprisingly, income and/or wealth distribution has increasingly become more uneven in recent years (Table 4.2). As Henry Blodget (2013) of *Business Insider* has shown, the already extremely unequal distribution of economic resources shown in Table 4.2 has become even more lopsided since 2009, the year for which the resource data are shown in this table.

There is strong evidence that redistribution of national resources in favor of the affluent is brought about more by heartless, cynical policy designs than by the spontaneous dynamics of market mechanism. Specifically, the redistribution is accomplished through a subtle and insidious economic policy of deliberately creating debt and/or deficit, thereby "justifying" and forcing cuts on social spending. While the escalating debt and/or deficit is blamed on social spending, especially on the so-called entitlements, the major culprits lie elsewhere: Pentagon/security spending, tax giveaways to the super wealthy and (in recent years) costly rescue plans to major banks and other Wall Street financial institutions. A major, perhaps the major, source of national debt and deficit has been the drastic change in the nation's taxation structure since the early 1980s: making it much less progressive than any time prior to 1980. Viewed in this light, a substantial portion of the staggering national debt of nearly $16 trillion represents a subtle redistribution of national resources from the bottom 90 percent of the population to the top 10 percent, especially the top 1 percent. It represents unpaid taxes by the wealthy, compared to what they had to pay before President Reagan's tax breaks for the affluent, which has to be financed by cutting social spending. This means that the wealthy have successfully converted their tax obligations to credit

Table 4.2 Distribution of income and wealth (2009)

Households	*Income*	*Net worth*
Top 1%	21.3	35.6
Top 10%	47.1	75.0
Bottom 90%	52.9	25.0
Total	100%	100%

Source: Based on Allegretto (2011, p. 4, Table 1).

claims, that is, lending and earning interest instead of paying taxes, which is essentially a disguised or subtle form of robbery.

This mean-spirited policy of taking from the poor and giving it to the rich started in the late 1970s and early 1980s and continues to this day unabated, under both Republican and Democratic administrations. David Stockman, President Reagan's budget director and one of the main architects of his supply-side tax cuts, implicitly confirmed this cynical policy of simultaneously raising military spending and cutting taxes on the wealthy in order to force cuts in non-military spending:

> Cutting defense had never been my real ideological agenda. My aim had always been to force down the size of the domestic welfare state to the point where it could be adequately funded with the revenues after the tax cut. All my efforts to cut defense had been to provide political lubricant for the other cuts.
>
> (As quoted in Du Boff 1989: 10)

A frustrated liberal but powerless Senator Ernest Hollings bitterly complained in 1984 that the combination of raising the Pentagon budget and lowering tax rates on high incomes had "intentionally created a deficit so large that we Democrats will never have enough money to build the sort of government programs we want" (ibid.).

Naomi Klein (2007), author of *The Shock Doctrine*, has called the neoliberal strategy of taking advantage of crisis times to redistribute national resources in favor of the wealthy the "shock doctrine" of "disaster capitalism," a doctrine that views economic disasters or crises as opportunities to be exploited to carry out brutal austerity policies—metaphorically, after the model of administering a "shock therapy" to a critically ill patient. Severe crisis or disaster moments that tend to trigger economic "shock therapy" can be either natural or social. Recent examples of natural disasters include the 2004 Indian Ocean tsunami in South/South-East Asia and the 2005 Hurricane Katrina in New Orleans. Both of these tragedies were taken advantage of by real estate "developers" and other investors in the "entertainment" industry for self-enrichment at the expense of the communities, small businesses and residents of the disaster-stricken communities.

Social crises that, according to the neoliberal shock doctrine, would call for economic shock treatment can be either real, such as the 2008 market crash and the ensuing long recession, or manufactured, such as the 2011 debt-ceiling panic, or the 2012 "fiscal cliff" alarm or, more recently (and for the second time in two years), the 2013 debt-ceiling/government shutdown "crisis"—all designed to frighten the people into accepting the slashing of vital social programs and privatizing valuable public property as the alleged solution to what is portrayed as imminent budget or debt disasters. These types of crises can be called phony or manufactured because the central claim behind austerity policies that "there is no money" for jobs, education, health care, housing, pensions and the like—is a lie. Generous subsidies to major Wall Street players since the 2008 market crash has lifted financial markets to new highs, as evinced by the Dow Jones Industrial Average's new frontier above the 16,000 mark, which means that the financial elites are even more prosperous now than they were at the peak of the pre-crash cycle. Systematic cuts in labor costs have gradually restored corporate profitability, and CEO pay continues to soar. This means that there really is no need for brutal austerity cuts as there really is no shortage of financial resources. The purported lack of resources is due to the fact that they are concentrated in the deep pockets of the financial oligarchy. As shown in Figure 4.1, for example, while the richest 5 percent of Americans acquired 81.7 percent of all wealth increase between 1983 and 2009, 60 percent of the middle, lower-middle and impoverished classes gained negative (−7.5 percent) wealth during that period.

Most economists, including many among liberal/progressives, initially scoffed at Klein's *The Shock Doctrine* as an overstatement of her case. Having witnessed the neoliberal use of the crisis conditions to implement brutal austerity cuts, a number of them seem to have come around to acknowledge the fact that economic policy makers have, indeed, taken advantage of the crisis situation to carry out economic shock therapy. For example, Nobel Laureate economist Paul Krugman purported that "The drive for austerity was about using the crisis, not solving it. It still is" (as quoted in Zacune 2013).

Application of "shock therapy" economic policies has been even more brutal in Europe than in the U.S. European countries have responded to the severe long recession by implementing relentless austerity measures, making punitive cuts to crucial public services and welfare benefits. Powerful financial interests and their political elites are using the crisis "as a pretext to deepen neoliberalism and remove obstacles, including workers' rights and much of the welfare state...."

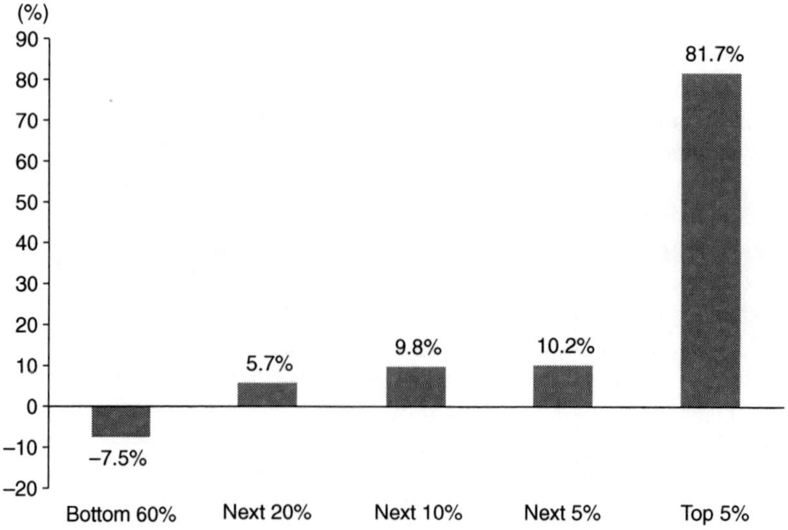

Figure 4.1 Share of total wealth gain (1983–2009) (source: Based on Mishel 2011).

A major thrust of the austerity policy has been a "systematic attempt by the European Commission and Central Bank (backed by the IMF) to deepen deregulation of Europe's economy" and privatize public assets and services—often at fire sale prices. Public assets targeted for privatization include various sectors such as public utilities, including water services, state buildings, national banks, energy, transport infrastructure, health and postal services. "The dark irony is that an economic crisis that many proclaimed as the 'death of neoliberalism' has instead been used to entrench neoliberalism," wrote Joseph Zacune (2013) at the Transnational Institute.

Notes

1 This statement by Henry Ford is quoted in many places; see, for example, "Famous Quotations on Banking" in *The Money Masters*, available at: www.themoneymasters.com/the-money-masters/famous-quotations-on-banking/; or "Business and Economics/Selected Quotes" in Wikipedia, available at: http://en.wikipedia.org/wiki/Portal:Business_and_economics/Selected_quote.

2 Today, nearly five years after the 2008 Wall Street crash, still nobody knows the colossal magnitude of the U.S. derivatives market; some say it is $60 trillion, some say it is $200 trillion, others say it is as high as $700 trillion, more than ten times the GDP of all countries combined. For an informative account see, for example, Thomas Kostigen, "There's a $700 trillion elephant in the room and it's time we found out how much it really weighs on the economy," *Wall Street Journal*'s online *MarketWatch.com*, March 6, 2009 available at: www.marketwatch.com/story/the-700-trillion-elephant-room-theres.

3 This statement by Rothschild is widely quoted; it can be viewed, among many places, at: http://investmentwatchblog.com/there-are-two-ways-to-conquer-and-enslave-a-nation-one-is-by-the-sword-the-other-is-by-debt-john-adams-1826/; or at: http://therookiecynic.wordpress.com/2010/10/06/one-central-bank-to-rule-them-all/, for example.

4 This statement by President Wilson is quoted in numerous places; see, for example here: http://peoplesconference.org/federal_reserve.htm and here: www.unc.edu/~ltolles/illuminati/moneycontrol.html. A number of commentators have argued that some of the damning words used in this much-quoted statement are either not Wilson's own, or taken out of context. Nobody denies, however, that regardless of the exact words used, he had serious reservations about the formation of the Federal Reserve Bank, and the policy of delegating the nation's money supply and/or monetary policy to a cabal of private banks or bankers.

5 It is quite likely that, in light of the interdependence of global markets, the chronic recession that has afflicted the "core" capitalist countries be transmitted to the hitherto healthy economies of other countries. How deep or severe the contagion effects would be, is hard to say a priori.

References

Allegretto, A. S. (2011). The state of working America's wealth, 2011: Through volatility and turmoil, the gap widens. Working Paper, Economic Policy Institute, Washington, DC. March 23.

Blodget, H. (2013). America today: 3 million overlords and 300 million serfs. *Business Insider*, April 10. Retrieved fromwww.businessinsider.com/wealth-and-income-inequality-in-america-2013–4?op=1 (accessed June 26, 2013).

Brown, E. (2013a). How the Fed could fix the economy—and why it hasn't. *Global Research*, February 25. Retrieved from www.globalresearch.ca/how-the-fed-could-fix-the-economy-and-why-it-hasnt/5324184 (accessed June 24, 2013).

Brown, E. (2013b). It's the interest, stupid! Why bankers rule the world. *Global Research*, February 15. Retrieved from www.globalresearch.ca/its-the-interest-stupid-why-bankers-rule-the-world/5311030 (accessed July 18, 2013).

Brown, E. (2012). Exploring the public bank option. *CounterPunch*, December 7. Retrieved from www.counterpunch.org/2012/12/07/exploring-the-public-bank-option/ (accessed December 18, 2012).

Deutsche Bank (2011). Revenue, competition, growth—potential for privatisation in the euro area. December 1. Retrieved from www.dbresearch.com/PROD/DBR_INTERNET_EN-PROD/PROD0000000000281545/Revenue,+competition,+growth%3A+Potential+for+privatisation+in+the+euro+area.pdf (accessed October 18, 2013).

Du Boff, R. (1989). What military spending really costs. *Challenge 32*, September/October: 4–10.

Epstein G. and Crotty, J. (2011). How big is too big? Unpublished paper, Department of Economics, University of Massachusetts, Amherst.

Finger, B. (2010). The limits of state intervention. *Against the Current*, July–August. Retrieved from www.solidarity-us.org/site/node/2927 (accessed October 18, 2013).

Hilferding, R. (1981 [1910]). *Finance capital: A study of the latest phase of capitalist development*. Tom Bottomore (Ed.). London: Routledge & Kegan Paul.

Hudson, M. (2012a). Scenarios for recovery: How to write down the debts and restructure the financial system. Institute for New Economic Thinking (INET), Berlin, April 13. Retrieved from http://ineteconomics.org/sites/inet.civicactions.net/files/hudson-michael-berlin-paper.pdf (accessed May 25, 2012).

Hudson, M. (2012b). How the banks broke the social compact, promoting their own special interests. *Global Research*, January 28. Retrieved from www.globalresearch.ca/how-the-banks-broke-the-social-compact-promoting-their-own-special-interests/28938 (accessed May 11, 2012).

Kindleberger, C. P. (2000). *Manias, panics, and crashes: A history of financial crises*. Hoboken, NJ: Wiley.

Klein, N. (2007). *The shock doctrine: The rise of disaster capitalism*, New York: Metropolitan Books.

Liberto, J. (2012). Wall Street set to break spending records this election. *CNNMoney*, September 5. Retrieved from http://money.cnn.com/2012/09/05/investing/wall-street-elections/index.html?iid=HP_LN (accessed June 24, 2013).

Marx, K. (1967). *Capital*. (Vol. 3) New York: International Publishers.

Mishel, L. (2011). Huge disparity in share of total wealth gain since 1983. Economic Snapshot/Report, Economic Policy Institute, Washington, DC, September 15. Retrieved from www.epi.org/publication/large-disparity-share-total-wealth-gain/ (accessed October 15, 2013).

Reeves, J. (2013). Too-big-to-fail financials might pose a bigger risk now than in 2008, *investorplace.com*, June 14. Retrieved from http://slant.investorplace.com/2013/06/too-big-to-fail-banks-financial-stock (accessed June 25, 2013).

Roberts, P. C. (2009). The rich have stolen the economy. *CounterPunch*, October 16–18. Retrieved from www.counterpunch.com/roberts10162009.html (accessed June 23, 2013).

Toporowski, J. (2010). *Why the world economy needs a financial crash and other critical essays on finance and financial economics*. London: Anthem Press.

Tremblay, R. (2013). A more than questionable Bernanke Fed monetary policy. *Global Research*, March 5. Retrieved from www.globalresearch.ca/the-feds.-monetary-policy-of-zero-interest-rates/5325258 (accessed June 24, 2013).

Weeks, J. (2010). *Capital, exploitation and economic crisis*. London and New York: Routledge.

Zacune, J. (2013). Privatizing Europe: Using the crisis to entrench neoliberalism. Working Paper, Transnational Institute (TNI), March 13. Retrieved from www.tni.org/sites/www.tni.org/files/download/privatising_europe.pdf (accessed June 23, 2013).

5 Marxian views of financial crises

Karl Marx on finance capital

While paying homage to Marx for his profound understanding of "the laws of motion of the capitalist mode of production," most left/radical economists argue that, nonetheless, his analysis cannot be of much service when it comes to the study of modern banking and big finance, since these are post-Marx developments. I will argue in this chapter that, in fact, a careful reading of his work on "fictitious capital" reveals keen insights into a better understanding of the instabilities of today's financial markets. It is true that his discussions of fictitious capital remained brief and fragmented. Nonetheless, what he wrote (in broad outlines) on the distinction between "money capital and real capital," between productive and unproductive labor and between speculative and real investment can be of significant interest in relations to the rise of finance capital and its destabilizing effects on the advanced market economies of our time (1967, Chapters 25–33).

The Marxian theory of value, as the product of human labor generated in the process of production, and its twin theory of surplus value—value over and above the cost of production—as the source of profit, interest and rental incomes implies that, to have a viable economy, the monetary sum of these various types of incomes and/or profits cannot deviate much from the total surplus value created in the process of production. In other words, the overall sum of money incomes and/or profits in an economy is limited, ultimately, by the total amount of real values produced in that economy; this also means that, in the long term, the *wealth of Nations*, to borrow Adam Smith's words, is determined or regulated by their productive capacity. Policy implications of this theory in terms of what really sustains an economy are enormous; since it can readily alert policy makers to the dangers of an impending economic crisis when deviations of monetary magnitudes from real-value magnitudes tend to become too big, and therefore unsustainable.

This stands in sharp contrast to the neoclassical economic theory that, instead of labor, views ownership and management as sources of profits, or economic surplus. Accordingly, there are no systemic limits to the amounts of income/profits made by smart capitalist managers and financial experts; it all depends on how creative they are, including all sorts of clever "financial innovations" that could create paper or electronic wealth out of thin air, without being limited by any underlying real values, or submerged boundaries. Not surprisingly, most mainstream economists did not see a problem with the astronomical growth of fictitious capital (relative to industrial capital) in the immediate period preceding the 2008 financial implosion. Indeed, not long before the market crash, these economists were cheerfully predicting that "there would be no more major crisis [*sic*] of capitalism. The end to crisis was because financial capital had developed the means to ensure itself against all forms of risk and uncertainty" (Weeks 2010: 140). As most mainstream economists, largely oblivious to the impending implosion, were euphorically celebrating "the end to crises" projections, they were altogether mystified when the supposedly "indefinite" financial expansion collapsed. Not surprisingly, they have also proven altogether inept in terms of suggesting constructive, humane or effective solutions to the crushing problems of unemployment and economic hardship on the overwhelming majority of citizens—it is, of course, an aphorism that one cannot expect an effective prescription without a sound diagnosis.

The Marxian theory of financial instability (and of economic crisis in general) goes beyond simply blaming either the "irrational behavior of economic agents," as neoliberal economists do, or "insufficient government regulations/controls," as Keynesian economists do. Instead, it focuses on the built-in dynamics of the capitalist system that fosters both the behavior of the market agents and the policies of governments. It views, for example, the 2008 financial meltdown as the logical outcome of the over-accumulation of the fictitious finance capital relative to the magnitude of the industrial or productive capital, or more precisely, relative to the aggregate amount of surplus value produced by labor in the process of production.

Instead of simply blaming "evil" Republicans or "neoliberal capitalism," as many left, liberal or Keynesian economists do (Kotz 2009, for example), it focuses on the dynamics of "capital as self-expanding value," as Marx put it, that not only created the huge financial bubble that imploded in 2008, but also subverted public policy in the face of such an obviously unsustainable bubble. In other words, it views public policy not simply as an administrative or technical matter but, more importantly, as a deeply political affair that is organically intertwined with the class nature of the capitalist state, which has increasingly become dominated by powerful financial interests.

While blaming policies or strategies of deregulation, securitization, and other financial innovations as factors that facilitated the financial bubble is not false, it masks the fact that these factors are essentially instruments or vehicles of the accumulation of fictitious finance capital. No matter how subtle or complex, they are essentially clever tools or strategies of transferring surplus value generated elsewhere by labor, or of creating fictitious capital out of thin air. Marx characterized this subtle transfer of (real/labor) value from productive to unproductive fictitious capital as "an extreme form of the fetishism of commodities" in which the real, but submerged, source of surplus-value is concealed.

In discussing how fluctuations in the magnitude of fictitious capital, or financial asset prices, may not necessarily reflect changes in the real economy, Marx wrote:

> To the extent that the depreciation or increase in value of this paper is independent of the movement of value of the actual capital that it represents, the wealth of the nation is just as great before as after its depreciation or increase in value.... Unless this depreciation reflected an actual stoppage of production and of traffic on canals and railways, or a suspension of already initiated [productive] enterprises ... the nation did not grow one cent poorer by the bursting of this *soap bubble* of nominal money-capital (emphasis added).
>
> (1967: 468)

Most critics of the increasing "financialization" of the more-developed market economies lament the disproportionate growth of money or finance capital relative to industrial capital as an "abnormal" growth, or an unfortunate expansion of finance capital beyond its "logical" limits. Finance capital, they argue, is supposed to grease the wheels of production, that is to serve as the means of circulation of goods and services, or as the funding source of investment in productive industrial undertakings. Accordingly, they recommend containment or control of the destabilizing financialization through policies of regulation and control.

The rise to prominence of finance capital in a mature market economy, however, represents no anomalous development; it is a fundamental characteristic of an advanced stage of capitalism. Finance capital is the ideal and quintessential form of capital, or capitalist property—independent of physical forms of value, or of the often cumbersome processes of producing goods and services. Indeed, as Marx points out, in the circuit of capital (M...C...P...C′...M′), that is, in the process of capitalist production/reproduction, productive and commodity forms of capital are essentially incidental to the goal of accumulating finance capital—or "capital as such," as he put it. This shows the absurdity of views that call for a "reasonable" proportion between industrial and finance capital, between "virtual wealth" and "real wealth," as if financial wealth were less real than tangible physical wealth (Gowan 2010: 49).

Marx prefaces his discussion of the relationship between finance capital, which he calls "loanable money-capital," and industrial or productive capital by posing this question: "to what extent does the accumulation of capital in the form of loanable money-capital coincide with actual accumulation, i.e., the expansion of the reproduction process?" (1967: 494).

The answer, he points out, depends on the stage of the development of capitalism. In the earlier stages of capitalist development, that is, before the rise of modern banks and the credit system, growth of finance capital was regulated or determined by the growth of industrial capital. For, in the absence of, or prior to the modern credit system, the dominant form of credit consisted of commercial credit. Under the commercial credit system, where one person lent the money to another in the reproduction process (for example, the wholesaler lent to the retailer, or the retailer lent to the consumer), finance capital could not deviate much from the industrial capital: "When we examine this credit detached from banker's credit it is evident that it grows with an increasing volume of industrial capital itself. Loan capital and industrial capital are identical here" (1967: 481).

But at higher stages of capitalist development, where banks scoop up or centralize and control national savings, the growth of finance capital no longer moves in tandem with the growth of industrial capital. Under these conditions, "Profit can be made purely from trading in a variety of financial claims existing *only on paper*.... Indeed, profit can be made by using only *borrowed capital* to engage in (speculative) trade, not backed up by any tangible asset." Such transactions represent "an extreme form of the fetishism of commodities in which the underlying source of surplus-value in exploitation of labor power is disguised."[1]

These brief passages reveal that Marx makes a clear distinction between real profit and profit from financial bubbles, or fictitious profit and/or capital. While real profit is rooted in, and therefore directly limited by production of surplus value, profit from fictitious capital is not—not directly, immediately, or in the short-term. Marx distinguishes between a variety of profits and/or incomes—all dependent, *ultimately*, on surplus value, created by human labor in the process of production. The main and the obvious category is profit that results from manufacturing or real production, or profit of "enterprise," as Marx called it.

According to his labor theory of value, profit of "enterprise" is essentially unpaid labor. Starting from production, he expresses the value of total gross national product (GNP) by this simple equation: GNP=C+V+S, where C stands for "constant" capital (or depreciation and inputs, including raw materials), V stands for "variable" capital, which is the equivalent of (production) wages, and S stands for surplus value, which is the basis of (production) profits, or profit of "enterprise." Interest payments for borrowed (and invested) capital as well as rental payments for the space rented for doing business would be deducted from profit of enterprise, or surplus value. Part of the remaining profit of enterprise would normally be set aside for reinvestment and/or expansion—which is called "retained earnings" in today's business vernacular—and the rest would become dividend income and/or entrepreneurial/managerial income. (In the above equation, Marx calls C "dead" labor, that is, labor ossified or congealed in the machinery or means of production; (V+S) "live" or "living" labor, that is, total labor (hours) performed, or total value created; which is today called net national product or value added.)

A second category of profits, according to Marx, is "profit upon alienation or expropriation," which comes from capitalists' appropriating part of the workers' income or wage in the form of interest or rent. When workers' pay (V in the above equation) is below the "subsistence" level, i.e., they are not paid a living wage, they often resort to borrowing to supplement their inadequate earnings, which frequently leads to indebtedness and, therefore, the appropriation of part of their income by bankers and other money-lenders. This "financial expropriation is based on re-dividing existing flows of money income, and thus amounts to a zero-sum game": lenders gain what borrowers lose. Marx characterizes this type of financial gain by lenders at the expense of borrowers profit from "secondary exploitation"—as distinct from profit from "primary exploitation," or profit of "enterprise," which as mentioned in the previous paragraph, is based on the extraction of surplus value in the process of production (Lapavistas and Levina 2011).

Both the profit of "enterprise" and profit upon "alienation" are made within the sphere of production; they both come from net national product, or value added (S + V in the above equation). However, there is also another type of profit whose connection to real values is indirect or submerged, and whose scope for expansion is, accordingly, much wider; it is the profit from fictitious capital, that is, profit that is made on paper or computer keyboards in the financial sector through trading or speculation in financial assets. This type of profit, and its accumulation into more fictitious capital, is the main source of financial bubbles and bursts.

It follows from this distinction between various types of profits/incomes that exploitation in production—as measured by the ratio of surplus value and necessary value (S/V), or approximately profit–wage ratio, which Marx calls the rate of exploitation—and exploitation upon "expropriation," or "alienation," go hand in hand: as the former intensifies so does the latter. For example, the rise in the profit–wage ratio in the U.S. over the past several decades has been accompanied by a corresponding rise in indebtedness, or in a larger and larger share of working people's income/wage being expropriated (in the form of debt servicing) by lenders. So, the distinction between different types of profits/incomes is not simply an academic exercise, or a radical (but "impractical") Marxian concept. More importantly, it finds close relevance to actual economic categories, developments, and trends. Not only does it show, for example, the sources of various types of incomes/profits, that is, how national resources are appropriated or distributed, but also the material foundations and limits to real economic growth, as well as the sources and limits to bubbles.

This transparent delineation of various types and sources of profits and/or incomes stands in sharp contrast to the mainstream theory of income distribution which tends to be more confusing and mystifying than clarifying. According to this theory, which is called "functional distribution of income," each of the four contributors to production (labor, capital, management and landlords) receives a share of output or income that is *by default* fair and equitable. The rationale for this spontaneous, guaranteed and fair distribution of income is that, the theory maintains, the share of each "factor of production," whether it is wage or salary or profit or interest or rent, is automatically determined by market mechanism in a way that it ends up to be exactly equal to that factor's contribution (at the margin) to the production of output/income.

As noted earlier, most economists, including many on the left, believe or argue that, since Marx lived and wrote in an era prior to the rise of big finance, he could not have foreseen the destabilizing influences of financial bubbles on an economy. A careful reading of his work on "money capital and real capital" (1967: 476–519) reveals that he did, indeed, discuss scenarios of systematic outflows of finance capital (which he interchangeably called "money hoards," "surplus-capital," or "money-capital") from the "sphere of production" into the realm of speculation in pursuit of higher returns; thereby paving the way for the rise of financial bubbles at higher stages of capitalist development.

> As for the other portion of profit, which is not intended to be consumed as revenue, it is converted into money-capital only when it is not immediately able to find a place for investment in the expansion of business in the productive sphere in which it has been made. This may be due to two causes. Either because this sphere of production is saturated with capital [i.e., there is overcapacity], or because accumulation must first reach a certain volume before it can serve as capital, depending on the investment magnitudes of new capital required in this particular sphere. Hence it is converted for a while into loanable money-capital and serves in the expansion of production in other spheres.... But if this new accumulation meets with difficulties in its employment, through a lack of spheres for investment, i.e., due to a surplus in the branches of production and an over-supply of loan capital, this plethora of loanable money-capital merely shows the limitations of *capitalist* production.
>
> (1967: 507)

"This plethora of loanable money-capital," which Marx also calls "surplus capital," is more or less what today's neoclassical economists call excess savings (S) over real investment (I), that is, S minus I. As discussed in Chapters 2 and 3, these economists do not view this imbalance between S and I as problematic because it would be only temporary as it would be rectified either automatically by the forces of supply and demand (neoliberals), or by government intervention (Keynesians). Marx, by contrast, argues that this discrepancy, or the "plethora" of finance capital, "shows the limitations of capitalist production," as it is an indication of overcapacity and/or overproduction, which often prompts retrenchment and/or downsizing by capitalists, thereby ushering in a cycle of high unemployment and economic contraction.

Marx further argues that while an abundance of "surplus capital" in the face of overcapacity or overproduction "shows the limitations of capitalist production," it does not necessarily show the limitations of the accumulation of capital in general—only of "production," or productive/industrial capital. For, under such circumstances in the sphere of production, "surplus capital" tends to abandon the "circuit of capital," or the "production–reproduction process," in pursuit of higher returns in financial markets, or speculation:

> The subsequent credit swindle proves that no real obstacle stands in the way of the employment of this surplus-capital. However, an obstacle is indeed immanent in its laws of expansion, *i.e.*, in the limits in which capital can realize itself as capital. A plethora of money-capital as such does not necessarily indicate over-production, not even a shortage of spheres of investment for capital.
>
> (Ibid.)

Together, the above two passages quoted from Marx reveal a number of important points. First, Marx considers two types of limits or boundaries to the accumulation of capital: (1) limits to productive/industrial capital, or "capitalist production," as he puts it, and (2) limits to finance capital—both boundaries are regulated or determined *ultimately* by real values produced in an economy. Limits to productive capital, which are directly determined by profitability imperatives within the sphere of production, are narrower than those to (fictitious) finance capital whose regulation or governance by real values is indirect and, therefore, more flexible. To simplify to put in the vernacular of today's business world, this means that the magnitude of fictitious capital, often represented by financial bubbles, can be, and it usually is, much larger than the magnitude of real values that are supposed to prop up such bubbles. Of course, a gigantic bubble on a narrow base of real values can expand only to a certain extent; it is bound to burst beyond that extent. To repeat Marx's statement (above): "However, an obstacle is indeed immanent in its laws of expansion [of finance capital], *i.e.*, in the limits in which capital can realize itself as capital."

Second, Marx makes it clear that transmission or leakage of finance capital from the real to the financial sector does not necessarily indicate the presence of stagnation or a lack of profitable investment opportunities in the real sector: "A plethora of money-capital as such does not necessarily indicate over-production, not even a shortage of spheres of investment for capital" (above quotation). Such systematic outflow of "surplus capital" from the sphere of production to the sphere of speculation in pursuit of higher returns shows that, according to Marx, finance capital can and does expand independent of industrial capital—not "merely in reaction" to developments in the real sector, as some contemporary Marxist economists claim (Bellamy Foster and Magdoff 2010; Brenner 2009; Kliman 2011).

Third, Marx's discussion of the systemic and systematic outflow of finance capital from the sphere of production (in pursuit of higher returns) to the sphere of speculation also shows that, contrary to widespread perceptions among contemporary economists, Marx did, indeed, envision the prospects of the emergence of financial inflations and bubbles. The discussion further signifies the superiority of his analysis of the relationship between industrial capital and (speculative) finance capital over those of neoclassical economists, according to whom any outflow of savings-cum-finance capital from the sphere of production (or from the "circular flow" model, as they put it) would be temporary and non-problematic, as it would soon be reverted back to the "income–expenditure circular flow," either by the invisible hand of the market mechanism or by the state's visible hand *à la* Keynes.

Rudolf Hilferding on finance capital

As discussed in the previous chapter of this book, the current domination of advanced market economies by finance capital is similar to that of a century ago. The spectacular rise of the economic power and political influence of financial interests in the late nineteenth and early twentieth centuries prompted the renowned Austro-German Marxist theoretician Rudolf Hilferding to carry out a most rigorous and systematic study of those momentous developments, as reflected in his classic book *Finance Capital* (1981 [1910]). In this section of Chapter 5, I will examine the extent to which Hilferding's analysis of the dynamics of finance capital finds relevance to both the actual developments of today's financial markets and the related theories of the so-called "financialization" phenomenon.

Hilferding's treatment of finance capital, like those of other Marxist scholars of his time, was deeply historical: systematically tracing its evolution from the earlier stages of capitalist development, when finance capital moved in tandem with industrial capital, to the more developed levels of capitalism, when the expansion of finance capital gradually gained independence from that of industrial capital. He sets out his inquiry with a clear definition of finance capital: "A steadily increasing proportion of capital in industry," writes Hilferding,

> ceases to belong to the industrialists who employ it. They obtain the use of it only through the medium of the banks which, in relation to them, represent the owners of the capital. On the other hand, the bank is forced to sink an increasing share of its funds in industry. Thus, to an ever greater degree the banker is being transformed into an industrial capitalist. This bank capital, i.e., capital in money form, which is thus actually transformed into industrial capital, I call "finance capital". Finance capital is capital controlled by banks and employed by industrialists.
>
> (As quoted in Lenin 1916)

Hilferding also makes a clear distinction between the stage of monopolistic finance capital and the earlier competitive capitalism of the liberal era:

> With the development of banking, and the increasingly dense network of relations between the banks and industry, there is a growing tendency to eliminate competition among the banks themselves, and on the other side, to concentrate all capital in the form of money capital, and to make it available to producers only through the banks. If this trend were to continue, it would finally result in a single bank or a group of banks establishing control over the entire money capital. Such a "central bank" would then exercise control over social production as a whole.
>
> (1981: 180)

Hilferding characterized the centralization of national savings in the hands of the bankers as perverse or "fraudulent" socialization of financial resources in favor of the "knights of credit":

> In this sense a fully developed credit system is the antithesis of capitalism, and represents organization and control as opposed to anarchy. It has its

> source in socialism, but has been adapted to capitalist society; it is a fraudulent kind of socialism, modified to suit the needs of capitalism. It socializes other people's money for use by the few. At the outset it suddenly opens up for the knights of credit prodigious vistas: the barriers to capitalist production … seem to have fallen, and the entire productive power of society appears to be placed at the disposal of the individual. The prospect intoxicates him, and in turn he intoxicates and swindles others.
>
> (Ibid.)

In the concentration of money capital in the hands of a small number of the "knights" of finance, Hilferding envisioned an opening of a path to socialism from below:

> The socializing function of finance capital facilitates enormously the task of overcoming capitalism. Once finance capital has brought the most important branches of production under its control, it is enough for society, through its conscious executive organ—the state conquered by the working class—to seize finance capital in order to gain immediate control of these branches of production. Since all other branches of production depend upon these, control of large-scale industry already provides the most effective form of social control even without any further socialization. A society which has control over coal mining, the iron and steel industry, the machine tool, electricity, and chemical industries, and runs the transport system, is able, by virtue of its control of these most important spheres of production, to determine the distribution of raw materials to other industries and the transport of their products. Even today, taking possession of six large Berlin banks would mean taking possession of the most important spheres of large-scale industry, and would greatly facilitate the initial phases of socialist policy during the transition period, when capitalist accounting might still prove useful.
>
> (1981: 367–368)

Hilferding's argument that nationalization of major banks automatically meant control of major non-financial industries was based on the economic structure of Germany at the time (early twentieth century), when industrial capital in Germany (and to a lesser extent elsewhere in Europe) was largely controlled by the banking system. Thus, as Barry Finger points out, "A socialist government that could nationalize finance capital would have in one fell swoop also annexed large swathes of the productive apparatus of society" (2013).

Hilferding argues that socialization of big finance and other major industries could make socialization of farming enterprises and small-scale businesses unnecessary, because by controlling the commanding heights of the economy the state could indirectly influence the rest of the economy.

> There is no need at all to extend the process of expropriation to the great bulk of peasant farms and small businesses because as a result of the seizure

> of large-scale industry, upon which they have long been dependent, they would be indirectly socialized just as industry is directly socialized.
>
> (1981: 368)

Hilferding maintains that expropriating big finance and other large-scale businesses, which are structurally "ripe" for socialization, while allowing the numerous, decentralized and micro-scale enterprises to continue operating on the basis of market mechanism would have both economic and political advantages. Economically, it could allow for a gradual and relatively less painful or turbulent transition to socialist economy; while politically it could enlist the support of the overwhelming majority of the population, since it would entail the expropriation of only a tiny minority of super-rich.

> It is therefore possible to allow the process of expropriation to mature slowly, precisely in those spheres of decentralized production where it would be a long drawn out and politically dangerous process. In other words, since finance capital has already achieved expropriation to the extent required by socialism, it is possible to dispense with a sudden act of expropriation by the state, and to substitute a gradual process of socialization through the economic benefits which society will confer.
>
> (Ibid.)

The dominant role of monopolistic finance capital of the Austria–Hungary–German economies Hilferding wrote about nearly a century ago seems to be, more or less, similar to that of today's big finance in all advanced market economies. But while Hilferding viewed the destabilizing role of parasitic finance capital as integral to the growth of capitalist system in general, most of today's left/liberal economists attribute it to "neoliberal capitalism," or deregulation policies of "right-wing" policy makers (Kotz 2009, for example). Accordingly, whereas Hilferding viewed the solution to the recurring crises precipitated by finance capital in the systemic transformation of capitalism, many of today's liberal economists call for the revival of Keynesian economics and/or re-regulation of the financial sector; which even if successful, would be only temporary.

Vladimir Lenin on finance capital

Drawing heavily on the empirical findings of John Hobson (1965 [1902]) and Rudolf Hilferding (1981 [1910]) on the fantastic growth of finance capital in the late nineteenth and early twentieth centuries, Vladimir Lenin further elaborated on the rise to dominance of finance capital, both on national and international levels. He called the global expansion of finance capital in search of more profitable investment opportunities imperialism—imperialism, not simply because of the extension of finance capital beyond national borders but, more importantly, because of the use of military force (when/if necessary) in facilitating that extension. Imperialism thus represented the military and/or geopolitical manifestations and conquests in pursuit of ever larger share of global markets on behalf of transnational capital. Colonization represented, Lenin argued, only one feature of this perpetual pursuit of economic gains. His book on this issue, *Imperialism: The Highest Stage of Capitalism* (1916), represents a classic Marxist analysis of imperialism—as a force of aggression driven worldwide largely by the imperatives of the accumulation of capital.

True to the Marxian tradition of a holistic approach to the study of socioeconomic developments, Lenin's economic analysis is profoundly historical, or evolutionary: characterizing the rise to dominance of finance capital as an inevitable outgrowth of the development of "capitalism in general":

> It is characteristic of capitalism in general that the ownership of capital is separated from the application of capital to production, that money capital is separated from industrial or productive capital, and that the rentier who lives entirely on income obtained from money capital, is separated from the entrepreneur and from all who are directly concerned in the management of capital. Imperialism, or the domination of finance capital, is that highest stage of capitalism in which this separation reaches vast proportions. The supremacy of finance capital over all other forms of capital means the predominance of the rentier and of the financial oligarchy; it [also] means that a small number of financially "powerful" states stand out among all the rest. The extent to which this process is going on may be judged from the statistics on emissions, i.e., the issue of all kinds of securities.
>
> (1916)

Citing extensive statistics on the fantastic growth of finance capital in the late nineteenth and early twentieth centuries, Lenin concluded that the twentieth century marked the turning-point from the old capitalism to the new, from the domination of capital in general to the domination of finance capital.

> On the threshold of the twentieth century we see the formation of a new type of monopoly: firstly, monopolist associations of capitalists in all capitalistically developed countries; secondly, the monopolist position of a few very rich countries, in which the accumulation of capital has reached gigantic proportions. An enormous "surplus of capital" has arisen in the advanced countries.
>
> (As quoted in Hunt 2002: 365)

After presenting wide-ranging statistics on the magnitude of major financial enterprises, Lenin set out to explain "how, under the general conditions of commodity production and private property, the business operations of capitalist monopolies inevitably lead to the domination of a financial oligarchy" (1916). In addition to its "normal" share of national income (in the form of interest earnings), Lenin cited a number of other ways through which finance capital absorbs the lion's share of economic surplus:

> Finance capital, concentrated in a few hands and exercising a virtual monopoly, exacts enormous and ever-increasing profits from the floating of companies, issue of stock, state loans, etc., strengthens the domination of the financial oligarchy and levies tribute upon the whole of society for the benefit of monopolists.
>
> (Ibid.)

Lenin further explained how big finance benefits not only from periods of economic expansion, but also from periods of contraction:

> During periods of industrial boom, the profits of finance capital are immense, but during periods of depression, small and unsound businesses go out of existence, and the big banks acquire "holdings" in them by buying them up for a mere song, or participate in profitable schemes for their "reconstruction" and "reorganization."
>
> (Ibid.)

Lenin characterized the powerful financial interests as a "financial oligarchy" because, he argued, a small group of bankers essentially controlled, or heavily influenced, both manufacturing/commercial enterprises and state authority. They did this through a complex network of relationships such as interlocking boards of directors, through the ownership of stocks and, of course, through the control of society's financial levers:

> At the same time personal link-up, so to speak, is established between the banks and the biggest industrial and commercial enterprises, the merging of one with another through the acquisition of shares, through the appointment of bank directors to the Supervisory Boards (or Boards of Directors) of industrial and commercial enterprises, and vice versa.
>
> (Ibid.)

Perhaps more importantly, Lenin also pointed out how the financial oligarchy controlled, influenced or swayed the authority of the state, and manipulated its power and institutional apparatus for its own interests:

> The "personal link-up" between the banks and industry is supplemented by the "personal link-up" between both of them and the government. "Seats on Supervisory Boards," writes Jeidels, "are freely offered to persons of title, also to ex-civil servants, who are able to do a great deal to facilitate (!) relations with the authorities."… The building and development, so to speak, of the big capitalist monopolies is therefore going on full steam ahead in all "natural" and "supernatural" ways. A sort of division of labour is being systematically developed amongst the several hundred kings of finance who reign over modern capitalist society.
>
> (Ibid.)

Today, the term "credit crunch" is used when banks and other financial intermediaries tend to deny or tighten credit to businesses in the real sector of the economy. Such a tightfisted policy of the financial system is usually characteristic of a period of economic stagnation, or market uncertainty. Under such adverse market conditions, banks and other financial institutions tend to further aggravate the lackluster market by resorting to a policy of retrenchment, or staying liquid, even though they may have plenty of cash at their disposal. As discussed in Chapter 3, neoliberal economists do not view this abundance of idle cash problematic since, according to their theory, the resulting oversupply of money would lead to a lower rate of interest, which would prompt a bigger demand for borrowing, thereby "restoring balance" between supply of and demand for money.

It is rather well-known that Keynes and his followers do not share the neoliberals' strong faith in the self-correcting powers of the market. Therefore, they recommend that, in the face of an excess supply of money-capital that may result from idle savings of a credit crunch situation, that is, when financial intermediaries tend to prefer liquidity to lending, a phenomenon Keynes called "liquidity preference," the government should step in to borrow and spend "on behalf" of those who are in possession of unutilized financial resources but not lending or investing them. Not only would this remove the imbalance between supply and demand in the financial/monetary markets, the Keynesians argue, but also create new purchasing power and a strong demand in the real sector of the economy; thereby (hopefully) ending economic stagnation and market uncertainty by thus prompting producers to invest and hire.

Also as discussed in Chapter 3, the Keynesian theory of "liquidity preference" is based on the assumption that, under conditions of a depressed economy and very low interest rates, those in possession of idle liquidity have no choice but to hold tight to their cash reserves in the hope of garnering higher returns in the future when interest rates rise. While this assumption (and, therefore, the theory of liquidity preference) may have had some validity when Keynes held it out in the context of the Great Depression, it does not seem to be valid anymore because, for one thing, in the age of finance capital, individuals or institutions in possession of financial or cash reserves no longer have to keep their "excess" liquidity idle, as Keynes maintained. Under conditions of highly "financialized" economies, they now have a multitude of lucrative investment opportunities in the financial sector: investment in financial assets, in real estate, in all kinds of derivatives or insurance schemes such "credit default swaps," and more. For another, the Keynesian concept of "liquidity preference" disregards investment opportunities in foreign markets, that is, investment of "excess liquidity" in other countries.

It is in this context that we can see how Lenin's treatment of finance capital, integrally intertwined with his theory of financial imperialism, is more instructive than that of Keynes—as well as those of many of contemporary Marxists. Whereas Keynes' theory of "liquidity preference," which he also called the "liquidity trap," characterized the "excess" liquidity as passively or "idly" sitting in the coffers of their owners/managers in the hope of higher returns in the future in domestic markets—thereby altogether disregarding financial speculation and globalization—Lenin, by contrast, viewed such cash reserves, which he called "surplus capital," as a driving forces behind the quest for foreign markets, including wars of conquest, which he called imperialism. After a lengthy analysis of the fierce competition among transnational finance capital of major capitalist powers of the time, he wrote:

> Thus finance capital, literally, one might say, spreads its net over all countries of the world. An important role in this is played by banks founded in the colonies and by their branches. German imperialists look with envy at the "old" colonial countries which have been particularly "successful" in providing for themselves in this respect. In 1904, Great Britain had 50 colonial banks with 2,279 branches…, France had 20 with 136 branches; Holland, 16 with 68 branches; and Germany had "only" 13 with 70 branches. The American capitalists, in their turn, are jealous of the English and German: "In South America," they complained in 1915, "five German banks have forty branches and five British banks have seventy branches…." The capital-exporting countries have divided the world among themselves in the figurative sense of the term. But finance capital has led to the *actual* division of the world.
>
> (Ibid.)

Lenin's analysis of finance capital, like his economic analysis in general, is deeply class-based: integrally connecting surplus capital to the lop-sided income or resource distribution, on the one hand, and imperialist aggressions in pursuit of higher profits, on the other.

> It goes without saying that if capitalism could … raise the living standards of the masses, who in spite of amazing technical progress are everywhere still … poverty-stricken, there could be no question of surplus capital.… But if capitalism did … [this], it would not be capitalism.… As long as capitalism retains what it is, surplus capital will be utilized not for the purpose of raising the standard of living of the masses in a given country, for this would be a decline in profits for the capitalists, but for the purpose of increasing profits by exporting capital abroad to backward countries. In these backward countries profits are usually high, for capital is scarce, the price of land is relatively low, wages are low, raw materials are cheap.
>
> (As quoted in Hunt 2002: 365–366)

Writing in the midst of WW I on the export of "surplus capital" from more- to less-developed countries, Lenin came to the conclusion that the war:

> was imperialist (that is, an annexationist, predatory, war of plunder) on the part of both sides; it was a war for the division of the world, for the partition and repartition of colonies and spheres of influence of finance capital, etc.
>
> (1916)

He repeatedly emphasized the class nature of external aggressions and global imperialist struggles over foreign markets:

> The *forms* of the struggle may and do constantly change in accordance with varying, relatively specific and temporary causes, but the *substance* of the struggle, its *class content*, positively *cannot* change while classes exist. Naturally, it is in the interests of … the … bourgeoisie … to obscure the substance of the present economic struggle (the division of the world) and to emphasize now this and now another *form* of the struggle.… The Capitalists divide the world, not out of any particular malice, but because the degree of concentration [of capital] which has been reached forces them to adopt this method in order to obtain profits.… To substitute the question of the form of the struggle and agreements (today peaceful, tomorrow warlike, the next day warlike again) for the question of the substance of the struggle and agreements between capitalist associations is to sink to the role of a sophist.
>
> (1916)

Policy and/or political conclusions of Lenin's analysis of "surplus" finance capital, and its social and political manifestations, both at home and abroad, were unmistakable: transformation of the poverty- and war-generating (capitalist) system into a superior civilization and a humane socioeconomic structure in which all citizen equitably (if not equally) benefited from the fruits of its labor and of the technological advances. Like Hilferding before him, Lenin argued that by creating big businesses and large scale production units, more-developed capitalist economies had practically paved the way for production on a socialistic basis because, while ownership remained private, production in such large scale enterprises had de-facto become social:

> Capitalism in its imperialist stage (the stage of monopolies and gigantic enterprises) leads directly to the most comprehensive socialization of production; it, so to speak, drags the capitalists, against their will and consciousness, into some sort of a new social order, a transitional one from complete free competition to complete socialization.… Production becomes social, but appropriation remains private. The social means of production remain the private property of a few. The general framework of formally recognized free competition remains, but the yoke of a few monopolists on the rest of the population becomes a hundred times heavier, more burdensome and intolerable.
>
> (Ibid.)

It is clear from these passages that the theoretical foundation of Lenin's book on imperialism, *Imperialism: The Highest Stage of Capitalism*, is grounded largely in finance capital. Perhaps a more suitable subtitle for the book would have been "*The Dominance of Finance Capital*," instead of "*The Highest Stage of Capitalism*," as it stands. His analysis of finance capital, and its dominant role in both domestic and international levels, stands in sharp contrast to those of many of the contemporary Marxist economists who, as shown below, tend to give short shrift to finance capital and/or financial sector; unduly arguing that financial developments are essentially incidental, secondary or merely reactions to industrial or real-sector developments (Kliman 2011; Brenner 2009; Kotz 2011a, 2011b; Bellamy Foster and Magdoff 2009).

Contemporary Marxist views of the financial crisis

As pointed out in Chapter 3 of this book, major financial bubbles of the magnitude of the bubble that imploded in 2008 have no place in the mainstream economic theory. For, according to the neoclassical near-barter general equilibrium and/or "circular flow" model, monetary or financial deviations from the underlying real values would be only temporary as such deviations would soon be reverted back by the market mechanism to their initial positions of equilibrium. In terms of the "circular flow" model, this means that "leakages" of savings from the income–expenditure flow would likewise be temporary as those "leakages" would soon be "injected" back into the flow of spending when they are borrowed (through banks and other financial intermediaries) by entrepreneurs in the real sector and spent for investment/production purposes.

In a similar fashion, though for different reasons, many contemporary Marxist economists also tend to give short shrift to monetary/financial categories in their explanations of the Great Recession that followed the 2008 market crash. Just as neoclassical economists seem incapable of extricating themselves from the elegant but abstract "circular flow" model, so too many Marxist economists seem reluctant to look beyond the "circuit of capital" model, which is discussed largely in Volumes 1 and 2 of Marx's *Capital*, and which like the neoclassical "circular flow" model is fashioned primarily on real, not financial, sector developments and categories.

This regrettably flawed treatment of finance capital by a great number of today's Marxist scholars represents not only an obvious departure from earlier views of Marxists like Lenin and Hilferding, but also from Marx's own treatment of finance capital. For, as discussed earlier in this chapter, Marx did, indeed, envision (in Volume 3 of *Capital*, Chapters 25–33) scenarios where part of the production or real-sector profits, which are today called "retained earnings," may permanently abandon or leak out of the production/reproduction circuit in pursuit of speculative gains, that is, for purely financial gains through buying and selling of assets. Calling the portion of finance capital that leaves the sphere of production in favor of the financial sector—in pursuit of independent, parasitic expansion—"surplus capital", Marx wrote, as quoted earlier in this chapter, "Profit can be made purely from trading in a variety of financial claims existing only on paper"; and that "The subsequent credit swindle proves that no real obstacle stands in the way of the employment of this surplus-capital. . . ." These and similar passages in part five of Volume 3 of *Capital*, which indicate that, according to Marx, finance capital can and does sometimes expand outside or independent of the real sector of the economy, are clearly at adds with the views of many contemporary Marxist economists who tend to perceive financial developments as mere reflections of, or reactions to, some supposedly undercurrent real developments.

By thus neglecting or trivializing the crucially important role of financial factors as sources of instability and crisis in today's advanced market economies, most contemporary Marxist economists have tended to either dismiss as "only monetary," or provide woefully insufficient explanations (almost always trying to find a "real," or non-monetary, cause) for either the 2008 financial crash or the Great Recession that followed the crash. Yet, an understanding of market cycles of boom and bust of the past several decades, as well as of the on-going chronic Great Recession, "requires us," as Professor Peter Gowan puts it, "to transcend the commonsense idea that changes in the so-called real economy drive outcomes in a supposed financial superstructure" (2010: 47).

A distinct advantage of Marxist theories of capitalist crisis over those of mainstream economists is that, contrary to mainstream theories (which blame the recurring crises of capitalism on "external" factors), they focus on the structural dynamics of the market mechanism that tend to periodically erode capitalist profitability from within the system itself; thereby precipitating a crisis. While rival Marxist theories have almost always disagreed on factors that precipitate a fall in profitability, they all have agreed that those factors operate within the sphere of production, or the real sector. A declining trend in profitability, which precede and/or drive a crisis, could thus be occasioned by factors such as insufficient aggregate demand, overcapacity, profit "squeeze," or a too high capital–labor ratio, which is more or less the same as Marx's too large of an "organic composition of capital" (Shaikh 1987).

Prior to the rise of finance capital to the stage of independent expansion (from industrial capital), Marxist proponents of these theories of crisis could safely disregard the role of the financial sector in the articulation of their theories. For, under such market conditions, finance capital moved more or less in tandem with industrial capital, as it was used or invested largely for commercial and manufacturing purposes. Thus, for example, Marxist theories of the 1970s recession could, as they actually did, justifiably discount or disregard the role of the financial sector and focus mainly on the role of the real sector developments in their explanations of that recession (ibid.).

Under market conditions of extensive financialization, however, the role of financial bubbles and bursts in bringing about economy-wide crises can no longer be ignored, or trivialized as of secondary importance. For, under these conditions, finance capital often finds more lucrative investment opportunities in the financial sector than the real sector. Larger and larger shares of credit creation are increasingly devoted to financial rather than real investment. Greatly facilitated by extensive deregulations of recent decades, these developments have in recent years led to a number of destabilizing financial bubbles, whose bursts have constituted the driving forces behind the ensuing recessions—recessions or crises of debt deflation.

These developments have posed serious challenges to contemporary Marxist theories of crisis. For, grounded in the sphere of production, or the real sector, they seem to fall short of providing satisfactory explanations for either the financial bubble that burst in 2008, or the Great Recession that followed the collapse of the bubble. With few exceptions (Gowan 2010; Mohun 2010; Dumenil and Levy 2011), most Marxist scholars argue that (a) the inflation of the bubble was a reaction to the undercurrent developments in the real sector, and (b) the impact of the bursting of the bubble on the ensuing long recession was a "triggering," not a causal effect. Viewing the bubble as having merely a "triggering" not a causal effect implies, obviously, that the main driver of the crisis, "a long period of a falling trend of profitability in the real sector," was already in place; all it needed to be expressed as the fully-fledged Great Recession was a triggering impact, which was provided by the financial collapse. To make this argument plausible, that is, to build a theoretical foundation that the "crisis-prone" conditions that escalated into the Great Recession by the financial collapse were already present in the real sector, a number of these scholars insist that the U.S. economy never really recovered from the 1970s contractionary cycle (Kliman 2011; Bellamy Foster and Magdoff 2010; Kotz 2009; Brenner 2009).

For example, radical proponents of the underconsumption theory of economic stagnation tend to attribute every crisis in the financial sector to a crisis of profitability in the real sector. Thus, John Bellamy Foster and Fred Magdoff, two of the leading advocates of this theory, wrote (in the immediate aftermath of the 2008 financial crash), "Our argument in a nutshell is that both the financial explosion in recent decades and the financial implosion now taking place are to be explained mainly in reference to stagnation tendencies within the underlying [real] economy" (2010: 81). Acknowledging and then rejecting alternative explanations of the crash, Bellamy Foster and Magdoff, further wrote:

> the root problem went much deeper, and was to be found in a real economy experiencing slower growth, giving rise to financial explosion as capital sought to "leverage" its way out of the problem by expanding debt and gaining speculative profits.
>
> (Ibid.: 82)

In other words, financialization, or the expansion of the financial sector, is precipitated largely by stagnation and lower profitability in the real sector; which means that financial implosions and crises are also ultimately caused by crises of profitability in the real sector. "Since financialization can be viewed as the response of capital to the stagnation tendency in the real economy, a crisis of financialization inevitably means a resurfacing of the underlying stagnation endemic to the advanced capitalist economy" (ibid.: 90).

Bellamy Foster and Magdoff's stagnation argument that the 2008 market crash in the U.S. was preceded by nearly four decades of economic inertia, that is, the argument that the U.S. economy never really recovered from the 1970s fatigue, is based on the theory of monopoly-finance capitalism, expounded by

Kalecki (1997), Steindl (1952) and Baran and Sweezy (1966). According to this theory, at higher stages of capitalist development, monopolistic and/or oligopolistic market structures tend to gradually replace competitive market structures. As this change in market structure erodes price competition, it also reduces the dynamic impetus to investment on new innovations. At the same time, "monopoly" capitalism also reduces purchasing power and consumer demand as it further aggravates poverty and inequality. Reduced demand for both capital and consumer goods means, obviously, narrowed opportunities for profitable investment in manufacturing, or stagnation in the real sector of the economy. It also means a steady outflow of investible funds, or retained earnings, from the sphere of production to the sphere of speculation (in the financial sector) in pursuit of more profitable investment outlets. Thus, not only the financial bubble and its burst (in 2008) but also the ensuing Great Recession all had their roots in capitalist tendencies to monopoly and stagnation.

Robert Brenner, another radical scholar, likewise explains the credit expansion and financialization of recent years as a reaction to the "declining profitability" and the resulting stagnation in the real sector—developments that were, in turn, precipitated by a persistent tendency to overcapacity, or a chronic problem of insufficient demand since the early 1970s. However, contrary to the Monthly Review theory of underconsumption (discussed above), which attributes the problems of insufficient demand and stagnation to "monopoly capitalism" and the lopsided distribution of income, Brenner attributes these problems to the systemic tendency to constantly produce/supply more than it can consume/demand. In the 1970s, when the Japanese and European economies were doing well while the U.S. economy was grappling with the crisis of "stagflation," Brenner argued that the suffering of the U.S. economy at the time was because by the late 1960s and early 1970s it had lost considerable share of its global markets to Japan and Europe. Now that the stagnation has also engulfed Japan and Europe Brenner argues that the problem of insufficient demand has become global—it is both systemic and global.

> The long term weakening of capital accumulation and of aggregate demand has been rooted in a profound system-wide decline and failure to recover the rate of return on capital, resulting largely … from a persistent tendency to over-capacity, i.e., oversupply, in global manufacturing industries.
>
> (2009: 3)

According to Brenner, manufacturers responded to "overcapacity" and weak demand in two ways. The first response was to retrench: to curtail investment, employment, wages and social spending, all of which (in the manner of a vicious cycle development) aggravated and/or perpetuated the stagnation that had started in the early 1970s. Indeed, Brenner argues that, with the exception of several years in the second half of the 1990s, the 1973–2007 represented a long, continuous stagnant cycle. The second response was reflected in the monetary policies of credit expansion and indebtedness, or loan pushing, designed to offset the declining demand in the real sector through debt and asset price inflation. However, the intractable structural weakness continued to hound the economy, until it eventually collapsed in 2008.

> From the start of the long downturn in 1973, economic authorities staved off the kind of crises that had historically plagued the capitalist system by resort to ever greater borrowing.... But they secured a modicum of stability only at the cost of deepening stagnation....
>
> (Ibid.)

Just as Brenner cannot envision an independent expansion of the financial sector from the real sector—developments in the former sector are always reactions to those in the latter sector—so he rejects the view (and the evidence) that a declining financial cycle can precipitate and lead a declining real sector; in other words, he denies that an independent crisis in the financial sector can be transmitted and spread to an otherwise healthy real sector. To the extent that a financial crisis can or does affect the real sector it would have only a triggering effect on the already anemic or stagnant economy ready to collapse: "Lacking an engine to drive it once the housing bubble had begun to deflate, the [real] economy was sliding toward recession *well before* the banking-cum-credit market crisis struck with a vengeance in mid-summer 2007" (ibid.: 7). Again: "What suddenly turned the specter of *a severe cyclical downturn* or worse into the reality of catastrophic systemic crisis was a development in the financial sector of which few were aware" (ibid.: 4).

David Kotz, another radical economist, likewise, rejects the arguments that the long chronic recession that followed the 2008 financial collapse was transmitted from, or driven by, the financial sector:

> One common view is that the severity of the real sector crisis is a result of the financial sector crisis.... This paper argues that the real sector crisis that began in 2008—the so-called "Great Recession"—is not primarily a result of the banking collapse.
>
> (2011b: 1)

Instead, "It is argued that the current crisis can be understood as a particular kind of over-investment crisis" (2011a: 2). Specifically, Kotz argues that the easy credit and the strong, asset-bubble-induced demand that preceded the 2008 crash led manufacturers to invest and expand production capacity. Once the bubble burst and the bubble-induced demand faded, however, producers found themselves saddled with "overcapacity" and falling profits, which Kotz calls the "crisis of over-investment"—not of the debt deflation that, after significantly reducing purchasing power/demand, appeared as over-investment (2011a, 2011b).

There is an obvious weakness in Kotz's argument: at the heart of the real sector crisis was over-investment; at the heart of over-investment was the artificially-elevated strong demand that was, in turn, prompted by what has come to be known in recent years as financialization, that is, by the financial and/or asset price inflation—so far, so good. However, once the financial/asset-price bubble burst and almost instantly unleashed a devastating crisis of deleveraging, or debt deflation, the connection or the causal relationship between the crisis in the financial sector that led to the crisis in the real sector, suddenly disappeared. The glaring inconsistency here seems to be lost on Professor Kotz: debt or asset-price inflation, boosting demand, drives an expanding cycle, such as the one that preceded the 2008 market crash; but debt or asset-price deflation, dampening demand, does not drive a declining cycle. In other words, the so-called "wealth effect" on demand and, therefore, on the economy works only in one direction, not two.

Andrew Kliman, another radical economist, is even more dismissive of the contributory role of the 2008 financial collapse in the Great Recession that followed the collapse, save for a "triggering" effect. He is also dismissive of the views and evidence that, starting with 1983, the U.S. economy did, indeed, recover from the long stagnation that lasted from the early 1970 to early 1980s:

> I will argue that the economy never fully recovered from the recessions of the mid-1970s and early 1980s.... I will argue that the persistently frail condition of capitalist production was among the causes of the financial crisis. And, most importantly, I will argue that it set the stage for the Great Recession.... In light of the frailty of capitalist production, *the recession and its consequences were waiting to happen* (emphasis added).
>
> (2011)

Kliman adamantly insists that the real-sector rate of profit (which he defines "as a percentage of the amount of money invested") in the U.S. economy has been either stagnant or in decline for the past forty years. The following is the proffered explanation for this alleged four-decade-long stagnation.

Prior to government intervention in market developments, that is, before the Great Depression and WW II, periodic crises of capitalism were let to run their course; which meant widespread bankruptcies and extensive value or capital destruction. While brutal (since no business was "too big to fail"), those earlier crises also had salutary, "market-cleansing" effects; as they wiped out inefficiencies and excess capacities and paved the way for fresh beginnings and robust profitability. As Kliman puts it, "Paradoxically, these processes also restore profitability and thereby set the stage for a new boom, such as the boom that followed the Great Depression and World War II" (ibid.). Demand management policies of government since the Great Depression and WW II, designed to prevent "value destruction" and/or "market-cleansing," however, have made both recessions and expansions less pronounced: post-WW II economic/business cycles have not been as long or as gyrating as previous ones.

> During the global economic slumps of the mid-1970s and early 1980s, however, much less capital value was destroyed than had been destroyed

> during the Depression and the following World War.... But since so much less capital value was destroyed during the 1970s and early 1980s than was destroyed in the 1930s and early 1940s, the decline in the rate of profit was not reversed. And because it was not reversed, profitability remained at too low a level to sustain a new boom.
>
> (Ibid.)

It is true that government demand-management policies since the Great Depression have made market fluctuations less severe than those before the Depression. It does not follow, however, that "since so much less capital value was destroyed during the 1970s and early 1980s than was destroyed in the 1930s and early 1940s," the U.S. economy did not, therefore, recover from the 1970s slump, as Kliman claims. Although he backs up his claim by his own calculations of the rate of profit, those calculations—using historical cost valuation for capital stock and before-tax, both direct and indirect, before-interest profit flow—are highly questionable. Not surprisingly, the outcome of his calculations, that is, his measure of the rate of profit, displaying a constantly declining trend for the entire post-WW II period, flies in the face of reality: it is at odds not only with the official rates of profit, but also with those of many independent scholars, including a number of Marxists (Shaikh 2010; Mohun 2010; Dumenil and Levy 2011).

A detailed evaluation of these economists' views of the Great Recession, is beyond the purview of this discussion; nor is such a thorough assessment essential to the discussion. Suffice it to say that, as pointed out above, their main claim that the recession was not caused by the 2008 financial collapse and/or the ensuing debt deflation; and that it was, instead, precipitated by a long period of chronic stagnation and a falling trend in profitability is not supported by facts. Evidence shows that, contrary to such claims, the 2008 financial collapse and/or the ensuing Great Recession were not preceded by a pattern of declining profits in the real sector of the economy. Empirical data indicates that the declining profitability trend that had started in the late 1960s and early 1970s was reversed and/or halted in 1983–1984. Since then the real sector profit rate on a macro level went through a number of zigzags, but the overall profit trajectory from 1983 to 2008 displayed a rising trend. The most noteworthy of those zigzags were the two relatively short-term declining cycles of the early 1990s and the early 2000s, on the one hand; and the three longer term rising cycles of the 1983–1987, 1993–2000 and 2002–2008, on the other (Figure 5.1).

> The main conclusion that we can derive from inspecting the time-series plots of various measures of the rate of profit for the U.S. economy (Figures 1–12) is that, other than one case, all the measures display similar trends: there is a break in the declining trend of profitability in the early 1980s; the subsequent period is marked by either a trendless or a slowly rising trend in profitability.... The weight of evidence thus suggests clearly that the current crisis was not preceded by a prolonged period of declining profitability. In

> fact, the current crisis was preceded by a period of rising profitability, buoyed by favourable trends in both the profit share and technology.
>
> (Basu and Vasudevan 2013: 83, especially Figure 21)

These findings confirm those of the renowned Marxist economist Anwar Shaikh who has, likewise, demonstrated empirically that the relatively long cycle of stagnation that had started in the late 1960s and early 1970s turned into a new cycle of expansion in 1983–1984 that, with the exception of a few short downturns along the long expanding cycle, continued until it was turned into the Great Recession by the 2008 financial crash. Shaikh highlights a number of contributing factors to that expansion: drop in wages and other labor costs, drop in interest rates, extensive deregulations, and asset price/debt-driven strong demand (2010, especially Figures 1 and 6). (Interestingly, Shaikh also characterizes the role of the 2008 market collapse in the ensuing Great Recession as "triggering," but in an entirely different sense: whereas for him "triggering" obviously means turning the pre-crash long cycle of expansion to the post-crash Great Recession, for Kliman, Bellamy Foster, Magdoff, Kotz, and Brenner it means turning the pre-crash "long cycle of stagnation" to the post-crash Great Recession.)

One would hope that in light of this evidence those Marxist economists who have so far tended to give short shrift to the role of finance capital in precipitating economic crises would now be willing to expand their traditional theories of

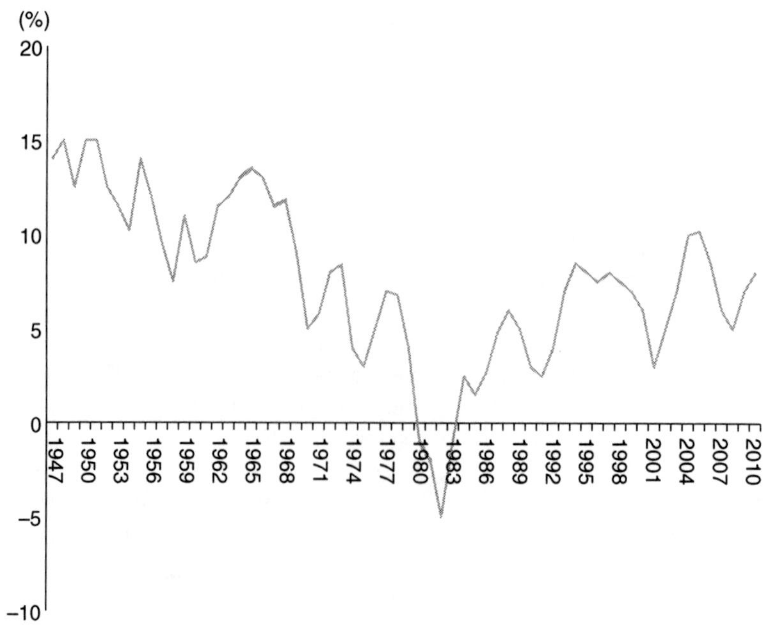

Figure 5.1 Rate of profit U.S. non-financial corporations (1947–2010) (source: Based on Shaikh 2010: 52, Figure 6; Basu and Vasudevan 2013: 83, Figure 21).

crisis, and acknowledge the fact that, in the era of finance capital, financial cycles can and do sometimes lead real cycles. For example, just as the debt-leveraged asset-price inflation of the 2002–2007 years boosted the purchasing power and helped expand the overall economy during those years, so did the debt deflation mechanism that set in following the 2008 financial implosion greatly contributed to the spread of the ensuing Great Recession.

Alas, in a regrettably rigid and ahistorical fashion these economists continue to insist that the role of finance capital is essentially secondary or incidental to that of industrial capital. It is true that a number of these economists have written extensively on the so-called financialization of most of the advanced market economies, and the havoc that parasitic finance capital has inflicted on these economies. Nonetheless, they tend to explain every development in the financial sector by an undercurrent or submerged "cause" in the real sector, that is, by a reaction to changes in the profitability imperatives in the non-financial sector—as if financial factors cannot affect profitability imperatives in the non-financial sector. It is one thing to say that the expansion of fictitious finance capital in an economy is *ultimately* bound by the aggregate magnitude of the real values that are produced in that economy; it is quite another, however, to view finance capital as largely shadowing industrial capital (more or less, like pre-capitalist or early stages of capitalism), as these economists seem to do.

It is not clear (it is, indeed, puzzling) why these radical scholars (implicitly) believe that the "wealth effect" on demand, and therefore on the entire economy, works only in one direction: debt and/or asset-price inflation can boost demand and cause or magnify an expanding real cycle; but debt and/or asset-price deflation cannot cause or aggravate a real-sector recession. Of course, the effects of debt deflation on purchasing power and/or demand would be manifested in a number of ways: underconsumption, overcapacity, and/or falling rate of profit. This allows Robert Brenner and David Kotz, for example, to argue that the Great Recession has been a crisis of overcapacity; it also allows the proponents of underconsumption theory to claim that it has been a crisis of underconsumption; and it further allows Andrew Kliman and those who think like him to argue that the crisis validated the theory of "the tendency of the rate of profit to fall." But all these problems (insufficient demand, overcapacity/overproduction and falling profits) were/are symptoms or effects of the crisis, not its causes. They were driven primarily by the 2008 financial implosion and the ensuing debt deflation; which means that not only was the Great Recession triggered by the financial collapse, but that it was also driven largely by the resulting debt deflation.

Note

1 This passage is based on Marx's discussion of "Speculation and fictitious capital," as quoted in Wikipedia, retrieved from http://en.wikipedia.org/wiki/Fictitious_capital#cite_note-1 (accessed July 7, 2013).

References

Baran, P. and Sweezy, P. (1966). *Monopoly capital.* New York: Monthly Review Press.

Basu, D. and Vasudevan, R. (2013). Technology, distribution and the rate of profit in the US economy: Understanding the current crisis. *Cambridge Journal of Economics, 37* (1), 57–89. Retrieved from http://cje.oxfordjournals.org/content/37/1/57.full.pdf+html (accessed July 1, 2013).

Bellamy Foster, J. and Magdoff, F. (2010). Financial implosion and economic stagnation. In M. Chossudovsky and A. G. Marshall (Eds.). *The global economic crisis: The Great Depression of the XXI century.* Montreal, Canada: Center for Research on Globalization.

Bellamy Foster, J. and Magdoff, F. (2009). *The great financial crisis: Causes and consequences.* New York: Monthly Review Press.

Bellamy Foster, J. and McChesney, R. W. (2009). Monopoly-finance capital and the paradox of accumulation. *Monthly Review, 61*(5) October. Retrieved from http://monthlyreview.org/2009/10/01/monopoly-finance-capital-and-the-paradox-of-accumulation.

Brenner, R. (2009). What is good for Goldman Sachs is good for America: The origins of the current crisis. Unpublished paper, Center for Social Theory and Comparative History, University of California (Los Angeles). April 18. Retrieved from www.sscnet.ucla.edu/issr/cstch/papers/BrennerCrisisTodayOctober2009.pdf (accessed November 10, 2012).

Dumenil, G. and Levy, D. (2011). *The crisis of neoliberalism.* Cambridge, MA: Harvard University Press.

Finger, B. (2013). Economic recovery from below: Notes on the insufficiency of "taxing the rich." *New Politics, 54* (2). Retrieved from http://newpol.org/content/economic-recovery-below-notes-insufficiency-taxing-rich (accessed August 2, 2013).

Gowan, P. (2010). The Crisis in the Heartland. In M. Konings (Ed.). *The great credit crash.* London and New York: Verso.

Hilferding, R. (1981). *Finance capital: A study of the latest phase of capitalist development.* Tom Bottomore (Ed.). London: Routledge & Kegan Paul.

Hobson, J. A. (1965) *Imperialism: A study.* Ann Arbor: University of Michigan Press.

Hunt, K. E. (2002). *History of economic thought: A critical perspective.* (Updated 2nd edn.). New York and London: M. E. Sharpe.

Kalecki, M. (1997). *Collected works of Michal Kalecki.* Oxford: Oxford University Press.

Kliman, A. (2011). *The failure of capitalist production: Underlying causes of the great recession.* Retrieved from www.marxisthumanistinitiative.org/economic-crisis/new-book-the-failure-of-capitalist-production.html (accessed July 8, 2013).

Kotz, D. M. (2011a). The current economic crisis in the U.S.: A crisis of over-investment. Unpublished paper, University of Massachusetts, Amherst. Retrieved from www.icape.org/f5-kotz.pdf (accessed December 9, 2012).

Kotz, D. M. (2011b). Overinvestment and the crisis of 2008. Unpublished paper, University of Massachusetts, Amherst. Retrieved from http://people.umass.edu/dmkotz/Over-Investment_and_the_Crisis_11_01.pdf (accessed October 15, 2012).

Kotz, D. M. (2009). The financial and economic crisis of 2008: A systemic crisis of neoliberal capitalism. *Review of Radical Political Economics, 41*(3), 305–317.

Lapavistas, C. and Levina, I. (2011). *Financial profit: Profit from production and profit upon alienation.* Discussion Paper 24, University of London. Retrieved from http://researchonmoneyandfinance.org/media/papers/RMF-24-Lapavitsas-Levina.pdf (accessed July 18, 2013).

Lenin, V. I. (1916). *Imperialism, the highest stage of capitalism*. Moscow: Progress Publishers (Public Domain: Modern History Sourcebook). Retrieved from www.fordham.edu/halsall/mod/1916lenin-imperialism.html#bm1 (accessed July 8, 2013).

Marx, K. (1967). *Capital* (Vol. 3). New York: International Publishers.

Mohun, S. (2010). *The crisis of 2008 in historical perspective*. Working Paper, Queen Mary University.

Shaikh, A. (2010). The first Great Depression of the 21st century. In L. Panitch *et al.* (Eds.). *The crisis this time*. London: Merlin Press.

Shaikh, A. (1987). The falling rate of profit and the economic crisis in the U.S. In Robert C. *et al.* (Eds.) *The imperiled economy* (Book I). New York: Union for Radical Political Economy.

Steindl, J. (1952). *Maturity and stagnation in American capitalism*. New York: Monthly Review Press.

Weeks, J. (2010). *Capital, exploitation and economic crisis*. London and New York: Routledge.

6 Debt cancelation—learning from biblical jubilee

> We must pierce the smoke-screen of creditors and re-establish the historical truth. Repeated and generalized debt cancelation has occurred throughout history.
>
> Eric Toussaint

> The spirit of the Lord is upon me
> because he has anointed me;
> he has sent me to announce good news to the poor,
> to proclaim release for prisoners
> and recovery of sight for the blind;
> to let the broken victims go free,
> to proclaim the year of the Lord's favour [the Jubilee year, or the year of debt relief and land restitution].[1]
>
> Isaiah 61 (declared by Jesus in his hometown synagogue in Nazareth as the intent of his ministry)

It is, of course, altogether axiomatic that the first step in the treatment of a bleeding patient is to stop the bleeding. In a similar fashion, the bleeding economies under the crushing burden of debt overhang need to, first, cast the albatross of indebtedness and, then, seek preventive measures to fend off the recurrence of the plague of debt. Otherwise, debt servicing can drain the resources of the debtor without even stopping the snowballing process of the debt—just as nonstop bleeding can condemn the patient to death.

In this chapter I will first provide a brief overview of the history of debt cancelation; and then offer alternatives to today's widely debated schemes of debt servicing that, along with a number of vaguely-suggested regulations of the financial system, are supposed to mitigate economic crises that are plaguing many economies around the world.

Debt cancelation in Bronze-Age Mesopotamia (2400–1400 BC)

Historical records show that debt cancelation in Bronze Age Mesopotamia took place on a fairly regular basis from 2400 to 1400 BC. Indeed, archeological evidence indicates that periodic acts of debt relief were viewed more as rules than exceptions. Ancient documents decoded from cuneiform inscriptions have led many historians to believe that the Bronze Age tradition of debt cancelation in the Near/Middle East may have served as the setting or model for the biblical pronouncements of debt relief. Careful studies of those records indicate that, contrary to today's perceptions (shaped largely by the influential financial interests) that debt cancelation may lead to economic disorder, as epitomized by the slogan "too big to fail," those earlier practices of debt relief were carried out precisely for the opposite reasons: to restore economic revival and social harmony by undoing the ravages of debt wrought on the economy and the overwhelming majority of the population. Freedom in those days meant real, economic freedom—freedom from debt bondage—not the abstract concept of freedom promoted today.

> The type of economic freedom being referred to was the royal act of cancelling back taxes and other personal debts, restoring traditional family landholding rights and freeing citizens who had been enslaved for debt. These royal interventions ensured rather than encroached on general economic freedom.
>
> (Hudson 1993: 15)

In those earlier times of periodic debt cancelation, economic, political and social life was organized mainly around the temple and the palace. The peasantry was provided with land (which they rented), tools, draught animals, livestock, and water for irrigation so that they could grow food for the royal families and dignitaries, their armies, their servants and workers of all type. In addition to the land they cultivated for the palace and the temple, the peasants owned their own land, home, livestock, and tools. When the harvest was poor, they incurred debt. They also accumulated debt through loans granted privately by high-ranking officials and other money lenders eager to get rich and to seize the peasants' property in case of default. If peasants were unable to pay off their debts, they could find themselves reduced to the condition of serfs or slaves. In order to ensure social peace and stability, and especially to prevent peasants' living conditions from deteriorating too far below tolerable levels, the authorities periodically canceled all debt and restored peasants' rights (Toussaint 2012).

While the most radical instances of debt cancelation and land reform in Bronze Age Mesopotamia/Near East are known to have been those carried out during the reign of King Hammurabi (1792–1750 BC), the history of such enlightened policies of debt relief goes further back in time to the Sumerian *Amargi* (royal declaration of land-based deb cancelation) in the city-state of Lagash in 2400 BC. Enmetena, a ruler of Sumer's southeastern city of Lagash from 2404 to 2375 BC:

> Promulgated the earliest Sumerian debt cancellation on record, *c.*2400 BC, after his military victory over the neighboring city of Umma. Like many subsequent such records, this edict is inscribed on a foundation brick for a

> local temple which he dedicated. Some 4,500 years later, archaeologists unearthed the inscription. Its first translator, Maurice Lambert (1972), rendered its wording as follows: Enmetena "instituted liberty in Lagash. He restored the child to its mother, and the mother to her child; he cancelled interest, and probably the debts themselves."
>
> (Hudson 1993: 15)

Another notable Sumerian ruler of Lagash was Gudea who, according to economic historian Michael Hudson, has left a number of valuable statues with important documents inscribed on them. He has also left a number of cylinders one of which contains the longest surviving Sumerian poem (1,400 lines) commemorating his rebuilding of the city-temple and how he restored order by canceling the land-related debts at the New Year festival celebrating this occasion in 2130 BC. The idea behind New Year festivals was to put "the world back in order," which "involved cancelling the debts which, above all other factors, disturbed traditional economic balance and self-sufficiency on the land" (ibid.: 16–17).

From the time of Enmetena's proclamation of *Amargi* in Sumer's city-state of Lagash in 2400 BC to Hammurabi's announcement of *misharun* (also meaning debt cancelation) in Babylon in 1792, upon his coronation as the king of Babylonia, some fourteen declarations of debt cancelations by various Sumerian and Babylonian kings are recorded (ibid.: 8–9). A detailed account of that long and fascinating history is beyond the purview of this study. Suffice it to say that, as mentioned earlier, periodic debt modifications in those days were viewed as essential to social health and economic revival.

The Hammurabi dynasty in Babylonia (approximately 1900–1600 BC) carried out periodic debt relief and agrarian reform programs (called *misharum* acts, or edicts) that were even more wide-ranging than those carried out earlier by the Sumerian rulers in Lagash. During his long rule of 42 years (1792–1750), Hammurabi alone carried out four such reforms or restructurings: in 1792, 1780, 1771 and 1762. These *misharum* edicts, Hudson points out,

> [M]aintained widespread land tenure for Babylonia's indebted soldier-peasantry, by saving the land from passing out of the hands of the population at large to creditors on more than just a temporary basis.... The designated occasion for clearing Babylonia's financial slate was the New Year festival, celebrated in the spring. Babylonian rulers oversaw the ritual of "breaking the tablets," that is, the debt records, restoring economic balance as part of the calendrical renewal of society along with the rest of nature.... Persons held as debt pledges were released to rejoin their families. Other debtors were restored cultivation rights to their customary lands, free of whatever mortgage liens had accumulated.
>
> (1993: 20)

Hammurabi's successors continued the tradition of periodic debt cancelations until the end of his dynasty in approximately 1600 BC. The last debt relief was carried out by Ammisaduqa, the last ruler of his dynasty, who came to power in 1646. Ammisaduqa's Misharum, decreed in 1636, proclaimed:

> Official creditors and tax collectors who had expropriated peasants should compensate them and return their property.... In cases where a creditor had taken some item of property using pressure, unless he gave it back and/or repaid its worth in full, he would be put to death.... In the wake of this decree, commissions were set up to review all real estate contracts and to eliminate all those which fell under the terms of the debt cancellation proclamation with a view to restoring the prior situation, *status quo ante*.
>
> (Toussaint 2012)

Historical records show that, in all, about 30 instances of debt cancelation took place in Mesopotamia from 2400 to 1400 BC. Such times of relief from debt bondage and economic hardship signified joyous occasions for widespread festivities, usually in conjunction with the annual celebrations of the New Year and/or the beginning of the spring (Alexander 1938, Hudson 1993). Today, such liberating economic reforms, which would bring financial relief to the overwhelming majority of the people, are considered taboo because they are portrayed as transgressions into the sacred domain of market mechanism.

The end of the reign of the Hammurabi dynasty in Babylonia, which came in 1595 when the Hittites conquered Babylon, also marked the end of the nearly 1000-year tradition of periodic agrarian reform and debt cancelation in Mesopotamia. This ushered in an inauspicious period in the history of the region that came to be known as Mesopotamia's "Dark Ages" (1400–800 BC). During this period "no further act of debt cancellation has been found ... inequality increased and intensified. Land was taken over by big private land-owners and debt enslavement became commonplace" (Toussaint 2012). However, the magnificent Bronze Age tradition of periodic debt relief and land redistribution in Babylonia that was thus lost after the Hammurabi dynasty was later revived in other parts of the region: in Judah/Canaan/Palestine in the Middle and Near East, as well as in the Pharaonic Egypt in North-East Africa. In both places, the revival and diffusion of the Babylonian practices took place after approximately 800 BC.

Debt cancelation in the Pharaonic Egypt

The first recorded instance of debt cancelation in Egypt seems to have taken place in the late eighth century BC, during the reign of Pharaoh Bocchoris (717–711). What makes the periodic practice of debt cancelation in Pharaonic Egypt undeniable is the discovery of the Rosetta Stone (an ancient Egyptian granodiorite stele) in 1799 by members of Napoleon's expedition to Egypt. The Stone's inscription, deciphered in 1822 by Jean-François Champollion, leaves no doubt that the tradition of debt cancelation was upheld in Egypt by the pharaohs from the eighth century BC, before Alexander the Great conquered the country in the fourth century BC. The Stone bears the same text in three languages: Ancient Egyptian, Egyptian demotic, and the Greek of Alexander the Great's era. As a major historical document, a lot has been said and written about the Rosetta Stone. What is less known, however, is the fact that the inscription memorializes a debt cancelation proclamation by King Ptolemy V (204–180 BC), issued at Memphis in 196 BC:

> Ptolemy V's debt cancellation reflects a declining economy plagued by pressure of taxes, rapid accumulation of arrears and … confiscations, prisons full of criminals and public and private debtors … fugitives scattered all over the country and living by robbery, and compulsion applied in every sphere of life, including military conscription. The natural results were scarcity of labor, gradual depopulation of villages, abandonment of fields, deterioration of land, neglect of dikes and canals, and … an atmosphere of war and unrest.
>
> (Hudson 1993: 31)

Ptolemy V's strategy of economic revival (through debt cancelation and financial relief to the public) in the face of widespread indebtedness and economic stagnation stands in sharp contrast to the practices of today's economic policy makers in the U.S. and other advanced market economies who have embarked on a counterproductive, recession-generating austerity course that, instead of economic recovery, is deepening the relentless recession.

Debt cancelation in the Canaan/Judah/Palestine—biblical passages on debt relief

> To the later prophets and Biblical compilers, the most important laws were the Sabbath year (*shemitta*) of Deuteronomy freeing debt-servants and the Jubilee Year cancelling debts and redistributing the land to its traditional user-holders every fifty years. Yet today, although many Christians, Jews and Moslems look to the Old Testament for guidance on what is morally right, these economic sanctions have been all but ignored as representing utopian sentiments.
>
> (Michael Hudson, economic historian, 1993)

Numerous passages in the Old Testament dealing with issues of economic equity and social justice are truly revolutionary, as they call for periodic rebalancing of socioeconomic arrangements that would include debt cancelation and land restitution:

> The laws of Exodus 21–23 (the Book of the Covenant), the Holiness Code of Leviticus and the laws of Deuteronomy place interest-bearing debt, land tenure and the periodic renewal of economic freedom from debt at the center of their economic program.
>
> (Ibid.: 38)

A careful reading of many passages of the Old Testament reveals that the major biblical codes and laws regarding economic issues continued the age-old tradition of periodic land reform and debt restructuring practiced in Bronze Age Mesopotamia.

It is a well-established historical fact that the "year of the Lord's favor," recited by Jesus from Isaiah 61 (see prologue to this chapter), refers to the year of debt relief and/or land restitution, known as the year of the Sabbath and/or Jubilee. The term Sabbath, derived from the Hebrew word *Shabbath* (or *Shabbat*), literally means "time/day of rest." Just as in a weekly cycle the seventh day has come to be known (in a number of religions and/or traditions) as the day of rest from work, so does the seventh year in a seven-year agricultural cycle, according to the biblical sources, refer to the year of refraining from tilling and cultivating, as this would give rest not only to the farmers but also the land. "For six years you are to sow your fields and harvest the crops, but during the seventh year you let the land rest unplowed and unused" (The Book of the Covenant in Exodus 23: 9–13). There are a number of similar passages in the Old Testament.

Perhaps the most important point in the biblical requirement of the observation of the year of the Sabbath (which is outlined in Deuteronomy 15, Exodus 21:2 and 23:10–11) is that the required "rest" is not limited to relief from work; it also includes relief from indebtedness and debt servitude.

> At the end of every seven years you must cancel debts. This is how it is to be done: Every creditor shall cancel any loan they have made to a fellow Israelite. They shall not require payment from anyone among their own people, because the Lord's time for canceling debts has been proclaimed.
>
> (Deuteronomy 15: 1–11)

Likewise, in Exodus 21: 1–11 The Lord instructs Moses that, "These are the rulings you are to set before them: If you buy a Hebrew servant, he is to serve you for six years. But in the seventh year he shall go free without paying anything."

More important (and much better known) than the biblical year of the Sabbath is the year of Jubilee, defined in Leviticus 25–26, which mandates not only debt cancelation every fifty years, as does the year of Sabbath every seven years, but also land restitution or redemption:

> Count off seven Sabbath years—seven times seven years—so that the seven sabbath years amount to a period of forty-nine years. Then have the trumpet sounded everywhere on the tenth day of the seventh month; on the Day of Atonement sound the trumpet throughout your land. Consecrate the fiftieth year and proclaim liberty throughout the land to all its inhabitants. It shall be a jubilee for you; each of you is to return to your family property and to your own clan.
>
> (Leviticus 25: 8–11)

As Rev. Tim Atwater points out, "It was no accident that rebels against colonial authority chose a line from Leviticus 25: 10 ('Proclaim liberty throughout the land to all the inhabitants…') as the inscription for their liberty bell" (2012).

The biblical "liberty throughout the land" has a much deeper meaning than today's overblown, superficial notion of democracy, which is largely devoid of economic freedom. It calls for radical periodic overhauls of the economy: freedom from debt-bondage, poverty and insolvency. In Jubilee all the debts are canceled, those enslaved because of debt are set free, the property lost due to indebtedness is restored to pre-foreclosure owners, and prices of land and labor are adjusted to "reasonable" levels "based on proximity to the next Jubilee." In short, harmony and balance is restored to the socioeconomic structure of the community—a design akin to today's notion of "sustainable development" (Atwater 2012). The following are a few examples or passages of the biblical themes of the Jubilee-Sabbath mandates:

> In this Year of Jubilee everyone is to return to his own property.
>
> The land must not be sold permanently, because the land is mine and you are but aliens and my tenants. Throughout the country that you hold as a possession you must provide for the redemption of the land.
>
> If one of your countrymen becomes poor and sells some of his property, his nearest relative is to come and redeem what his countryman has sold.… But if he does not acquire the means to repay him [the buyer], what he sold will remain in the possession of the buyer until the Year of Jubilee. It will be returned in the Jubilee, and he can then go back to his property.
>
> (Leviticus 25: 13, 23, 24, 25)

For a long time, many readers of these biblical passages on debt relief and land redistribution argued that they were probably wishful products of the utopian imaginations of the prophets, without real-world antecedents. As discussed earlier in this chapter, however, recent historical/archeological discoveries (such as the Rosetta Stone in Egypt, or ancient records of debt cancelation in Bronze Age Mesopotamia) leave no doubt that such passages were actually grounded in real-world precedents. Indeed, as noted earlier, it is quite likely that they were inspired by the history of debt relief and agrarian reforms of the earlier times in Sumer and Babylonia:

> What confirms their [Biblical economic laws'] historicity is the discovery of Bronze Age Mesopotamian legal antecedents. These discoveries have wrought a revolution in Biblical studies in recent decades. Indeed, what turns out to be ironic in studying the history of Near Eastern legal practices is that precisely those parts of the Biblical narratives that hitherto have been most in doubt—the laws cancelling debts, freeing debt servants and redistributing the land to its traditional users—turn out to be the most clearly documented Bronze Age legacy. However, they are attested more in the Babylonian core than in Israel. Indeed, the Babylonian experience survives

today primarily in the transmuted form that has come down to us through the Bible.

(Hudson 1993: 13)

Many of the biblical passages regarding land tenure and debt forgiveness were written or proclaimed by the Social Prophets (Isaiah, Jeremiah, Ezekiel, Amos, and others) during the eighth and seventh centuries BC. Many others were written during the nearly 150-year period following the liberation of the people of Judah from Babylonian captivity in 539 BC. The exile of Jews to Babylonia (following the latter's takeover of the kingdom of Judah in 598) formally ended in 538, when the Persian-Median king (and conqueror of Babylonia) Cyrus the Great gave the Jews permission to return to Palestine.

Upon returning home from exile in 444 BC, Nehemiah, a Jewish official at Persian-dominated Babylon, who had risen to the position of cupbearer under Artaxerxes, set out to rebuild Jerusalem and carry out certain economic and/or land reforms in favor of the poor and indebted farmers who had lost their land to native money lenders and land-grabbers. "He won popular support by cancelling the debts and redistributing the lands that had been forfeited to local creditors." Having gained popular support for his reforms, Nehemiah thus paved the way for the work of Ezra the scribe, and other compilers of the Bible, to give the final form to the first five books of the Old Testament in late fifth century BC. During this period, Ezra and his associates "reworked the Holiness Code of Leviticus into the idea of nothing less than a covenant with the Lord to promote economic justice in the land." It is not surprising that, to this day, the Jews and Christians who advocate meaningful economic justice—that is, justice beyond charity—still look back to that period (the sixth and fifth centuries BC) as the source of their convictions and/or inspirations (Hudson 1993: 13, 37).

Starting with the fourth century BC, that is, not long after Nehemiah's reforms, however, the religious/biblical emphasis on economic justice gradually shifted from reform, reconstruction and justice here-and-now to promises of the other-worldly, to righteous preaching of abstract justice and charity—essentially marking the transition from the Old Testament to the New Testament. Along with the rise of the influence of the Roman Empire in the region, which gave preference to creditors and landlords over debtors and farmers, the native elites and religious leaders of Judah/Canaan/Palestine also gradually abandoned the long-cherished ideals of Jubilee and debt cancelation, as the rise of aristocratic/private land ownership gradually eclipsed royal/temple ownership.

> By Roman imperial times, Judaism too had become dominated by representatives of the wealthy—the very class against whom the great prophets and reformers had preached from the eighth through fifth centuries BC.... The Biblical commandments cancelling agrarian debts and redistributing lands which had been forfeited to absentee holders were superseded by Rabbi Hillel's *prosbul*, a legal clause by which borrowers signed away their rights to avail themselves of the Jubilee Year [and the Sabbatical Year debt

> cancellations].... The fact that Hillel could establish the *prosbul* waiver as part of Jewish religion showed how far Israel had moved with the same tide of privatization that was sweeping the rest of antiquity into a new Dark Age.
>
> (Hudson 1993: 39)

These inauspicious developments, which started in the fourth century BC, meant that by the time of the arrival of Jesus interpretations and teachings of the Bible had already been significantly diluted and degraded, very much different from the Old Testament, which had taken shape largely from the eighth to the fifth centuries BC. Outraged by these deviations, Jesus set out to revive the debt relief and/or land reform teachings of the Social Prophets and the Old Testament. His reading from Isaiah 61 at the Nazareth Synagogue (as his first public act upon his return home) is an example of this "defiant" mission. He also expressed outrage at the deviances from the path of the Social Prophets when he angrily overturned the money/jewelry dealers' table who had taken over Jerusalem's temple—a "rebellious" act for which he ultimately paid with his life. The story is rather well-known as it is told in all four gospels (Luke 19, Matthew 21, Mark 11 and John 2).

From then onward, while biblical and church teachings of piety and righteousness continued to give lip service to compassion for the poor, and even occasionally condemn plutocracy, such exhortations remained largely abstract pronouncements devoid of actual policy measures of debt relief, or land redemption. Indeed, as Professor Hudson points out, "The papacy itself sponsored the Italian bankers to drain money to Rome." To justify interest charges in contradiction to the Old Testament, "Canon Law was developed largely to rationalize the charges of Lombard bankers sponsored by the papacy to transfer royal tribute in the twelfth and thirteenth centuries." (Canon Laws, or simply canons, began with guidelines approved by the Apostles at the Council of Jerusalem in the first century, that is, not long after the death of Jesus.) Since there are many passages in the pre-Christian Bible that forbid interest charges on lending (for example, Ezekiel 18, verses 8, 13 and 17), the Revised Standard Version of the Bible commits an obvious distortion in order to justify interest charges:

> [It] translates this sanction anachronistically as referring to "excessive" interest, i.e., to usury over and above the legal rate approved by civil authorities. This perverts the text's original meaning, for neither Hebrew, Greek nor Latin had separate words to distinguish between "interest" and "usury." That distinction is a product of Canon Law seeking to carve out a form of financial gain (*interesse*) that could be taken by Christians legitimately in the face of the Biblical strictures against *neshek* (Hebrew), *tokos* (Greek) and *Faenus* (Latin) [synonym words for interest].
>
> (Hudson 1993: 43)

Now, the question is: why were the economic teachings of the Old Testament regarding the Sabbath and Jubilee years of debt cancelation, as well as the

Bronze Age tradition of actual debt relief and land redistribution, lost or abandoned?

The answer needs to be sought not in the different temperaments of various rulers, or varying degrees of their generosity (or lack thereof), but in the actual socioeconomic developments and structures of the respective societies. Prior to the fourth century BC, the dominant form of landownership in the Mesopotamia/Near East region was public, or considered public, as the bulk of land belonged to palaces and temples. Just as the overwhelming majority of the people were thus dependent on the religious and political leaders for land tenure and other means of subsistence, so were the rulers dependent on their subjects for farming, as well as for defense or military service. Not surprisingly, the palaces and temples—as both land owners and ruler or leaders—found it essential to periodically carry out agrarian reforms and debt cancelations in order to relieve their subjects from debt-servitude and abject poverty—thereby also safeguarding their own rule from decline and degradation, through economic revival and social recovery. What made implementation of such reforms relatively facile was the fact that, at the time, the political and economic powers or entities were often the same: state and temple authorities, their debt collectors, tax officials, and other functionaries. Perhaps more importantly, land was only minimally commercialized in those days; which meant that land and real estate in general were used primarily for the provision of foodstuff and shelter on a non-commercial basis.

Beginning with approximately the fourth century BC, however, this socioeconomic picture had somewhat changed: by this time in the history of the region, the majority of land had gradually fallen into private hands, as had most of the commerce and financial business. From then forward, the laboring masses of farmers and workers became more and more dependent on private owners, the landed aristocracy and money-lenders, for farming, employment and credit than on the public or state sector. Since the state and the temple had also increasingly become dependent upon and, therefore, intertwined with, or beholden to, the financial elites and the wealthy landlords, their long-standing ability to carry out economic reforms in favor of the masses had drastically declined. These fundamental changes in the social and economic structures also signified the ensuing drastic shift from the relatively radical economic teachings of the Old Testament to the revised and attenuated versions of it—versions that continue to be dominant today—and from economic justice and redistribution here-and-now to charity and reward in the hereafter.

The following is Professor Hudson's description of the extent to which modern texts and interpretations of the Bible are at variance with the more compassionate teachings of the Old Testament:

> So far has the modern idea of market efficiency and progress gone that today, although the Bible remains our civilization's defining book, it is perceived largely as a composite of stories, myth and wisdom literature best epitomized perhaps in spirituals and hymns, not economic laws. The Ten Commandments and the Golden Rule have become so dissociated from the

> economic legislation of Exodus, Leviticus and Deuteronomy that whoever takes these laws in earnest is considered utopian and anachronistic if looking backward nostalgically, or radical if adopting them as a guide for current activism. Yet these laws formed the take-off point for Christ upon his return to Nazareth's synagogue, and for his denunciation of the money-changers who had taken over Jerusalem's temple.... To dismiss these laws is thus to remove much of the Bible from the context of its times, above all from its Bronze Age Near Eastern matrix.
>
> (Hudson 1993: 5–6)

Such is the pernicious impact of the profit-driven market mechanism on religion. Indeed, as pointed out in the first chapter of this study, while gutting out the economic, compassion or welfare contents of celestial religions, market mechanism creates its own religion: market religion; which in place of the compassionate ethos of godly religions promotes greed, self-interest and the worship of material objects or possessions.

Recent instances of debt default: The cases of Iceland and Argentina

Powerful financial interests (and their "experts" among economists and policy makers) have in recent decades created the impression that canceling or writing down the oppressive debt burden on the productive capacity of our society, that is, on both labor and industrial capital, would be calamitous. Their apocalyptic "too big to fail" ploy is designed to inculcate this message of panic in the public psyche.

Empirical evidence from both distant and recent pasts shows, however, that it is often economic recovery, not collapse, which results from canceling or writing down the oppressive debt burdens. The preceding sections of this chapter recounted many such instances of social and economic revival (in the ancient Near East/Mesopotamia) through periodic debt cancelation, which were often branded as creating a "clean slate," or a debt-free fresh start. This section will highlight two such instances of debt modification in our own time, Iceland in 2008 and Argentina in 2001, both with equally successful results for economic revival and social well-being.

The case of Iceland

> Iceland's journey from financial ruin to fledgling recovery is a case study in roads not taken and choices not made by other countries faced with economic calamity in recent years.
>
> (Dennis 2012)

The financial meltdown of the 2008 struck Iceland very hard. The country's three largest banks, whose fictitious capital had skyrocketed to nearly ten times the nation's GDP, were allowed to go bankrupt as they became practically insolvent. The amount of debt that the financial sector had accumulated was so huge that any attempt at their rescue would have condemned the entire nation to bankruptcy for generations to come. Contrary to the U.S.–EU policy makers whose motto is that the big banks are "too big to fail," the Icelanders realized that they were "too big to be rescued." Recognizing "the peril, and perhaps the fallacy, of trying to rescue the banks ... Iceland did what the United States chose not to do—allow its biggest banks to fail and force foreign creditors to take a hike" (Dennis 2012). As the angry citizens filled the streets in protest, Prime Minister Geir Haarde invoked God's help, and declared (in October 2008) the bankruptcy of the big banks: "No responsible government takes risks with the future of its people, even when the banking system itself is at stake" (ibid.).

Following the collapse of the speculating giant banks, the government guaranteed the deposits of the Iceland citizens but refused to pay off many financial investors from abroad. The administration also "created new banks made up of the domestic operations of the failed firms. The old banks, which held foreign assets, are being dismantled and their assets sold, with proceeds going to pay off creditors" (ibid.).

Although in the aftermath of the financial implosion the country's debt rose to more than 100 percent of its GDP, economic policy makers adopted expansive, not tight, fiscal policies: while cutting only "non-essential" spending, it maintained spending on the country's already generous economic safety net programs: "adding and expanding programs targeted to the most vulnerable groups." (This is, incidentally, very much reminiscent of the New Deal economic policies of the United States in response to the Great Depression). In an effort to offset the expanded social spending, "the country put in place new taxes on the banking system and on wealthy individuals" (ibid.). Iceland's policy makers also adopted a pro-growth monetary policy:

> Allowing the krona to remain weak has hastened Iceland's return to stability. The country's exports, which feature fish and aluminum, were running about 11 percent higher last year, and the tourism industry also showed an 11 percent increase through November.... But struggling countries bound together by the euro, such as Greece and Portugal, don't have the ability to let their currency fluctuate to more favorable levels.
>
> (Ibid.)

The combined result of defaulting on the fraudulent, un-payable debt and simultaneously carrying out stimulating or expansive fiscal and monetary policies has been an amazing economic recovery:

> Three years later, the unemployment rate has fallen. Tourism has increased. The economy is growing. The government successfully raised money from investors in the summer for the first time since the crisis.... Iceland completed its IMF program in the summer. Inflation has fallen. Consumers are

> spending more money. There are new investments in geothermal energy, and the fishing waters remain plentiful. Hammers and power saws have become a familiar sound again in Reykjavik.
>
> (Ibid.)

Even the IMF officials, whose "structural adjustment programs" are usually diametrically opposed to what Iceland did, acknowledged the success of the country's "unorthodox" adjustments: "For a country whose entire financial system collapsed, Iceland is doing remarkably well," confessed Julie Kozack, the IMF's mission chief for Iceland.

True, there are still lingering problems in the aftermath of the cataclysmic financial collapse of 2008. Unemployment, which has come down considerably, and which is much lower than that of many countries plagued by the financial crisis, is still somewhat high, at around 7 percent. While significantly lightened by government's reform and restructuring programs, the reduced but persistent debt on businesses and consumers continues to be burdensome. Despite the lingering maladies, however, the economy and consumer/societal confidence are on the rise: "Judging by economic data and by the workaday scenes of life in the capital, the economic engines are turning again.... Slowly but surely, recession inched toward recovery"(Dennis 2012).

The case of Argentina

Argentina experienced a series of economic turbulences in the 1990s which culminated in the major recession of the 1998–2002 years. During the nearly four-year crisis, while inflation and unemployment skyrocketed, the country's Gross Domestic Product (GDP) plummeted by nearly 5 percent and its external debt rose to the oppressive levels of more than $100 billion. The traditional IMF-neoliberal prescriptions of more austerity cuts in exchange for more credit/debt only aggravated the crisis, which further added to the debt burden. As angry riots, called "IMF riots," became persistent and widespread, the government fell and the new policy makers changed course: they shunned the IMF/creditors' prescription of perpetual debt and austerity and, instead, charted new economic strategies of growth and debt repudiation.

Assured of the public support (indeed, largely driven by people's demand and/or pressure), the new government declared default in late 2001 on its "unpayable" debt, and embarked on an expansive, not austere or tight, economic policy. Although the shock of this bold policy, combined with the punishing reaction of the IMF/transnational capital, further aggravated the crisis during the first quarter of 2002, economic recovery began after only that one quarter of shrinkage and, by the first quarter of 2005, real GDP had expanded to its pre-recession level, surprising all experts and observers. The thus revitalized economy continued to expand at annual growth rates of above 8 percent until the 2008 financial meltdown in major market economies of the world, which also briefly and insignificantly contaminated the Argentine economy. After a brief slowdown in late 2008 and early 2009, "The economy then rebounded, and the IMF now projects growth of 8 percent for 2011" (Weisbrot *et al.* 2011: 3).

As noted, the 1998–2002 crisis was the culmination of a series of economic disorders that had plagued the Argentine economy for at least a dozen years previously. During that agonizing period, a number of factors converged to precipitate the crisis. Some of the "usual" culprits such as corruption, tax evasion, money laundering and off-shore banking are rather well-known. There was also the misguided currency policy of pegging the Argentine peso to the U.S. dollar, on a one-to-one basis. As this policy artificially overvalued the peso, it hurt the country's external balances; since the strong peso meant easy or more imports and difficult or less exports.

The critical factor behind the economic disorders of the 1990s, however, is known to have been the neoliberal policies of debt and austerity—led or encouraged by the IMF and its satellite of international financial institutions (IFIs). Since the early 1990s, Argentina had relied on the IMF to provide the country with access to credit, as well as to lead its "structural adjustment programs." At every turn of an economic disturbance and payments problems in the early 1990s (and there were at least half a dozen of such disturbances), the IMF called for more debt in return for more belt-tightening. This is obviously akin to trying to cure a poisoned patient with more of the same poison. The notorious, "one-size-fits-all" IMF prescription of debt and austerity worked like a double-edged sword: one edge drained national resources through the escalating debt-servicing payments, the other stinted economic growth through cutting essential social and developmental spending. As this deadly combination incrementally worsened both external debt and economic hardship to intolerable levels, Argentinians said: *bastar* (enough)! By the time street protests became widespread and the government declared default on its external debt and spurned the IMF policies in late 2001, the nation's external debt had snowballed to the tune of $132 billion. In that year alone the country's GDP plunged by 4 percent, while unemployment rose to 18.4 percent by the end of the year (Weisbrot, *et al.* 2011).

In the course of the year leading to the default on foreign debt, the Argentine government (at the behest of the IMF) carried out "seven rounds of austerity measures … including 13 per cent cuts in pensions and salaries," according to Sophie Arie of *Guardian* (December 9, 2001). Reporting from Buenos, she further wrote, "As the country hurtles into bankruptcy, its people are suffering stress, panic attacks and a wave of suicides." Arie also noted, "Corner shops and lampposts carry flyers for group therapy and anti-stress massages while national newspapers are scattered with adverts for bankruptcy litigation and sexual impotence cures." Not surprisingly, she continued:

> Public discontent has been simmering with protests most days and angry piqueteros blocking roads across this vast country for months. Unions are planning a national strike on Thursday.… But Argentines are not disappointed only in their President. In the October [2001] legislative elections, a

> record 40 per cent of voters chose to cast blank or spoiled votes rather than support any of the candidates.
>
> (Ibid.)

Economic crisis and public outrage further intensified in late 2001 when (on the fifth of December) "the IMF refused to release a US$1.3 billion tranche of its loan, citing the failure of the Argentinean government to reach previously agreed-upon budget deficit targets, and demanded further budget cuts, amounting to 10% of the federal budget" (*New York Times*, December 10, 2001[2]).

In late 2001, Argentina suffered a run on banks as people withdrew money from their bank accounts, converted it into dollars and other hard currencies and sent it abroad. The government reacted by effectively freezing bank accounts, allowing only small withdrawals. Enraged, large numbers of people took to the street, often in violent protests. Protest demonstrations included clashes with the police and property destruction, frequently directed at banks, IMF-sponsored privatized and foreign-owned entities, as well as big American and European companies. President De la Rúa declared a state of emergency but the situation deteriorated, precipitating the violent protests of December 20 and 21 in Plaza de Mayo, where clashes between demonstrators and the police resulted in several deaths. The rapid spread of demonstrations, leading to the escalation of violence, eventually led to the fall of the government. On December 21, De la Rúa fled Casa Rosada (the Presidential palace) in a helicopter, and Adolfo Rodríguez Saá, then governor of San Luis, was appointed as the new interim president.[3]

With no money or foreign reserves to spare, and literally broke, Argentina had no choice (short of liquidating more of its national assets) but to default on most of its foreign debt—specifically, on $93 billion out of $132 billion, the largest defaulted in debt history. Transnational capital stampeded; foreign investment and other types of capital flows toward Argentina came to a halt. The country's exports, especially agricultural products, were banned from a number international (mainly creditors) markets. The U.S. Department of Agriculture placed restrictions on Argentine food and drug exports. At the behest of powerful U.S. and European banks/creditors, Argentina was effectively excluded from the international financial markets for nearly four years.

Not deterred by the harsh responses of the IMF and other international financial institutions, or daunted by the geopolitical threats of their imperialist governments, Argentina boldly eschewed the neoliberal policies of austerity and indebtedness; and opted, instead, for an expansive policy of social and economic growth:

> Social spending nearly tripled in real terms, and rose from 10.3 to 14.2 percent of GDP. In 2009, the government expanded the reach of its social programs, launching the "Universal Allocation per Child" (*Asignación Universal por Hijo*) with the goal of reducing poverty and improving the welfare of children. This was a conditional cash transfer program for low-income households, similar to Brazil's *Bolsa Familia* and Mexico's

> *Progresa-Oportunidades* programs, which have won widespread international praise, but is significantly larger relative to GDP.
>
> (Weisbrot, *et al.* 2011: 3–4)

Despite adverse international conditions, generated due to economic/financial sanctions imposed by creditor powers following the default, Argentina began to grow barely three months after the default and the nearly-collapsed economy. Its economy grew "94 percent for the years 2002–2011 ... among the highest growth rates in the world" (ibid.: 5). Argentina has also seen considerable progress on social indicators since its independence from the IMF and/or neoliberalism:

> Poverty has fallen by over two-thirds from its peak, from almost half of the population in 2001 to approximately one-seventh of the population in early 2010.... Income inequality has also fallen dramatically. In 2001, those in the 95th percentile had 32 times the income of those in the 5th percentile. By early 2010, this fell by nearly half, to 17. Perhaps more importantly, this change is due in large part to improving incomes among the poor and not just diminishing incomes among the rich.... Unemployment has fallen by over half from its peak, to 8.0 percent.... There were also significant reductions in infant and child mortality over the last nine years, somewhat more than in similarly situated countries.
>
> (Ibid.: 3–4)

Policy implications of the success stories of debt repudiation by Argentina and Iceland for the indebted countries in Europe and elsewhere are unmistakable: the solution to un-payable debt is not taking on more debt but debt modification/repudiation—a clean break from the vicious cycle of debt, austerity, economic devastation, and misery.

Conclusion

Heavily indebted nations face two diametrically-opposed options: either follow the dictates of the creditors and try to pay the (often un-payable) debt through austerity and more debt; or follow the examples of Iceland and Argentina and default on the devastating debt. The former option is a recipe for a vicious cycle of debt, austerity and socioeconomic decay: with economic decline under the burden of debt and austerity, and more borrowing on top of it, it is highly unlikely that these nations' debt-servicing efforts would ever catch up with the continuous snowballing of their debt obligations (Hudson 2012, Ch. 2). The latter option would entail discarding the deadweight of the oppressive debt, creating a *clean slate* and embarking on a debt-free path of economic revival.

The specter of economic sanctions and financial restrictions imposed by powerful international creditors in reaction to debt cancelation could, of course, be a daunting prospect for nations contemplating debt default. The actual shock of the immediate impact of such sanctions, reducing a country (at least in the short-term) to a pariah status in international markets, can likewise be traumatic. But if Iceland and Argentina (and other countries before them: UK 1932, Germany 1948, France 1812, Denmark 1813, Turkey 1982, Sweden 1812, Portugal 1890, Poland 1981, Greece 1932, Austria 1945, Japan 1942 and China 1939) survived the creditors threats and actual sanctions, and lifted their economies from the path of debt and stagnation to that of growth and development, so could other countries, such as Greece, Spain and Ireland, whose external debt seems equally un-payable.

The rationale behind the idea of debt cancelation/modification goes beyond moral issues of compassion and justice. Perhaps more importantly, it is grounded on broader and longer-term considerations of socioeconomic revival and/or sustainability. This chapter's brief discussion of the periodic debt cancelations in the Bronze Age Mesopotamia revealed that such considerations certainly served as primary grounds for those often rejuvenating debt cancelations. As historian Eric Toussaint points out, the rulers of those "societies of 3,000 to 4,000 years ago … sought to maintain social cohesion by preventing the constitution of big private domains, and took measures to ensure that peasants enjoyed direct access to the land." Accordingly, "They limited the rise of inequality while overseeing the development and maintenance of irrigation systems (2012).

Likewise, the chapter's brief review of the biblical principles of Sabbath and Jubilee revealed that the main rationale behind such principles, or commandments, was to periodically rejuvenate social and economic structures by cleansing them from the crushing debts, and restoring landownership from money-lenders and land-grabbers to the status quo ante, that is, to the original owners and/or cultivators. Indeed, according to certain passages of the Old Testament, land is the "Lord's gift" that can be owned on a "temporary" basis: "Land must not be sold in perpetuity, for the land belongs to me and you are only strangers and guests. You will allow a right of redemption on all your landed property," and restore it to its customary cultivators every 50 years (Leviticus 25: 23–28, 54).

Under capitalism, too, "value destruction" and debt nullification were considered until recent times as "normal" outcomes of major economic crises, or market collapses. While such painful experiences of "market cleansing," or liquidation of the destabilizing financial speculators, may seem and feel traumatic in the short-run, over time they would be advantageous as they can bring about a clean break from debt overhang, thereby relieving debt-burdened societies and their economies from chronic indebtedness, stagnation and economic hardship. In recent decades, however, as colossal financial institutions and interests have grown so powerful as to elect governments and appoint policy makers, that earlier tradition of "market cleansing" debt liquidation has been blocked in favor of scandalous policies of bailing out financial speculators at the expense of the public, both present and future generations.

Notes

1 There is a wide variety of slightly different wording, or expression, of this passage from Isaiah 61; but the essence or spirit of all the various versions is the same.
2 As quoted in Wikipedia: http://en.wikipedia.org/wiki/Argentine_economic_crisis_%281999%E2%80%932002%29 (accessed October 3, 2013).
3 These developments were reported on daily basis in the *New York Times*, *The Telegraph* and *BBC News*, among others. Some of these reports, as well as a number of reports in Spanish directly from Buenos Aires, are available online at: http://en.wikipedia.org/wiki/Argentine_economic_crisis_%281999%E2%80%932002%29#cite_note-26.

References

Alexander, J. B. (1938). A Babylonian year of Jubilee? *Journal of Biblical Literature*, *57*: 55–79.

Arie, S. (2001). Argentina hits rock bottom. *Guardian*, December 9. Retrieved from www.guardian.co.uk/world/2001/dec/09/globalisation.argentina (accessed May 15, 2013).

Atwater, T. (2012). Debt cancellation: Biblical norm, not exception. Jubilee USA Network. Retrieved from www.jubileeusa.org/get-active/jubilee-congregations/faith-worship-resources/debt-cancellation-the-biblical-norm.html (accessed May 12, 2013).

Dennis, B. (2012). The Iceland experiment. *Washington Post*, January 17; reprinted by Global Association of Risk Professionals. Retrieved from www.garp.org/risk-news-and-resources/risk-headlines/story.aspx?newsid=40962 (accessed July 12, 2013).

Hudson, M. (2012). *The bubble and beyond*. Forest Hills, NY: Institute for the Study of Long-term Economic Trends (ISLET).

Hudson, M. (1993). *The lost tradition of biblical debt cancellation*. New York: Social Science Forum, Henry George School of Social Science. Retrieved from http://michael-hudson.com/wp-content/uploads/2010/03/HudsonLostTradition.pdf (accessed January 10, 2013).

Toussaint, E. (2012). Debt cancellation in Mesopotamia and Egypt from 3000 to 1000 BC. *Global Research*, September 4. Retrieved from www.globalresearch.ca/debt-cancellation-in-mesopotamia-and-egypt-from-3000-to-1000-bc (accessed July 13, 2013).

Weisbrot, M., Ray, R., Montecino, J. and Kozameh, S. (2011). The Argentine success story and its implications. Center for Economic and Policy Research. Retrieved from www.cepr.net/documents/publications/argentina-success-2011–10.pdf (accessed July 12, 2013).

7 The case for public banking

The fact that profit-driven commercial banks and other financial intermediaries are major sources of financial instability is hardly disputed. It is equally well-known that, due to their economic and political influence, powerful financial interests easily subvert government regulations, thereby periodically reproducing financial instability and economic turbulence. By contrast, logic suggests and empirical evidence confirms that public-sector banks can better reassure depositors of the security of their savings, as well as help direct those savings toward productive credit allocation and investment opportunities. Ending the recurring crises of financial markets requires, therefore, placing the destabilizing financial intermediaries under public ownership and democratic control. This is not necessarily a radical or socialist proposal; it makes sense even within the general framework of a capitalist economy.

It is necessary to emphasize at the outset that public banking does not always mean 100 percent public ownership. Traditionally, it has meant majority shares or assets owned by the government. Accordingly, the dominant role of public-sector banking in a country is defined not in terms of 100 percent ownership but on the basis of government ownership of major banks, or its control of the main bulk of credit for allocation to strategic industries or major infrastructural projects of national importance. In general, the dominant status of public banking in a country refers to a situation where over 50 percent of the banking system's assets are in possession of banks that are publicly owned.

Why public banking—advantages over private banks?

It is only logical that public, not private, authority should manage people's money, or savings. Since commercial banks' money originates primarily from people's savings, it stands to reason that they should be public entities. This explains, in part, why commercial banks are publicly-owned and/or directed, wholly or partially, in many countries around the world. These include China, Russia, India, Brazil and, to a lesser extent, Germany. As shown in the next section of this chapter, there is a consensus among experts that the health and stability of the economies of these countries (relative to core capitalist countries whose banks have not been subject to regulatory constraints) is largely due to public supervision of their banks, and the calculated or targeted allocation of their nation's financial and/or credit resource. Whereas the unrestrained financial sector in the main capitalist countries of the United States, Europe and Japan have doomed their economies to a protracted long recession, less-financialized economies of countries such as China, Brazil, Russia, and India, where there is a significant public ownership and/or supervision of the banking system, have weathered the global crisis somewhat better—despite the fact that they too are infected, or bound to be infected, by the global plague of capitalist crisis.

As pointed out in Chapter 5 of this study, the late German Economist Rudolf Hilferding argued that the system of centralizing people's savings and placing them at the disposal of profit-driven private banks is a perverse kind of socialism, that is, socialism in favor of the few:

> In this sense a fully developed credit system is the antithesis of capitalism, and represents organization and control as opposed to anarchy. It has its source in socialism, but has been adapted to capitalist society; it is a fraudulent kind of socialism, modified to suit the needs of capitalism. It socializes other people's money for use by the few.[1]

Contrary to profit-driven private banks that create financial bubbles during expansionary cycles and credit crunch during contractionary ones, government-owned banks can provide steady, reliable financial resources as dictated by a nation's industrial and/or commercial needs. Despite the purported efficiency of competitive markets, the safety and stability of credit and/or banking system requires that fierce and high-risk competition in pursuit of highest returns in the shortest time possible be restricted. National policies of careful allocation of financial or credit resources to growth- and employment-generating investments are of critical social and economic importance. "Thus public ownership of the credit and banking system is rational and, indeed, necessary, along with democratic control." Many people would probably be surprised to learn that even today "the bulk of the German banking system remains in public hands, through savings banks and *landesbanken*." To an even larger extent, "The Chinese financial system is overwhelmingly centered on a handful of huge, publicly-owned banks and the government does indeed steer the credit strategies of these banks" (Gowan 2010: 64).

That public-sector banks tend to be more stable and, therefore, more reliable is reflected in public reaction to moments of financial turbulence. Experience shows that during such periods of financial instability people frantically rush to transfer their savings from private to government-owned (or government-backed) banks. Ironically, this also includes people who are ordinarily contemptuous of public ownership on the ideologically dubious ground that the "government cannot do anything right."

> At the beginning of the second wave of the crisis in October 2008, Northern Rock was the only government owned bank in the UK. It experienced a very sudden influx of funds because it was considered a safe haven for depositors while privately owned banks were not. While we did not observe depositors

> in other banks queuing to withdraw their deposits—as had happened to Northern Rock before it was nationalized a year earlier—a bank run was in fact happening in the background. Institutional investors were trying to shift their cash from the major banks to government backed investments including Treasury Bills. That was precisely the time—and in all likelihood the trigger—for the UK government putting together the bailout package for the four major banks. Only then did the panic recede.
>
> (Andrianova *et al.* 2010)

There is a widespread perception that public-sector banks are inefficient and are, therefore, not conducive to optimum levels of economic growth. Evidence suggests, however, that such concerns are far from warranted. There are, indeed, compelling reasons not only for higher degrees of reliability but also higher levels of efficacy of public-sector banking and credit system when compared with private banking—both on conceptual/theoretical and empirical grounds.

Nineteenth century neighborhood savings banks, Credit Unions, and Savings and Loan associations in the United States, Jusen companies in Japan, Trustee Savings banks in the UK, and the Commonwealth Bank of Australia all served the housing and other credit needs of their communities well. Perhaps a most interesting and instructive example is the case of the Bank of North Dakota, which has continued to be owned by the state for nearly a century—and is widely credited for the state's budget surplus and its robust economy in the midst of harrowing economic woes in other states. Ellen Brown, author of *The Web of Debt*, describes the "miracle" of the Bank of North Dakota as follows:

> A total of 49 states and the District of Columbia have all reported net job losses.... In this dark firmament, however, one bright star shines. The sole state to actually gain jobs is an unlikely candidate for the distinction: North Dakota. North Dakota is also one of only two states expected to meet their budgets in 2010. (The other is Montana.).... Since 2000, the state's GNP has grown 56 percent, personal income has grown 43 percent and wages have grown 34 percent. The state not only has no funding problems, but this year it has a budget surplus of $1.3 billion, the largest it has ever had.
>
> (2009)

Brown then asks, "Why is North Dakota doing so well, when other states are suffering the ravages of a deepening credit crisis? "Its secret," she answers,

> [may] be that it has its own credit machine. North Dakota is the only state in the Union to own its own bank. The Bank of North Dakota (BND) was established by the state legislature in 1919, specifically to free farmers and small business owners from the clutches of out-of-state bankers and railroad men. The bank's stated mission is to deliver sound financial services that promote agriculture, commerce and industry in North Dakota.
>
> (Ibid.)

Explaining how the Bank of North Dakota utilizes people's savings for productive credit and/or investment, Eric Hardmeyer, president of the bank, points out, "Really what separates us [from private banks] is that we plow those deposits back into the state of North Dakota in the form of loans. We invest back into the state in economic development type activities." The bank president further indicates that in the course of the last dozen years or so "we've turned back a third of a billion dollars just to the general fund to offset taxes or to aid in funding public sector types of needs."[2]

North Dakota's gains from interest-free credit go beyond the actual dollars saved, or not paid as interest: by productively investing the monies thus saved it can also enrich its public capital, both human capital such as health and education, and physical capital such as roads, schools, hospitals and the like. By contrast, burdened by interest payments and other financial obligations to private banks, nearly all other states are forced to cut investment on public capital formation, to slash jobs and liquidate state-owned properties or state-sponsored services—often at fire-sale prices. Consider California, for example. At the end of 2010, it owed private banks and other bondholders $70 billion in interest only—44 percent of its total financial obligations of $158 billion. "If the state had incurred that debt to its own bank," writes Ellen Brown, "California could be $70 billion richer today. Instead of slashing services, selling off public assets, and laying off employees, it could be adding services and repairing its decaying infrastructure" (2013b).

At the national level, in 2011 the U.S. federal government paid a sum of $454 billion in interest on its debt—the third highest budget item after the military and Social Security outlays. This figure amounted to nearly one-third of the total personal income taxes ($1,100 billion) collected that year. This means that if the Federal Reserve Bank was publicly owned, and the government borrowed directly from it interest-free, personal income taxes could have been cut by a third (ibid.). Alternatively, the savings could be invested in social infrastructure, both human and physical, thereby drastically augmenting the productive capacity of the nation and elevating the standard of living for all.

The research work carried out by Lietaer *et al.* (2012) on the French experience with public banking shows that if a government borrowed from its own publicly-owned central bank interest-free, it might even be able to do without any national debt. Citing this fascinating empirical research, Brown writes:

> The Treasury borrowed interest-free from the nationalized Banque de France from 1946 to 1973. The law then changed to forbid this practice, requiring the Treasury to borrow instead from the private sector. The authors include a chart [reproduced here as Figure 7.1] showing what would have happened if the French government had continued to borrow interest-free versus what did happen. Rather than dropping from 21 percent to 8.6 percent of GDP, the debt shot up from 21 percent to 78 percent of GDP.
>
> (2013b)

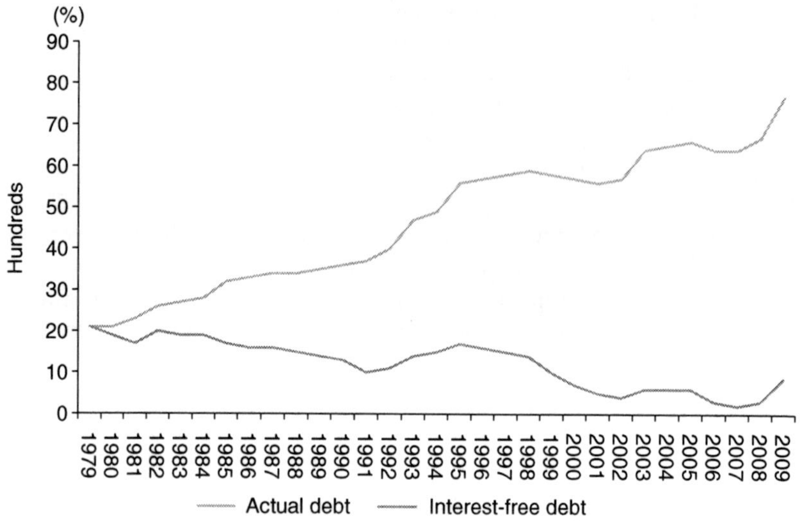

Figure 7.1 Actual debt (borrowed at interest from private banks) vs. interest-free debt (borrowed from nationalized Banque de France), 1979–2009b (source: Based on Lietaer *et al.* 2012, as cited in Brown 2013).

Under the feudal mode of production, peasants were frequently allowed to cultivate plots of land for themselves on a rental basis. However, those tenant farmers rarely succeeded in becoming landowners in their own right because a major share of what they harvested was taken by landlords as rent, often leaving them with a bare subsistence amount of what they produced. Today, under conditions of market dominance by finance capital, a similar relationship can be discerned between the powerful financial interests (as feudal lords of our time), on the one hand, and the public at large (as peasant population of today), on the other. Just as in the past feudal lords extracted rent by virtue of their ownership of land, so today the financial oligarchy extracts interest and other financial charges by virtue of having concentrated the major bulk of national resources in their hands in the form of finance capital.

In the latest edition of her book, *Occupy Money*, Professor Margrit Kennedy (2012) shows that between 35 percent and 40 percent of all consumer spending is appropriated by the financial sector: bankers, insurance companies, non-bank lenders/financiers, bondholders, and the like. Commenting on Professor Kennedy's findings, Ellen Brown writes, "This hidden tribute" to the financial sector "helps explain how wealth is systematically transferred from Main Street to Wall Street. The rich get progressively richer at the expense of the poor, not just because of 'Wall Street greed' but because of the inexorable mathematics of our private banking system" (2013b).

Writing on the success of the Bank of North Dakota, and on how a number of other states are trying to follow this bank's model to establish their own state-owned banks, Alf Young of the *Scotsman* writes, "it's little wonder that twenty American states, some of them close to bankruptcy, are at various stages of legislating to form their own state-owned banks on the North Dakota model." Young further points out, "There's a long-standing tradition of such institutions elsewhere too. Australia had a publicly-owned bank offering credit for infrastructure as early as 1912.... Up until 1974, the federal government in Canada borrowed from the Bank of Canada, effectively interest-free" (2012).

Compelling empirical data from numerous cases of public-sector banking worldwide suggests that the success story of Bank of North Dakota is by no means an exception, or a coincidence. In 2009, a group of economists at the universities of Leicester and Brunel carried out a relatively comprehensive study of the efficacy of government-owned banks in a large number of countries for a period of 12 years (1995 to 2007). The researchers concluded, "We have provided new evidence which suggests that the view that government ownership of banks is harmful to economic growth lacks empirical grounding. If anything," they added, "our findings suggest that recently government ownership of banks has been associated with better long-run growth performance" (Andrianova *et al.* 2009: 17). The authors further wrote:

> [W]e have found that ... countries with government-owned banks have, on average, grown faster than countries with no or little government ownership of banks.... This is, of course, a surprising result, especially in light of the widespread belief—typically supported by anecdotal evidence—that "...bureaucrats are generally bad bankers."
>
> (Ibid.: 11)

The researchers provided a number of explanations for the relatively superior performance of public banks compared with private ones. These included the "moral hazard behavior," or the tendency of the profit-driven private banks to divert both finance and human capital from long-term, development-oriented projects toward short-term, high-yield investments:

> Specifically, unchecked extreme moral hazard behavior by opportunistic bank insiders poses an extreme, yet real, threat to the growth promoting role of banks. Such behavior diverts bank resources towards short-term enrichment of insiders at the expense of maximizing shareholder wealth and may also be responsible for the misallocation of human capital by attracting talented individuals to unproductive speculative activities. Our findings suggest that even in the 21st century, government owned banks can continue to play a "developmental" role, not only in developing but also in industrialized countries by containing extreme moral hazard behaviours that have a capacity to undermine long term economic growth.
>
> (Ibid.: 17)

The authors further pointed out that, contrary to popular perceptions, private banking situations tend to be more conducive to corrupt or collusive relationships between bankers and politicians than public banking settings:

> We provide a novel political economy explanation for our findings. We suggest that politicians may actually prefer banks not to be in the public sector. When banks are—in theory—controlled by their shareholders, in practice they are more likely to be controlled by their top managers because of agency problems. Conditions of weak corporate governance in banks provide fertile ground for quick enrichment for both bankers and politicians—at the expense ultimately of the taxpayer. In such circumstances politicians can offer bankers a system of weak regulation in exchange for party political contributions, positions on the boards of banks or lucrative consultancies. Activities that are more likely to provide both sides with quick returns are the more speculative ones, especially if they are sufficiently opaque as not to be well understood by the shareholders such as complex derivatives trading.
>
> Government owned banks, on the other hand, have less freedom to engage in speculative strategies that result in quick enrichment for bank insiders and politicians. Moreover, politicians tend to be held accountable for wrongdoings or bad management in the public sector but are typically only indirectly blamed—if at all—for the misdemeanors of private banks. It is the shareholders who are expected to prevent these but lack of transparency and weak governance stops them from doing so in practice. On the other hand, when it comes to banks that are in the public sector, democratic accountability of politicians is more likely to discourage them from engaging in speculation. In such banks, top managers are more likely to be compelled to focus on the more mundane job of financing real businesses and economic growth.
>
> (Andrianova *et al.* 2010)

Perhaps the strongest testimonials favoring the case for public banking come from the experiences of the so-called BRIC countries: Brazil, Russia, India and China. The relative health of the economies of these countries is credited, at least in part, to the critical role that public banking plays in their economies. While the United States and other core capitalist countries have been mired in recession since 2008, the BRIC countries have been enjoying respectable rates of economic growth. "Between 2000 and 2010, BRIC's GDP grew by an incredible 92.7 percent, compared to a global GDP growth of just 32 percent, with industrialized economies having a very modest 15.5 percent" (*China Daily*, April 14, 2011).

The share of public-sector banks in the BRIC countries ranges from 75 percent in India, to 70 percent in China, 60 percent in Russia and 45 percent in Brazil. Professor Kurt von Mettenheim of the Sao Paulo Business School of Brazil explains how government-owned banks helped temper the effects of the global financial meltdown on BRIC economies:

> Government banks provided counter cyclical credit and policy options to counter the effects of the recent financial crisis, while realizing competitive advantage over private and foreign banks. Greater client confidence and official deposits reinforced liability base and lending capacity. The credit policies of BRIC government banks help explain why these countries experienced shorter and milder economic downturns during 2007–2008.
>
> (Mettenheim 2010)

Banking business is qualitatively different than any other business as it involves control and management of a nation's savings, or economic surplus. As such, it appropriately belongs in the public sector. As Ellen Brown points out: "By taking banking back, local governments could regain control of that very large slice (up to 40 percent) of every public budget that currently goes to interest charged to finance investment programs through the private sector" (2012).

A basic public utility model—not necessarily socialism

The idea of bringing the banking industry, national savings and credit allocation under public control or supervision is not necessarily socialistic or ideological. In the same manner that many infrastructural facilities such as public roads, school systems and health facilities are provided and operated as essential public services, so can the supply of credit and financial services be provide on a basic public utility model for both day-to-day business transactions and long-term industrial projects. As pointed out above, this is, indeed, how financial/credit services are provided in many countries around the world. Provision of financial services and/or credit facilities after the model of public utilities would allow for lower financial costs to both consumers and producers. By thus freeing consumers and producers from what can properly be called the financial overhead, or rent, similar to land rent under feudalism, the public option credit and/or banking system can revive many stagnant economies that are depressed under the crushing burden of never-ending debt-servicing obligations.

Even in the core capitalist countries public banking has occasionally been used to save capitalism from its own systemic crises. For example, in the face of the Great Depression of the 1930s, and following the Hoover administration's unsuccessful policy of trying to bail out the insolvent banks, the FDR administration was compelled to declare a "bank holiday" in 1933, pull the plug on the terminally-ill banks and (temporarily) take control of the entire financial system. The Emergency Banking Act of 1933, introduced by President Roosevelt (four days after he declared a nationwide bank holiday on March 5, 1933) and passed by Congress on March 9, guaranteed full payment of depositors' money, thereby effectively created 100 percent deposit insurance. Not surprisingly, when the banks reopened for business on March 13, 1933, "depositors stood in line to return their stashed cash to neighborhood banks" (Silber 2009). A discussion of how the government restored trust and normalcy in the banking/financial system by controlling and managing the system—without bailing out the failed speculators, as was done in the financial meltdown of 2008—is beyond the purview of this study. Suffice it to say that the government takeover of control and management of the banking system was instrumental in restoring both the stability of the system and, therefore, of people's trust in it.

Similarly, in the face of the collapse of its banking system in the early 1992, the Swedish state assumed ownership and control of all insolvent banks in an effort to revive its financial system and prevent it from bringing down its entire economy. While this wiped out the existing shareholders, it turned out to be a good deal for taxpayers: not only did it avoid costly redistributive bailouts in favor of the insolvent banks, it also brought taxpayers some benefits once banks returned to profitability.

Both in Sweden and the United States, once profitability was returned to insolvent banks their ownership was returned to private hands. It is perhaps this kind of commitment by capitalist governments to powerful financial–corporate interests that has prompted a number of critics to argue that one definition of capitalism is that it is a system of socializing losses and privatizing profits.

Both Germany and Japan successfully used their banking resources and services as public utilities for funding the industrialization and re-building of their economies following their devastation during WW II. Publicly owned banks in Germany—dominant sources of credit creation and financial allocation to this day—consist of 11 regional banks, *landesbanken*, each of which is connected to thousands of savings banks that are owned by municipalities. Together, they focus "on serving the public interest rather than on maximizing private profits. After the Second World War, it was the publicly owned Landesbanks that helped family-run provincial companies get a foothold in world markets" (Brown 2011). Peter Dorman provides a succinct description of the structure and operations of Landesbanks:

> They are publicly owned entities that rest on top of a pyramid of thousands of municipally owned savings banks. If you add in the specialized publicly owned real estate lenders, about half the total assets of the German banking system are in the public sector. (Another substantial chunk is in cooperative savings banks.) They are key tools of German industrial policy, specializing in loans to the *Mittelstand*, the small-to-medium size businesses that are at the core of that country's export engine. Because of the *landesbanken*, small firms in Germany have as much access to capital as large firms; there are no economies of scale in finance. This also means that workers in the small business sector earn the same wages as those in big corporations, have the same skills and training, and are just as productive.
>
> (As quoted in Brown 2011)

Although the public utility model of *landesbanken* has in recent years come under fierce attack for takedown by private banks, the model continues to be the major source of credit creation and financial provision for both consumers and manufacturers.

In the absence of incestuous business–political relationships between Wall Street and the government apparatus, nationalization of banks and other financial intermediaries is not as complicated or difficult as it may sound; since banking laws already empower regulators to impose extraordinary controls and close supervision over these institutions. It is certainly easier than public ownership and management of manufacturing enterprises that require much more than record keeping and following regulatory or legal guidelines. Indeed, in the immediate aftermath of the 2008 financial implosion, the U.S. and British governments became de facto owners of the failed financial giants such as Citibank, A.I.G, the Royal Bank of Scotland, and Anglo-Irish Bank. Through the provision of enormous amounts of public funds, these governments effectively became the main investors in the collapsed institutions. Were it not because of political and/or ideological reasons, they could have easily made their de facto ownership legal ownership, and provided both consumers and producers with credit and financial services at the mere cost of such services, instead of at profits. "The FDIC [Federal Deposit Insurance Corporation] could readily have taken over insolvent banks and saved insured depositors with their existing loan portfolios," points out economist Michael Hudson of the University of Missouri, Kansas City. Hudson further writes:

> The FDIC (and similar government agencies abroad) could have become major shareholders in the "systemically important" Too Big to Fail banks. After wiping out their superstructure of bad debt claims, it could have written down bad or outright fraudulent mortgages to realistic prices based on current rental values.
>
> (2012b)

Not only did the government/FDIC have the financial means to take control and ownership of the failed banks, but also the right to do so:

> We have a resolution process that we've used for decades, and when we put a bank into receivership, we have the right to break all contracts, we can fire people, we can take away bonuses and we don't get into this kind of problem,

Sheila Bair (Chairperson of the FDIC at the time) pointed out in an interview with the *New York Times* reporter Joe Nocera. Bair further related in the same interview how the authorities at the Treasury and the Federal Reserve Bank:

> [A]lways had the view that the F.D.I.C. was not in the same league as Treasury and the Fed.... As a result, we were rarely consulted. They would bring me in after they'd made their decision on what needed to be done, and without giving me any information they would say, "You have to do this or the system will go down." If I heard that once, I heard it a thousand times. "Citi is systemic, you have to do this." No analysis, no meaningful discussion. It was very frustrating.
>
> (*New York Times Magazine*, July 9, 2011)

Following the dictates of big finance, Wall Street proxies in the Treasury Department and the Federal Reserve Bank heavy-handedly overruled Ms. Bair. Instead, they "made a political decision to recognize claims by existing stockholders, bondholders and counterparties at public expense. For the economy at large, all countries kept the bad debt overhead on the books as far as debtors were concerned" (Hudson 2012b).

In the same interview with the *New York Times* reporter, Ms. Bair explained how the government opted to save the bondholders and other financial elites, instead of the public, or the overall economy, when they decided to bailout the failed banks. She (rhetorically) asked: "What was it James Carville used to say?" The answer, she pointed out: "'When I die I want to come back as the bond market.'" She further asked: "Why did we do the bailouts?" The answer: "It was all about the bondholders," she said. "They did not want to impose losses on bondholders." We kept saying:

> "There is no insurance premium on bondholders," you know? For the little guy on Main Street who has bank deposits, we charge the banks a premium for that, and it gets passed on to the customer. We don't have the same thing for bondholders. They're supposed to take losses.

The fraudulent compensation of Wall Street's gambling losses at the expense of everyone else is testament, once again, to the demagogical pretentions of the champions of austerity and neoliberalism that the government should stay out of the market's affairs.

Necessary but not sufficient

While public banking is necessary for socially-beneficial utilization of national savings and/or financial resources, it is not sufficient. Perhaps more important is democratic management of the publicly-owned banks. Bureaucratic management of the widely nationalized industries in Western Europe in the immediate aftermath of WW II, along with the equally bureaucratic management of the centrally planned economies of the Soviet Union and Eastern Europe, created a regrettably negative connotation of public ownership that continues to this day. Of course, the flawed record of that unsavory model of public ownership and/or management has been greatly exaggerated by the relentless ideological assault of neoliberalism. It must be acknowledged, nonetheless, that the heavy-handed, top-down style of managing public enterprises, which ultimately condemned those enterprises to becoming notoriously wasteful and inefficient, made them more vulnerable to the supply-side attacks pioneered by Ronald Reagan and Margaret Thatcher in the 1980s—neoliberal ideological attacks that continue unabated to this day.

Any discussion or advocacy of public banking, or of public ownership in general, must therefore provide an explanation for those failed experiences with public ownership. A discussion of the flaws of the centrally planned economies of Eastern Europe, including the Soviet Union, which greatly contributed to their ultimate collapse, is beyond the scope of this study. I will therefore briefly focus on the failed experiences of the Social-Democratic model of management of the publicly-owned enterprises in Western Europe, as it was carried out, for example, in Great Britain.

Ample evidence shows that the main reason for the failure of the Social-Democratic projects of public ownership was that, despite the sincere intentions on the part of many participants, such projects were not (on the whole) really intended to be socialistic enough to include genuine workers participation in the organization and management of publicly-owned industries. Instead, the extensive nationalization of key industries in the immediate post-WW II were driven largely by objectives or plans that were designed to revive and preserve capitalism, badly shaken by the Great Depression, by WW II and, perhaps more importantly, by the widespread protest movements and labor unrest of the time (Cumbers and McMaster 2012: 360). The traumatic devastation wrought by the depression, followed by the war, prompted extensive grassroots movements that often called for radical or revolutionary transformations, thereby seriously threatening the status quo. "To fend off revolution from below," President Roosevelt famously declared, "we need to carry out reform from above" (paraphrased). Such was the essence of and the impetus behind the New Deal/ Social-Democratic reforms and/or nationalizations.

To this end, a major thrust of public ownership in the immediate aftermath of the war was growth and industrialization as these were considered crucial to the goal of reviving and rescuing capitalism. Cumbers and McMaster point out that, "[I]n reality, postwar forms of nationalization were part of social democratic attempts at capitalist modernization, undertaken by national states, with little attempt to develop more radical forms of economic governance" (2012: 362). The authors further write: "Indeed, capitalist modernization agendas could often be driven more effectively under state ownership than might have been possible under fragmented forms of private ownership," where large sums of initial capital outlays needed for investment in major infrastructural projects or key industries were often lacking.

Thus, extensive postwar nationalizations and other reforms were driven primarily by long-term utilitarian considerations of capitalist revival. As such, the reforms were focused chiefly on the goals to be reached; the fact that the means or methods to meet those ends were essentially capitalist—albeit state capitalist—did not matter. Not surprisingly, public ownership did not essentially transform the capitalist model of labor–management power structure, save for the fact that the management apparatus now consisted primarily of state-appointed administrators and secondarily of union bureaucrats, while at the same time keeping the workers at an arm's length from any meaningful decision-making or democratic participation (Hyman and Egler 1981).

Theory suggests and empirical evidence confirms that the top-down, neither socialist nor capitalist, model of management is a recipe for inescapable bureauscratization, inefficiency, wastefulness, and ultimate failure. Extensive post-WW II nationalizations could not escape this fate. After the initial successes (from the late 1940 to late 1960s) in terms of industrialization and the rebuilding of the depression- and war-ravaged economies, the publicly owned and managed enterprises began to show signs of inefficiency and stagnation. Such signs of malaise began to emerge in the late 1960s and early 1970s, as the bureaucratic apparatus of the publicly owned and operated industries had become increasingly multi-layered, and the rank-and-file labor increasingly disillusioned with the immediate postwar promises of radical reforms, labor participation and democratic control. The following musings of a frustrated British coal-miner with the postwar promises of nationalizations, democratic control and socialism is revealing:

> I can remember standing at the pit with the banners, celebrating with my father and his friends. They thought, this was it. What a surprise they were going to get. They thought nationalization would bring everything they'd fought for. But within a very short space of time they found out that they'd swapped one boss for another. The first boss we got was a major from the Indian army, six months later followed by Captain Nicholson.... Later we had a banker!
>
> We really believed it would make a difference. We really thought it was the beginning of socialism, you know, almost time to hoist the red flag. I thought that we'd be working for ourselves, that we'd be in control. But in fact the supervision and bureaucratic administration became a hundred times worse. You'd get 10 foremen where you'd only have one. You'd always have to use 10 pieces of paper where before you'd only have one. You'd always have to go through many more channels to get anything done. That approach killed nationalization. A lot of us felt really frustrated. Mind, I still think nationalization is the only way, but next time it will have to be different.
>
> (As cited in Benyon and Wainwright 1979: 180)

Although anecdotal, the sentiments expressed here were widely shared by the rank-and-file of the labor unions, as well as by the public at large. Such disappointments made the neoliberal assault (formally commenced in the early 1980s with the "supply-side" economics of Ronald Reagan and Margaret Thatcher) on the New Deal and Social-Democratic safety-net programs painfully more effective. Similar sentiments of disappointment and frustration among labor ranks with the bureaucratic management of the nationalized and centrally-planned economies of Eastern Europe and the Soviet Union, likewise, played a crucial role in the inefficiency, stagnation and ultimate collapse of those economies. It is therefore crucially important to note that without democratic control and/or local participation public banking, or public anything, would not necessarily be a savory alternative to private banking.

Notes

1 Hilferding's book has gone through a number of prints/reprints. This quotation is from Chapter 10 of an online version of the book, retrieved from: www.marxists.org/archive/hilferding/1910/finkap/ch10.htm (accessed July 20, 2013).

2 Interview, as quoted by Public Banking Institute, retrieved from: http://publicbankinginstitute.org/ (accessed September 25, 2013).

References

Andrianova, S., Shortland, A. and Demetriades, P. (2010). There should be no rush to privatise government owned banks. Centre for Economic Policy Research. Retrieved from www.voxeu.org/article/don-t-rush-privatise-government-owned-banks (accessed June 25, 2013).

Andrianova, S., Shortland, A. and Demetriades, P. (2009). Is *government ownership of banks really harmful to growth*? Working Paper No. 09/11, University of Leicester, December. Retrieved from www.le.ac.uk/economics/research/RePEc/lec/leecon/dp09–11.pdf (accessed July 20, 2013).

Benyon, H. and Wainwright, H. (1979). *Worker's report on Vickers*. London: Pluto Press.

Brown, E. (2013). It's the interest, stupid! why bankers rule the world. *Global Research*, February 15. Retrieved from www.globalresearch.ca/its-the-interest-stupid-why-bankers-rule-the-world/5311030 (accessed July 18, 2013).

Brown, E. (2012). Exploring the public bank option. *CounterPunch*, December 7. Retrieved from www.counterpunch.org/2012/12/07/exploring-the-public-bank-option/ (accessed December 18, 2012).

Brown, E. (2011). What we can learn from Germany: How countries with publicly owned banks do better than America. *AlterNet*, October 18. Retrieved from www.alternet.org/story/152736/what_we_can_learn_from_germany%3A_how_countries_with_publicly_owned_banks_do_better_than_america?page=0%2C0 (accessed February 16, 2012).

Brown, E. (2009). Cutting Wall Street out. *CounterPunch*, November 2. Retrieved from www.counterpunch.org/brown11022009.html(accessed January 10, 2013).

China Daily (2011). BRICS: Working together to shape the future. April 14. Retrieved from www.chinadaily.com.cn/cndy/2011-04/14/content_12322993.htm.

Cumbers, A. and McMaster, R. (2012). Revisiting public ownership: Knowledge, democracy and participation in economic decision making. *Review of Radical Political Economics*, *44*(3), 358–373.

Gowan, P. (2010). The crisis in the heartland. In M. Konings (Ed.). *The Great Credit Crash*. London and New York: Verso.

Hilferding, R. (1981). *Finance capital: A study of the latest phase of capitalist development*. Tom Bottomore (Ed.). London: Routledge & Kegan Paul.

Hudson, M. (2012). Scenarios for recovery: How to write down the debts and restructure the financial system. Institute for New Economic Thinking, Berlin, April 13. Retrieved from http://ineteconomics.org/sites/inet.civicactions.net/files/hudson-michael-berlin-paper.pdf (accessed May 25, 2012).

Hyman, R. and Egler, T. (1981). Job controls, the employers' offensive, and alternative strategies. *Capital and Class*, *15*: 115–149.

Kennedy, M. (2012). *Occupy money: Creating an economy where everybody wins*. Gabriola Island, BC (Canada): New Society Publishers.

Mettenheim, K. V. (2010). Observations on government banking and BRICs in the recent financial crisis. Unpublished paper, Sao Paulo Business School of Brazil. Retrieved from http://academia.edu/1679005/Observations_on_Banking_in_BRIC_Countries (accessed July 15, 2013).

Nocera, J. (2011). Sheila Bair's Bank Shot. *New York Times*, July 9. Retrieved from www.nytimes.com/2011/07/10/magazine/sheila-bairs-exit-interview.html?pagewanted=all&_r=0.

Silber, W. L. (2009). Why did FDR's bank holiday succeed? New York: Federal Reserve Bank of New York Economic Policy Review, July.

Young, A. (2012). Cashing in on state-owned banking. *Scotsman*, November 24. Retrieved from www.scotsman.com/news/alf-young-cashing-in-on-state-owned-banking-1–2654306 (accessed January 14, 2013).

8 Beyond regulation and public banking[1]

While nationalization of commercial banks, as discussed in the previous chapter, could mitigate or do away with market turbulences that are due to financial bubbles and bursts, it will not preclude other systemic crises of capitalism. These include profitability crises that result from very high levels of capitalization (or high levels of the "organic composition of capital" *à la* Marx), from insufficient demand and/or underconsumption, from overcapacity and/or overproduction, or from disproportionality between various sectors of a market economy.

Historically, calls to nationalize the banks were made at a time (the first few decades of the twentieth century) when industrial capital, especially in Germany and to a lesser extent elsewhere, "was controlled by the private banking system. A socialist government that could nationalize finance capital would have in one fell swoop also annexed large swathes of the productive apparatus of society" (Finger 2013). Furthermore, demands to nationalize the banks

> [A]lso rested on the specific historic limitations of a means of circulation backed by tangible commodities (gold and silver). To nationalize the banks was to seize the national hoard of metal so that the socialist state could finance its economic operations and suppress other, alien, forms of accumulation and social activity, such as equipping and paying counterrevolutionary armies.
>
> (Ibid.)

Neither of these two conditions is present today. For one thing, while finance capital restricts industrial capital and retards manufacturing by draining resources away from real investment, it does not directly control industrial capital or manufacturing enterprises. For another, the prevailing money today is, of course, fiat (paper) money, not commodity money (gold or silver). Furthermore, as long as capitalism and, along with it, the lopsided distribution of economic surplus prevails, financial instability cannot be uprooted by nationalizing the banks. For, while nationalization of traditional banks may temper financial fragility, other types of financial intermediaries and institutions are bound to arise in order to avoid regulation and/or nationalization, thereby precipitating financial instability. These include all kinds of shadow banks and speculative enterprises such as private equity firms, derivative markets, hedge funds, and more. To do away with the systemic crises of capitalism, therefore, requires more than nationalization of banks; it requires changing the capitalist system itself.

Regulation, the liberal-Keynesian prescription to fend off financial instability, would not be an effective solution to the recurring crises of financial bubble and bursts either; because, for one thing, due to the political influence of powerful financial interests, financial regulations would not be implemented, as evinced, for example, by policy responses to the 2008 financial implosion and the ensuing Great Recession. For another, even if regulations are somehow implemented (for example, under the pressure from the grassroots, like the widespread protest demonstrations and militant labor actions in response to the Great Depression), they would provide only a temporary relief; for, as long as there is no democratic control, regulations would be undermined by the influential financial interests that elect and control both policy-makers and, therefore, policy. The dramatic reversal of the extensive regulations of the 1930s and 1940s that were put in place in response to the Great Depression and World War II to today's equally dramatic deregulations serves as a robust validation of this judgment. This shows, once again, that the need to end the recurring crises of the capitalist system requires more than financial regulation; it calls for changing the system itself, as pointed out above. Since the role of labor would be critical to such a systemic transformation, a brief analysis of trade unions and/or labor leaders' response to the 2008 financial crash and the ensuing Great Recession would, therefore, be a logical first section of this chapter.

Trade unions' response to the crisis

Creditor-sponsored attacks (carried out by the financial oligarchy's bagmen in Washington, Brussels, Berlin and London) on the working class since the 2008 financial implosion has taken dramatic dimensions: the loss of millions of jobs, destruction of social welfare systems, disappearance of millions of retirement pension plans, and massive cuts in food assistance programs, healthcare packages, public education programs, and more. According to recent reports, 26 million people within the European Union are without work. In Spain and Greece, the official unemployment rate is 27 percent, while among young people it is approaching 60 percent (Rippert 2013). The massive cuts in social spending have resulted in an enormous transfer of economic resources from the bottom up. The transfer has, indeed, more than made up for the 2008 losses of the financial speculators. In the U.S., for example, the wealthiest 1 percent now own 40 percent of the entire country's wealth; while the bottom 80 percent own only 7 percent. Likewise, the richest 1 percent now take home 24 percent of the country's total income, compared to only 9 percent four decades ago (Blodget 2013).

In the face of these brutal attacks on the living conditions of the working class, trade union leaders in the U.S. and Europe have, regrettably, offered no independent response to neoliberalism's global race to the bottom. They have, indeed, been actively collaborating with the neoliberal champions of the brutal austerity policies of their capitalist rulers against the class interests of the rank-and-file labor. Labor bureaucracy's collaboration with the creditor-sponsored austerity policies since the 2008 financial collapse is effected largely through the nominally socialist, Social Democratic, labor and democratic parties or governments such as Democratic Party in the U.S., Labour Party in the UK, Die Linke in Germany, SYRIZA in Greece, the Left and the New Anti-capitalist Party in France. Rooted largely in the various segments of the middle class, including the upper echelons of the labor bureaucracy, these left/liberal-sounding governments or parties tend to play a dual role: on the one hand, they pay lip-service to the notion of workers' right to employment and economic security; on the other, they use the illusion thus created to block independent mobilizations or actions of the working class.

In Greece, Spain and Portugal "popular resistance has been dissipated by means of one-day general strikes and protests in which the unions and pseudo-left organizations ensure that the mobilizations remain ineffective and never challenge incumbent governments or the European Union" (Rippert 2013). Rippert further writes, "The unions are integrating themselves ever more openly into the state apparatus. They defend the 'national interest' of their own ruling class and serve as business contractors to impose mass layoffs and cuts in wages and benefits." In a similar fashion, collaboration of union leaders, often through the political machine of the Labor Party, has been instrumental in the undermining of the social safety-net programs in the UK.

In the United States, leaders of the United Auto Workers (UAW) union, for example, forced an agreement on its members that included a six-year strike ban as part of the wage- and benefit-cutting contract dictated by the Obama administration's Auto Task Force in 2009. The agreement also included curtailment of wages and benefits of new workers to about 60 percent of what auto workers previously made, elimination of overtime pay, and the policing of the shop floor by union representatives on behalf of the bosses. It is not surprising, then, that rank-and-file members no longer look to union leaders, "with their legions of six-figure-salaried officials and joint union-management slush funds, as instruments of struggle" on behalf of the working class. This explains, at least in part, the dwindling numbers of union membership. The UAW once had over one million members and as recently as 2004 had 650,000 on its membership rolls. Today it has a membership of about 380,000 (White 2012).

Class collaborationist policies of the labor bureaucracy follow from a self-defeating philosophy that is called "national business unionism," or "union-management partnership." National business unionism accepts capital's needs for profitability as a precondition for labor's need for survival, advocates collaboration with the capitalist class on a national basis, and shoulders the burden of onerous economic sacrifices to maintain corporate profitability. A major outcome of this policy has been the change of many unions into labor syndicates: "They have become businesses that seek a cut in the profits sweated out of the workers. In the United States, The UAW is today a major holder of stocks in the Big

Three automakers. Its income is tied to driving up the profits and stock prices of the companies at the expense of the workers" (ibid.).

This explains why in the United States and many other industrialized countries labor bureaucracy's response to capitalist exploitation of labor has gradually changed "from pressuring employers to improve the wages and conditions of workers to pressuring the workers to improve the competitiveness of the corporations by means of layoffs, wage cuts and speedup" (ibid.). It also helps explain the relative ease with which the transnational capital has been able to heighten international labor rivalry, to exploit global labor markets and to more easily relocate production to countries with lower labor cost.

Inculcation of nationalist sentiments in the labor ranks (and the resulting international labor rivalry) is of, course, a boon for the ruling kleptocracy that loves to pit workers against their class brothers and sisters internationally. It is not surprising that, as the grueling economic conditions of the Great Recession continue unabated and the high rates of unemployment remain unrelenting, many politicians and policy makers are increasingly trying to whip up xenophobia and nationalist sentiments, especially economic nationalism, among workers. This includes not only the unabashedly right-wing or conservative politicians, but also the purportedly liberal Democratic President of the United States, Barack Obama, who has recently been promoting his new, nationalist approach—"made in America"—to "comfort" the jobless Americans. In an address to a gathering of the AFL-CIO Executive Council the President stated:

> So the message I want to deliver to our competitors … is that we are going to rebuild this economy stronger than before. And at the heart of it are going to be three powerful words: Made in America. (Applause.) Made in America.
>
> (as cited by Johnson 2010)

Note that Mr. Obama is careful not to use the openly nationalist/protectionist "buy American" slogan. Instead, he uses a more subtle, Orwellian version of it: "made in America." While prima facie reasonable, and perhaps pleasing to populist sentiments, the "buy American" or "made in America" policy suffers from a number of weaknesses. While the policy may save some jobs in import-competing industries, it would hurt employment in export industries, as it is bound to create protectionist retaliation among international trading partners. Furthermore, since the policy implicitly accepts the primacy of the needs of (national) capital, it heightens international labor rivalry, thereby making labor hostage to the profitability imperatives of national capital.

There is an insidious but subtle division of labor between liberal politicians, corporate media and labor bureaucracy in confusing and betraying the working class. While shedding crocodile tears for the plight of the unemployed, or half-heartedly dispensing populist utterances in "defense" of the economically hard-pressed working people, they do not propose effective strategies to save jobs or maintain living standards. On the contrary, as they pretend to be defending the workers' rights, they also tend to prepare them for "painful but necessary" hard economic times. For example, through its editorials and columnists such as Thomas Friedman, the *New York Times* has been playing a leading role in preparing the American public to accept the new, protracted phase of economic challenges, and to reconcile with lower standards of living:

> Welcome to the lean years. Yes, sir, we've just had our 70 fat years in America, thanks to the Greatest Generation and the bounty of freedom and prosperity they built for us. And in these past 70 years, leadership—whether of the country, a university, a company, a state, a charity, or a township—has largely been about giving things away, building things from scratch, lowering taxes or making grants.... Indeed, to lead now is to trim, to fire or to downsize services, programs or personnel. We've gone from the age of government handouts to the age of citizen givebacks.
>
> (Friedman 2010)

In a similar vein, the *Times* further opined:

> American workers are overpaid, relative to equally productive employees elsewhere doing the same work. If the global economy is to get into balance, that gap must close.... The global wage gap has been narrowing, but recent labor market statistics in the United States suggest the adjustment has not gone far enough.
>
> (Hadas *et al.* 2009)

Without using blunt words such as "the need to cut wages," President Obama also frequently preaches to the public to be prepared for the looming lean years:

> We must lay a new foundation for growth and prosperity—a foundation that will move us from an era of borrow and spend to one where we save and invest; where we consume less at home and send more exports abroad.

Obviously, by "we" Mr. Obama means the working class and the general public, not the ruling kleptocracy. And by "consume less" he obviously means "get used to a lower standard of living"—because wages, benefits, pensions and all kinds of social safety net programs are on the chopping board for austerity cuts (2009).

In their efforts to relentlessly push wages (and social spending) in the more developed countries down, the powerful financial interests (and their bagmen in the government) are pursuing multiple objectives. An obvious objective is, of course, to pay for the gambling losses of the Wall Street speculators. Another objective is to make U.S. producers more competitive in global markets, a strategy of export promotion that President Obama calls National Export Initiative: "Boosting America's exports strengthens our economic growth and supports millions of good, high-paying American jobs. That's why I set a goal during my State of the Union address to double our exports over the next five years." Stripped from its Orwellian veneer, the President's "national export initiative" simply means bringing U.S. wages and benefits down on a par with those of China, Vietnam, India, and other less-developed countries so that American manufacturers can compete more effectively in international markets (2010).

These are ghastly neoliberal policies of super exploitation that are sometimes called "the race to the bottom," or competing backward to the Dickensian days of working class misery. As discussed in Chapter 4 of this book, Naomi Klein (2007) has aptly called this sinister strategy "the shock doctrine," a strategy that takes advantage of the overwhelming crisis times to implement neoliberal austerity programs and redistribute national resources from the bottom up.

Of course, the neoliberal strategy of dismantling the welfare state and driving the labor pay down to slave wages is not limited to the United States. Downward competition is pursued in all core capitalist countries. Indeed, the competitive downward pressure of profitability and survival has driven almost all countries of the world to participate in this retrogressive (but capitalistically rational!) race to the bottom.

Is there a solution to this destructive international labor rivalry? What can the working class do to put an end to or, at least, temper to the downward spiraling of wages and benefits on a global level? Since cross-border unionization is often suggested as a potential solution, it is therefore necessary to briefly discuss international trade unionism.

International trade unionism

A logical strategy to counter neoliberalism's international race to the bottom would be the organization of international trade unions. If at an earlier stage of capitalist development "workers of the world unite" seemed an impossible dream articulated by the leading labor champion Karl Marx, internationalization of capital has now made that dream an urgent necessity. As capital and labor are the cornerstones of capitalist production, their respective organizations and institutions evolve more or less simultaneously, over time and space. Thus, when production was local, so was labor: carpenters, shoemakers, bricklayers, and other craftsmen organized primarily in their local communities. But as capitalist production became national, so did trade unions. Now that capitalist production has become global, labor organizations too need to become international in order to safeguard their rights against the profit-driven whims of the footloose and fancy-free transnational capital.

Prior to extensive globalization of production, labor confrontations with capital at the local or national levels were relatively more successful. Thus, for example, immigrant women workers strike in 1912, known as the "Bread and Roses" strike, against the American Woolen Company in Lawrence, Massachusetts, succeeded in securing important concessions from the company. This historic success was largely due to the fact that at the time the company had limited or no ability to move production elsewhere. Likewise, before the age of production mobility and outsourcing, auto unions successfully used selective strike tactics (as reflected, for instance, in the celebrated 1937 sit-down strike in Flint, Michigan) to safeguard their jobs and economic security. Indeed, the very formation and growth of labor organizations in times past, that is, before the wide-ranging internationalization of production, were significantly facilitated by the fact that there was a lack or limited mobility of production in those earlier times (Juravich 2007; Yates 2009).

Transition of labor organizations from the national to an international level is, of course, much more difficult than one that would evolve within national boundaries. While objective conditions—internationalization of production, communication, transportation and the like—are increasingly becoming conducive to cross-border organizing and solidarity, the capitalist nation state, working on behalf of the transnational capitalist class, is quite resourceful in erecting all kinds of political and cultural prejudices and barriers in the way of such efforts.

Despite these barriers, official international trade union organizations have already come to existence; they are called international trade secretariats (ITSs). They include, for example, the International Union of Food and Allied Workers (IUF) and the International Metalworkers Federation (IMF), with similar organizations for public employees, chemical workers, communications workers, etc. These are worldwide organizations to which the relevant national unions in each country can affiliate. ITSs have at times conducted effective international solidarity campaigns, such as the IUF's support of the Guatemalan Coca Cola workers' strike in 1984–1985. Because the ITSs are based on national unions, however, they are leadership-to-leadership organizations bound by the politics and bureaucracies of their affiliates. They could play an important role in getting affiliates to coordinate their bargaining internationally, but have not yet done so. Furthermore, local unions only have access to the ITSs through their national leaderships, which as discussed earlier, do not have salutary records in terms of effectively defending workers' right.

While international trade union bureaucracies, like their national affiliates, have so far pursued policies that favor collaboration with the ruling powers in their respective countries, and thus only partially served the interests of rank-and-file workers, the very fact that international labor networks and institutions already exist denotes an important step forward in the history of working class struggles. For it is perhaps easier to dismantle the structures and practices that insure the power of bureaucratic labor leaders, and to redirect the services and facilities of the international labor institutions so they serve the interests of labor, than to establish such institutions from scratch.[2]

As noted earlier, a retarding factor in the effectiveness of the official international labor organizations to defend the interests of their members has been the business unionist policies of the labor bureaucracy in major industrialized countries, especially in the U.S., which accept the primacy of capital's needs and, therefore, advocate collaboration with the capitalist class on a national basis. Also as mentioned earlier, leaders of organized labor in these countries have traditionally played a dual role: on the one hand, using labor leverage, they have at times defended trade unions' economic interests within the nation state;

on the other, they have at other times rallied workers to the side of transnational capital in its search for markets and investment opportunities abroad. Without this support, wars of an imperialist nature fought over global markets and resources would be very difficult, if not impossible. Organized labor in major industrialized countries, particularly in the United States, has been haunted by this experience. As Walden Bello points out,

> The extreme international mobility of corporate capital coupled with the largely self-imposed national limits on labor organizing by the Northern labor unions (except when this served Washington's Cold War political objectives) was a deadly formula that brought organized labor to its knees as corporate capital, virtually unopposed, transferred manufacturing jobs from the North to cheap-labor sites in the Third World.
>
> (Bello *et al.* 1994: 114)

While many in the "Northern" labor leadership continue to pursue the ideas and practices of national business unionism, there are signs of growing internationalist consciousness not only in the grassroots but also in a minority of the labor bureaucracy. Reflecting the changing views of the many rank and file union members in the United States, David Johnson, an organizer for the United Electrical Workers (UE), writes:

> The response of the labor movement [to NAFTA] has been terrible.... Some unions are still talking about "buying American." The problem with buying American, the problem with protectionism, is that it doesn't address who the enemies are. It is not the workers in Mexico who decide to move these plants down there.... Another response of the labor movement is what I call "solidarity by resolution." Trade unions get together, sometimes in a beautiful resort in a nice hotel, and they pass a lot of nice resolutions that say things like, "Workers have to stick together," and "By god its long past time we did something about it." I think we've all seen those resolutions and probably written some of them, and I know we've voted for some of them. It's our opinion in the UE that the time is really over for that stuff. A few years ago, maybe, we had the luxury of playing around with that stuff. It's time now to get beyond that.
>
> (1993: 8)

Expressing frustration with the official AFL-CIO policy, Johnson continues:

> With very few exceptions, the U.S. labor movement has a well-deserved reputation, not only in Mexico but throughout Latin America and through much of the world, of racism, of paternalism, of interference in their national sovereignty. Workers in Latin America have not forgotten the role of the international arms of the AFL-CIO, with their friends in the CIA. This is a terrible legacy we have to overcome if we're going to build up real

> solidarity across the borders, and it needs to be said right out that we're starting from way back.
>
> (Ibid.: 9)

While not widespread, the dissenting views among labor ranks are not exceptional either. The fact that during the national debate over the North American Free Trade Agreement (NAFTA) dozens of independent labor and other grassroots' organizations sprang up across the U.S., Mexico and Canada in opposition to the treaty is a clear indication of the changing views. These organizations, with their often meager resources, were able to establish cross-border contacts with their counterparts, exchange ideas on issues of international unionization such as wage and benefits coordination and, in a small number of cases, succeeded in organizing labor unions in U.S.-owned plants operating in Mexico. Examples of these initiatives include the IBT Local 912/Green Giant solidarity caravan, the UE-FAT (Mexican Authentic Workers' Front) Strategic Alliance, and the AFL-CIO-backed Coalition for Justice in Maquiladoras. Less official transnational solidarity organizations and networks such as Labor Notes and the Transnational Information Exchange succeeded in establishing tri-national exchanges and meetings of auto, telecommunications, and garment workers. Similarly, solidarity tours by members of the Ford Workers Democratic Movement of Mexico and by telecommunications workers, teachers, and others have taken place in the last few years. The formation of the North American Worker-to-Worker Network in the context of the North American Free Trade Agreement (NAFTA), which includes both labor and community organizations, has been another important step toward strengthening this new form of internationalist organizing.

In more recent years, as the escalating austerity attacks of transnational capital on labor and their communities have become more onerous, many in the labor movement and other anti-austerity forces have begun cross-border contacts in pursuit of coordinated strategies to safeguard their jobs, their economic safety-net programs and their environment. One of the very promising results of such efforts at international collaboration of labor and other grassroots was the historic opening (in New York City) of the Global Unions Conference in 2006. Entitled "Global Companies, Global Unions, Global Research, Global Campaigns," the conference attracted 560 representatives of trade unions, community leaders, non-governmental organizations and academics from fifty-three countries to explore coordinated and more effective "campaigns to support organizing and bargaining by unions and workers" worldwide (Bronfenbrenner 2007: 6).

Although the conference's agenda was somewhat modest (it did not challenge the rule of capital; it only sought to temper that rule), it was nonetheless a historic event because, for one thing, never before a group of that magnitude and diversity had assembled in one place; for another, it showed promising prospects for a worldwide labor movement. What is needed to effectively challenge the tyranny of capital, however, is a global movement beyond unions—a new labor movement.

A radical response to neoliberal austerity: A labor movement beyond unions

It is no mystery that in the age of widespread global capitalism international labor rivalry will continue to grow unless the logic that governs the demand and supply of labor under capitalist system is checked. It is also obvious that the existing trade union bureaucracies in more developed capitalist countries are tragically collaborating with their ruling classes (often through the nominally liberal, socialist or social democratic parties) according to the imperatives of national capital.

It is equally clear that non-labor varieties of radicals and/or progressives such as environmentalists, Greens, intellectuals, artists, students and the like—in short, radical groups working within the amorphous and "leaderless" coalitions such as Occupy Wall Street—are incapable of bringing about meaningful change. Despite all the good intentions, so far they have been able to serve more as pressure valves than forces of change. The history of social movements and societal changes shows that as long as the working class continues to work and produce, and therefore feed or nurture the production foundation of the capitalist system, the status quo would not be radically transformed. Movements like Occupy Wall Street in the U.S. and *Tamarod* (rebellion) in Egypt do a wonderful job in exposing the unjust and corrupting nature of the capitalist system. However, their self-imposed policy of "no specific demands," "no organization" and "no leadership"; that is, their tendency to restrict themselves to sporadic protest and occupation activities around general and abstract goals such as peace, democracy and social justice, tends to be self-limiting and, ultimately, self-defeating.

The Occupy movement shied away from making specific demands on grounds such as: concrete demands tend to narrow the movement's focus and limit its ideals and goals; focusing on specific demands is tantamount to focusing on trees while losing sight of the forest; demands may Balkanize the 99 percent and diffuse their energy as they tend toward the least common denominator; and the like. Far-reaching goals such as "democracy now," or essential grievances such as "banks got bailed out, we got sold out," may sound loftier and more important than specific demands such as "Medicare for all," "jobs for all," or "save Social Security"; but it is only through these kinds of specific demands that broader masses of the working people and other grassroots can be mobilized. More importantly, in the absence of such concrete, winnable demands it would become increasing more difficult to sustain a movement on the basis of general grievances, or lofty but amorphous ideals.

The Occupy and *Tamarod* movements have also avoided building systematic organizations or selecting/electing specific leaders out of a purported fear that doing so may lead to centralization and bureaucratization of power. This is a legitimate concern. But there is such a thing as being too cautious. We can no longer afford not to use automobiles out of fear of auto accidents; we must drive carefully, and not allow drunkards to sit at the wheel. The solution to the problem of centralization of power is not doing away with organization; it is guarding against it through democratic means and "appropriate" *checks and balances* (Hossein-zadeh 2012).

Decentralization does not necessarily mean "democracy," just as centralization does not necessarily mean authoritarianism. Occupy and similar movements need (and can have) both organization and leaders without losing democratic operations. Furthermore, claiming that the Occupy movement has no leaders, and that major decisions within the movement are made collectively is not really true.

> Leaders exist within Occupy regardless of intentions; saying that Occupy is a "leaderless movement" does not make it so. The inevitable leaders of Occupy are those who dedicate their time to the movement, organize events, are spokespeople, those who help set agendas for meetings or actions, those who set up and run web pages, etc. In reality there already exists a spectrum of leadership that is essential to keeping the movement functioning.
>
> (Cooke 2012)

Cihan Tugal points out that what we learn from the experiences of Occupy and *Tamarod* is that "when movements don't have (or claim not to have) ideologies, agendas, demands and leaders, they can go in two directions: they can dissipate (as did Occupy), or serve [others'] agendas" (2013), as does *Tamarod.*

What conclusions can be drawn from these experiences? What can the working people and other grassroots do to protect their jobs, their sources of livelihood, their communities and their environment? Is there a defense against these threats? Are there alternatives to the global capitalist agenda? What can communities do to undermine the strategies of multinational corporations that block progressive social and economic reforms?

A logical, first step deterrent to transnational capital's strategy of blackmailing labor and communities through threats such as destroying or exporting jobs by moving their business elsewhere would be to remove the lures that induce plant relocation, capital flight or outsourcing. Making labor costs of production comparable on an international level would be crucial for this purpose. This would entail taking the necessary steps toward the international establishment of wage and benefits, that is, of labor cost parity within the same company and the same trade, subject to (a) the cost of living, and (b) productivity in each country. A strategy of this sort would replace the current downward competition between workers in various countries with coordinated bargaining and joint policies for mutual interests and problem-solving on a global level. While this may sound radical, it is not any more radical than what the transnational capitalist class has been doing for a long time.

In the same fashion that, in their fight against the working class, the elites of the international capitalist class are not bound by territoriality or national boundaries, so does the working class need to coordinate its response internationally. Representatives of transnational capital and their proxies in capitalist governments routinely meet at international conferences in order to synchronize their cross-border business and financial policies—a major focus of which in recent years has been to implement global austerity measures and entrench neoliberal policies worldwide. These include the World Economic Forum in Davos, Switzerland, the World Bank and IMF annual meetings, the Periodic G20 meetings, the Aspen Institutes Ideas Festival, The Bilderberg Group annual geopolitics forum, and the Herb Allen's Sun Valley gathering of media moguls—to name only a handful of the many such international policy gatherings. Through its global strategies and operations, transnational capital has broken free from national constraints and commitments at home—especially from the traditional labor and environmental challenges at the national level—and successfully shifted the correlation of class forces and social alliances worldwide. Today's elites of global capitalism "are becoming a trans-global community of peers who have more in common with one another than with their countrymen back home," according to Chrystia Freeland Global Editor of Reuters, who travels with the elites worldwide. "Whether they maintain primary residences in New York or Hong Kong, Moscow or Mumbai, today's super-rich are increasingly a nation unto themselves" (2011).

Business and government representatives of transnational capital carry out their offensive against the living conditions of the overwhelming majority of the world's population largely through such organizations as the International Monetary Fund, the World Trade Organizations and the powerful international banking system. To counter this heartless (but capitalistically logical) offensive, popular and working class movements around the world also need to respond globally. An important step in this direction would be abandoning the current business unionist policies of the labor bureaucracy in major industrialized countries and, instead, organizing new labor organizations, both at the national and international levels. In other words, what is needed to reverse the decline of labor and the balance of class forces is a new type of union strategy and a new labor movement.

Crucial as they are in the struggle for labor rights (the right to organize, the right to strike, and the right to bargain collectively), trade unions have their limitations in the fight against the vagaries of a market economy: unemployment, alienation, and poverty. To begin with, they encompass only a small portion of the working class, usually the more skilled and better paid layers. Second, trade unionist politics is usually limited to economic demands such as wages and working conditions. While critical to the economic welfare of union members, broader social issues such as democracy, equality, universal health and education, and environmental concerns remain outside the purview of trade union politics.

Third, to the extent that trade unions defend the economic interests of the working class, their bargaining power is limited by a number of factors. One such factor, as discussed in Chapter 2, is the market's tendency (and capability) to create a "reserve army" of the unemployed which severely limits the power of unions to bargain with the employers. The second factor is workers' dependence on the requirements of capital accumulation. Since wages and profits share the economic surplus, increases in the share of wages cut down on profits and investment, and result in a slackening of growth and a rise in unemployment. As the late Stephen Hymer put it, "this makes the working class a hostage to the capitalist class on whom they depend for capital accumulation and to whom they must provide incentives in the form of profits and accumulation of capital" (as quoted in Cohen *et al.* 1979: 269). During periods of expansionary cycles and a labor shortage, a rise in the overall surplus can afford an increase in the shares of both wages and profits—like the immediate post-WW II period in the U.S. But the rise in automation of production and internationalization of capital are making a repeat of that experience increasingly less likely.

A third factor that limits the bargaining position of the national union is the fact that investment, production, and competition now take place on an international level. Labor is therefore constrained in its defense of wages and employment by the threat of international capital flight and plant relocation. Even if we assume that international capital mobility and outsourcing is somehow successfully blocked by a country's unions and their allies, the dilemma for national labor remains that any national policy to increase (or maintain) employment and wages will undermine a country's position within the competitive world market, thereby further threatening wages and employment. In fact, even if a socio-political movement representing the poor and the working class came to power, it would immediately face this dilemma. If it tries to break out of the global market, it will face capital flight, economic sanctions/boycotts orchestrated by major world powers, currency depreciation, balance of payment difficulties, and economic collapse. This explains why Karl Marx argued long ago that individual countries cannot break out of the grip of world capitalism. To be viable, socialism has to be global or, at least, encompass major industrialized economies of the world.

The solution to the woes and vagaries of capitalism lies, therefore, with the transformation of the transnational, not just national, economies. Fighting against the ills of the market system is crucial to labor and other social layers suffering from them. But it makes little sense to fight symptoms without challenging the system that produces them. Transforming the world economy in the interests of the majority of the people is, of course, not easy. It certainly cannot be brought about in one leap or an overnight uprising. It can come about only as the cumulative outcome of many steps along the path of a long and difficult journey of continuous social and economic change. If the ideal society in which we would all like to live is called Socialism with a capital S, achievement of that Socialism would evolve out of a series of socialisms, with small initial letters, along a transitional path—a series of ongoing experiments and struggles to constantly rectify the damage wrought by the existing social order. Nobody can tell a priori how long or what form such transitional steps or stages may take; nor would such speculation be very useful. It is clear, however, that to change the world economy in the interests of the majority of its inhabitants needs new politics and new organizations to articulate the struggle for change.

Many radicals have dropped class politics at exactly the moment it is needed most. Rosa Luxemburg's view that socialism is the only humane alternative to capitalist barbarism is as relevant today as when she expressed it (during the carnage of WW I). Barbarism stares us in the eye in many disguised forms. Yet, much of the left these days shy away from using words such as class struggle, organization, or the crucial role of labor for social and economic change. "It is fashionable these days," as Walden Bello puts it,

> [T]o describe the desired alternatives [to capitalism] as an equitable, democratic, and ecologically sustainable social and economic organization. But once one begins to attempt to spell out the concrete implications of this abstract ideal, one cannot avoid describing a system of social relations that checks or restrains the devastating logic of capitalism.... Whatever one wishes to call it, conscious cooperative organization must supplant both blind competition and monopolistic collusion as the strategic principle of production and exchange if the economy is brought back to its appropriate relationship to the community.
>
> (1994: 112–113)

To help initiate change in this direction, labor needs its own independent political organization(s) and its own class presence to influence the evolving one-world economy. A viable independent labor organization would be one that, as labor activist David Riehle put it, "advances the idea that workers should represent themselves, that workers would be candidates for public office, [and] that the working class itself can provide the solutions to the permanent crisis of present society" (1993: 12–13).

It is true that in the older industrialized countries the percentage of the labor force working in large manufacturing and mining enterprises has declined, compared to those working in the so-called service industries. But this is no more than diversification of the work force, which follows diversification of technology and economic activity; and the conclusion that it represents a decline in the overall weight or importance of the working class is unwarranted. The look of one's work uniform, the color of a wage earner's collar, or whether one's pay is called wage or salary does not make him or her more or less of a worker than other wage earners. In fact, statistics on wage and benefits of the work force show that, on the average, the so-called white collar workers are paid less and are much less secure economically than the traditional industrial/manufacturing workers. Growth of the service industries has also meant growth of minimum-wage and no-benefits workers. Concentration of large numbers of workers in telecommunications, transport, banks, hospitals, energy sector, and the like can today paralyze the capitalist economy as effectively as their "blue-collar" counterparts in the manufacturing sector. Furthermore, "professionals" and salaried employees such as teachers, engineers, physicians, and even middle and lower level managers are increasingly becoming wage workers, and are thus ruled by the supply and demand forces of the labor market. The tendency for wage work to become the dominant or universal form of work means that, overall, the ranks of the working class are expanding, not contracting, despite the relative decline in manufacturing employment.

> But while the overall percent of the labor force in the working class remained essentially unchanged (63 percent in 2010 compared with 62 percent in 1996), changes in details suggest two offsetting trends. The percent of the labor force engaged in traditional working class occupations has declined.... At the same time ... traditional middle class professions like teaching and nursing have come under the discipline of corporate management in substantial numbers, resulting in a class shift within the professions. When we take into account the growing fraction of teachers, nurses, and other professionals who once had the autonomy and authority that made them part of the middle class, but who have since become subject more closely to the type of supervision characteristic of the skilled working class, the overall fraction of the labor force in the working class remained virtually unchanged.
>
> (Zweig 2012: vii; see also Braverman 1974; Yates 2009)

More numerous than ever before, the working class can influence, shape, and ultimately lead the world economy if it takes on the challenge (a) on an international level, and (b) in the context of broader coalitions and alliances with other social groups that also struggle for equity, environmental protection, and human rights. This requires a new labor movement with independent politics and organization(s). Whatever the new labor organization is called (call it a party, a labor coalition, or anything you like), it has to be different not only from the U.S. business union model but also from the Social Democratic model of Europe, trade unions + party. It can certainly learn from models of labor movement in Latin America and South Africa where unions, grassroots' parties, and community-based organizations increasingly function as arms of a single working class movement (Moody 1994). This means that the new labor movement and/or organization has to represent the interests of the entire working class, not just organized industrial labor, nor only its singular economic interests. In addition, it must aim at defending the interests of all those who challenge the logic of the profit-driven market mechanism. As Susan George, of the Transnational Institute, puts it:

> If the labor movement stays separate from all the other progressive forces in the world, we will be picked off one by one. There are tremendous opportunities for building alliances with environmentalists, with church groups, with development organizations. There is a whole host of people out there, but one has to go about building those alliances consciously. That does not mean you have to give up your own identity. That does not mean you have to agree on every issue, but it does mean that if we are going to beat this free market, competitive economy we have to re-group our forces. It is curious that the majority in the world is losing by this system and yet we do not seem to be able to unite and make our own political points.
>
> (1994: 12)

The inadequacies and limitations of the existing major trade unions do not mean that a new independent labor organization should (or can afford to) bypass labor unions. Such a labor organization will have to grow out of, but go beyond, the existing labor institutions; it must expand its horizons from the industrial or trade level to the national level, and from purely economic to political action. In other words, it can no longer confine itself to the fight for wages but must fight for an equitable share of the aggregate economic surplus, a fair distribution and reasonable allocation of national income. As was pointed out earlier, these objectives cannot be truly achieved within a national framework, since no nation alone is able to break free from the grip of world capitalism. Therefore, new, independent labor organizations of various countries must shift their horizons from the national to the world level, to international solidarity and international coordination of policy and action.

As noted earlier, the road to a social structure not regulated by capitalist profitability imperatives is a long and tortuous one; it cannot be traveled in one leap, but rather through a series of transitional steps and stages. Only through a careful and timely formulation of transitional programs and demands can a bridge be built between the present and such a society. While based on the needs of the broad masses of the dispossessed and disaffected, such demands do (or should) not initially "transcend capitalism"; they must be based on "realistic transitional program for resistance," as Barry Finger puts it (2013). While the exact nature of transitional demands will depend on the concrete conditions of many specific movements along the way of this long struggle, the following seem to be some of the most logical demands for the present time.

1 The right to employment for all those able to work. Employers, their ideological allies, and their representatives in government will obviously cry out at this demand that "there are simply not enough jobs." The labor coalition can then respond by raising the following demand.
2 A sliding scale of working hours, which means that the new international labor movement should correlate the length of the work week to labor productivity so that, as productivity rises, the number of working hours will automatically fall, and no jobs will be lost. If it takes less time to produce the same commodities, we should all work less rather than eliminating some people's jobs. There is absolutely nothing outlandish or radical about this demand; it only makes sense.

   But capital has its own logic, and in the last half century or so, just the opposite has taken place. In the United States, for example, people are working longer hours as labor productivity has been steadily going up. A 1991 study by Professor Juliet Schor of Harvard University showed that productivity in the United States had risen about 2.7 times since WW II. If the gains in productivity had been directed into decreasing the work week, the professor observed, the amount of labor time required to maintain a constant standard of living would have declined to 20 hours per week. Instead, both men and women now devote more time to combined market and non-market labor than they did nearly 45 years ago.

3 A sliding scale, or indexing, of wages. This means adjusting wages to the rate of inflation so that workers' purchasing power and their standard of living will not fall as the prices rise. Closely related to this demand is the demand that the share of wages as a percentage of national income should not fall relative to the share of profit, rent, and interest. Studies of income distribution in the U.S. show that, for example, the relative share of interest earners as a percentage of national income has been steadily rising at the expense of the share of wage earners in the post-WW II period (Konczal 2011).
4 The right to a guaranteed universal, single-payer type health care system.

These and similar demands such as the right to affordable education, the right to pollution-free air and water, and the right to equal treatment of men and women regardless of gender and sexual preferences are certain to rally diverse segments of society behind the labor coalition, and thus help end the absolute rule of capital.[3]

Many people would view these proposals as unrealistic. What they mean by this is that these demands cannot be realized under the present socioeconomic and political structure. And they are right. But, as this structure is reorganized, many of the currently "impossible" alternatives will become possible. There is definitely no dearth of material resources for this purpose, certainly not in the U.S. and other industrialized countries. The evolving internationalization of capital and integration of world markets is pulling the workers of the world together to an unprecedented extent. "More and more workers around the globe not only work for the same 1,000 or so dominant multinational corporations (MNCs) or their contractors," as labor historian Kim Moody points out, "but are linked in common production or service delivery system" (1994). Rapid internationalization of production, technology, and information is increasingly creating favorable conditions for a humane alternative to capitalism. What is lacking is the political will and/or capacity to reorient the society's priorities and reallocate its resources. Whether or when these proposals would be realized, ultimately, comes down to the relationship of social forces and the balance of class struggle.

Others might reject these demands on philosophical grounds: that in the great contest between capitalism and socialism (as it prevailed in the Soviet Union and its counterparts elsewhere), capitalism has decisively triumphed, that the rules and the laws of market mechanism are eternal, and that, therefore, any talk of socialism or proletarian internationalism is anachronistic and/or passé. Let us examine these contentions more closely.

Prospects for international labor solidarity—and for globalization from below

As noted above, many would argue that these are not propitious times to speak of radical alternatives to capitalism. In a recent article titled "The Silent Death of the American Left," Jeffrey St. Clair, editor of *CounterPunch*, pointedly asked:

> Is there a counterforce to the grinding machinery of neoliberal capitalism and its political managers?... Where is our capacity to confront the daily horrors of drone strikes, kill lists, mass layoffs, pension raids and the looming nightmare of climate change?

Answering his own questions, St. Clair (2013) wrote,

> It is a bitter reality ... that the Left is an immobilized and politically impotent force at the very moment when the economic inequalities engineered by our overlords at Goldman Sachs who manage the global economy, should have recharged a long-moribund resistance movement back to life.
>
> "Instead", he further wrote, "the Left seems powerless to coalesce, to translate critique into practice ... powerless to confront rule by the bondholders and hedge-funders ... and incapable of confronting the true legacy of the man [Barack Obama) they put their trust in." In conclusion, St. Clair noted: "One looks in vain across this vast landscape of despair for even the dimmest flickers of real rebellion and popular mutiny, as if surveying a nation of somnambulists.... We remain strangely impassive in the face of our own extinction.

Admittedly, the present state of the socio-political landscape of our society appears to support such feelings of pessimism. The high levels of unemployment in most countries of the world and the resulting international labor rivalry, combined with the austerity offensive of neoliberalism on a global level, have thrown the working class on the defensive. The steady drift of the European socialist, Social Democratic, and labor parties toward the U.S.-style market economies and the erosion of their traditional ideology, power, and prestige have led to workers' confusion there. The collapse of the Soviet Union, however much some socialists have always distanced themselves from that system, haunts the specter of socialism, and is likely to do so for some time to come. These developments have understandably led to workers' and leftists' confusion and disorientation globally.

None of these, however, mean that there is no way out of the status quo. Capitalism is not only "destructive," it is also "regenerative," as Karl Marx put it (in his discussion of the impact of capitalism on colonies and other less-developed areas). As it captures world markets, universalizes the reign of capital, and disrupts the living conditions for many, it simultaneously sows the seeds of its own transformation. On the one hand, it creates common problems and shared concerns for the majority of the world population; on the other, it creates the conditions and the technology that facilitate communication and cooperation among this majority of world citizens for joint actions and alternative solutions. When this majority will come to the realization and determination to actually appropriate and utilize the existing technology for a better organization and management of the world economy, no one can tell. But the potential and the trajectory of global socioeconomic developments point in that direction. The distance between now and then, between our immediate frustrations and the superior but elusive civilization of our desire, can be traversed only if we take the necessary steps toward that end.

Internationalism is not a dogma invented by Marx but recognition of the laws of capitalist development, of the laws of the accumulation of capital as "self-expanding value" that is blind to physical or geographical borders. The need and the call for international labor solidarity stems from a recognition of this process: that if not labor, then capital would continue to rule the world.

A comparison between the early stages of the development of capitalism on a national level and its subsequent expansion to international level is instructive. In its early stages of development, capitalism consolidated and centralized all the petty states, principalities, and feudal domains into nation states in order to create a broader arena for the development of productive forces. Today a similar consolidation of markets is taking place on an international level. Just as in the early stages of capitalism, nation states facilitated consolidation of national markets by establishing national currencies, national business laws, national tax laws, and the like, today they perform a similar task through international agencies such as the IMF, the World Bank, European Union, World Trade Organization (WTO), and the Bank for International Settlements, which represents the unofficial international banking cartel.

Labor organizations too need to move from national to international arena—just as they moved from the local and/or craft level of early capitalism to the national level of today. The fact that earlier attempts at international labor solidarity failed by no means signals the end of the necessity of that solidarity—the growth of labor organizations has almost always lagged behind those of capital. Nor does it, therefore, detract in any way from the validity of the Marxian theory of history and/or proletarian internationalism. As a science, Marxism will have to deal with new developments by advances in its theory. But only the doctrinaire can perceive a crisis of Marxism and a doom of international labor solidarity from the unsuccessful international labor experiences of the past, or from the failure of economic planning experiments in the former USSR and its allies. From a Marxian perspective of history, the collapse of the Soviet system should have come as no surprise; on the contrary, the demise of that system gives striking confirmation to the scientific validity and continued relevance of Marxist theory. A crucial factor in Marx's view of the viability of a socialist society is its achievement to a higher productivity of labor than under capitalism. Without this condition, and without democratic decision making, revolutionary expropriation of the means of production and their placement at the disposal of the state would be, according to this view, a dramatic event without a future, since these revolutionary gains are bound to (sooner or later) succumb to the more competitive capitalist market forces. In the absence of these two key conditions, the collapse of the Soviet-type economies was inevitable.[4]

Those who refer to a crisis of Marxism and the "end of history" (Fukuyama 1992) see the conjunctural deviations of actual developments from theory, and an altering of conditions, as a loss of the general explanatory power of the theory. Some of the general conditions that have contributed to the failure of past efforts at international labor cooperation are: the prematurity of some of those efforts, including perhaps that of the First International; the corruption and/or ideological bankruptcy of the leadership of the working class; the successful promotion of the ideology of nation state and/or nationalism by the capitalist class; the divisive atmosphere of the Cold War era; and, perhaps most importantly, the immediate post-WW II economic boom in the United States and other core capitalist countries, which afforded the working class in these countries a decent standard of living, thereby fostering a policy of cooperation with the capitalist class at home and a cavalier attitude toward workers elsewhere. Whatever the reason or reasons, the fact is that most of these conditions have changed, or are changing, and new conditions that will prepare and/or favor international labor collaboration are replacing them—euphoric celebrations of the "triumph" of capitalism and the apparent confusion of the working class notwithstanding.

Chief among the emerging new conditions is the change in the U.S. international economic position and, with it, in the traditional labor strategies in the face of globalization of production. Until the early 1970s, the United States was the major world supplier of manufactured products. Furthermore, those products were largely produced at home. As long as the U.S. produced at home and sold abroad, its workers did not have to compete with those of other countries. It should therefore not be surprising that, during that era, the AFL-CIO pursued a policy of free trade and shunned international labor cooperation as these served its (temporary) economic interests.[5] World economic integration and globalization of production have changed this. Workers in the United States are beginning to realize that they can no longer afford to shun workers in other countries as this would be leaving corporations free to play them off against workers in low-wage parts of the world.

Signs of this welcome change toward internationalism were noticeably visible in the Global Unions Conference mentioned earlier in this chapter. During the conference, union leaders from the more-developed countries such as the United States, Western Europe and Canada remarkably acknowledged the need to rectify their past attitudes and expectations, that is, "unilateral" expectations toward the workers in the less-developed countries; expectations that "sought help from workers in the Global South or eastern Europe but did not reciprocate" (Bronfenbrenner 2007: 6):

> The large number of participants from unions from Europe and the full support from the GUFs [global union federations] also represented a significant change in the perception of where the European labor movement and the GUFs stood on the issue of comprehensive cross-border campaigns. In fact, the sessions were filled with stories of unions in Europe beginning to link with one another and with unions in other countries, as employers with whom they had heretofore had a stable labor relationship were now engaging in large-scale cutbacks in jobs and demands for concessions in wages and social benefits.
>
> (Ibid.: 7)

In the United States, shoots of a new politics in the labor ranks and in the independent unions are also reflected in domestic labor strategies of recent years. These include union reform activities, cross-union solidarity actions/organizations, community-based labor organizations, one-day work stoppages, efforts to build a labor party, and sporadic efforts at building independent worker cooperatives. In recent years, for example, there have been a number of one-day work stoppages around the country by retail and fast food workers targeting non-union chains like McDonald's, Taco Bell, Burger King, and TJ Max. Such tactically short-time strikes (designed not to incur the wrath or reprisal of company management) have taken place in cities such as New York, Chicago, Detroit, Milwaukee, and St. Louis. As labor and community activist Laura Flanders (2012) points out, "So far, they're succeeding in staging one day walk outs without dire reprisals from management." In light of the unfavorable job market, Flanders continues:

> That's a jaw-dropping thing, helped by visible community and church group support. And while the one day strikes may be involving only a minority of workers so far, they are clearly building support as the wave of actions shows.

There have also developed in recent years a number of sporadic instances of worker owned and managed cooperatives. A relatively well-known example of such cases has been the experience of the New Era Windows in Chicago, formerly called the Republic Windows and Doors. In 2008, the management of the Republic Windows and Doors factory gave the workers a stern ultimatum that if they did not consent to the drastic giveaways demanded by the management, they would be laid off. Instead of accepting draconian cuts of their wages and benefits, or succumbing to being laid off, the few hundred union workers voted to occupy their plant. The long story of the nearly five-year struggle of the workers against the factory owners/managers is beyond the scope of this discussion. Suffice it to say that, as Flanders relates, "Five years on, as some of those same workers cut the ribbon on their own cooperatively-run business," now called the New Era Windows, "it was yet another bold step by innovative workers in a season of daring by labor." Asked why he and his co-workers had decided to start a co-op, veteran window maker "Ricky" Maclin told Flanders, "it was because they were tired of their lives being in someone else's hands" (ibid.).

The New Era workers factory occupation was a rare act of labor militancy reminiscent of the 1930s sit-down strikes and factory occupations. Following the Great Depression and WW II, as the U.S. economy boomed and the American labor enjoyed respectable wages and benefits, without any serious competition from abroad, not only did labor unions balk at international cooperation with workers in other countries, they also did not support "radical" labor actions such as independent worker cooperatives at home. Today, however, the United Electrical, Radio and Machine Workers of America (UE), for example, "will be representing the New Era workers, and The United Steelworkers of America is working with the Basque co-ops of Mondragon to open industrial size co-ops in the U.S." (ibid.).

These instances of labor resistance and their occasional successes are, admittedly, fragmented and anecdotal. And while their near-term outcome is uncertain, the experiments themselves signify important long-term potentials.

Globalization of production, technology, and information has created not only favorable conditions for labor internationalism but also for broader grassroots forces that are likewise challenging capitalist regulation of their lives and communities. Although often submerged, there exist unmistakably hopeful signs that the global economic rollback policies of neoliberalism have begun to awaken the grassroots and working people everywhere. The result has been a widespread but little-recognized resistance to these policies. Massive uprisings in places like Egypt, Zapatistas' uprisings in the Chiapas, women's riots in the Nigerian oil belt, and urban riots in Spain, Greece or Brazil all represent one thing: grassroots' response to the neoliberal economic austerity programs. These initiatives have led to a series of international solidarity networks of trade unionists, environmentalists, women, consumer advocates, and other citizen activists. A full account of international coalitions of grassroots groups is beyond the scope of this study. A brief tour through some computer networks shows numerous such cross-border groups, despite the fact that not all of them are connected with electronic networks (Daly and Cobb 1994; Krimmerman and Lindfeld 1992; Shuman 1994; Danaher 1994).

Initially stunned by the dizzying shock-therapy style attack of neoliberalism on their living conditions in the aftermath of the 2008 financial collapse, citizens across Europe are now gradually building powerful campaigns to stop creditor-sponsored privatization of public properties and services.

> In parallel to the imposition of austerity measures and privatization, there are countless grassroots initiatives that amount to a counter-trend against this new wave of dangerous privatization. This backlash extends far beyond reactive resistance and highlights a real way forward for public services in Europe. New reinvigorated public services with genuine democratic participation can emerge and take root.... A "European Spring" characterized by actions, strikes and demonstrations can help to connect and multiply local resistance throughout the continent.
>
> (Zacune 2013)

The author of this passage further relate how in Paris, for instance, the transfer of water services from private companies to municipal authorities was a major success, resulting in savings of €35 million in the first year and improved service delivery. Similar trends of "re-municipalization" have taken place in Germany, Finland and the UK; as local public authorities re-establish control over energy, forests, water, transport, refuse and recycling sectors.

In Spain, popular struggles, known as "citizen waves," have been organized by the mass *Indignado* movement to fight the austerity cuts and privatization of public property and services spearheaded by what has come to be known as the Troika: the International Monetary Fund, the European Central Bank and the European Commission. These have included the "blue wave" against water privatization, "green" for education, "white" for healthcare, and "orange" for social services. "On 23 February 2013, the different 'waves' came together for a massive protest in Madrid" (ibid.).

In Portugal, a citizens' campaign initiative, called "Água é de todos" (Water for All), presented 40,000 signatures in March 2013 "opposing the privatization of the national water company." In Italy, an anti-privatization referendum in June 2011, resulting in 96 percent of the voting electorate (around 26 million voters), succeeded in "overturning laws promoting the privatization of the management of water and local public utilities." And in July 2012, following widespread public pressure, "the Italian Constitutional Court declared that legal attempts to reintroduce the privatization of local public services was unconstitutional" (ibid.).

In Athens, Greece, the "Save Greek Water" campaign was launched in July 2012 to oppose water privatizations and "promote the democratic control of water resources." Likewise, In Thessaloniki, Initiative 136, a citizens' movement, "is opposing the privatization of the Water and Sanitation Company and calling for social management through local cooperatives instead." The Pallini municipality has also "taken the decision not to allow the privatization of its water supplies." More broadly, the Greek public and trade unions (often defying the class collaborationist policies of their bureaucratic leaders) "have strongly resisted the privatization of Greek energy services, telecommunications and transport infrastructure" (ibid.).

"For a European Spring" is an anti-austerity resistance movement that coordinates international protest actions across Europe. Its mission statement, posted on the home-page of its Website (http://foraeuropeanspring.org), declares,

> The pan-European movement continues to grow and For a European Spring will use its website to spread the word of new mobilizations, actions, strikes and struggles that are helping to build a grass-roots resistance to the unjust and undemocratic policies being imposed by the European Commission, the International Monetary Fund (IMF) and the European Central Bank – a.k.a. the Troika.

The website lists numerous anti-austerity protest actions that are scheduled all across Europe.

It is true that, despite their significant growth in recent years, these grassroots movements remain largely fragmented, and their resistance to the austerity policies of the rentier class of transnational financial interests is still mainly defensive. To the impatient radicals, who are eager to see all their desired social changes take place in their own life time, this is frustrating. This feeling of disappointment is understandable because it is easy to focus on the individual droplets without seeing the wave or cascade that those droplets can gradually generate. The feeling of frustration is also understandable because it is equally easy to lose sight of the fact that historical periods of gestation for radical social transformations can be quite long, especially in core capitalist societies where forces of oppression and exploitations have become institutional, systemic and, therefore, invisible. The fragmented and the defensive status of labor and other grassroots' coalition networks does not detract from the importance of the potential and the opportunities that these movements represent for social and economic change in the interests of the overwhelming majority of world population—recently called the 99 percent. They show the potential of how globalization from above can create globalization from below; and are therefore reasons for hope and optimism. This is why I think the defeatist conclusion in the face of the brutal offensive by the transnational beneficiaries of war and austerity policies is wrong. The task of those who are convinced that capitalism is not the ideal summit of human civilization is therefore not *to wring their hands*, to paraphrase an old saying, *but to dust off their clothes and go to work*—patient, independent organizing for radical change in favor of working people.

Notes

1 This chapter draws heavily on an earlier paper of the author, titled "NAFTA and Labor: A global strategy for a global economy," which was published in *Political Economy of Globalization*, edited by Satya D. Gupta, Boston/Dordrecht/London: Kluwer Academic Publisher, 1997.

2 For a critical evaluation of international trade union bureaucracies, see Thompson and Larson (1978), Sims (1992), Waterman (1988), MacShane (1992) and Fraser (1991).

3 Among the many labor advocates who have written on these strategies and demands, the term "transitional demands" is most closely associated with or attributed to Leon Trotsky who systematically formulated these strategies in his *The Transitional Program for Socialist Revolution* (New York: Pathfinder Press, 1977); see also Weitzman (1984) and Gorz (1967).

4 Evidence shows that prominent Bolshevik leaders such as Lenin and Trotsky occasionally spoke of the ominous likelihood of the failure and/or reversal of their revolution in the absence of revolutionary outbursts in advanced capitalist countries. For example, in "A Letter to American Workers," dated August 20, 1918, Lenin wrote:

> We are now as if in a beleaguered fortress until other detachments of the international socialist revolution come to our rescue.... We know that help from you, comrades American workers, will probably not come soon.... We know that the European proletarian revolution also may not blaze forth during the next few weeks.... We stake our chances on the inevitability of the international revolution.... We know that circumstances brought to the fore our Russian detachment of the socialist proletariat, not by virtues of our merits, but due to the particular backwardness of Russia, and that before the outburst of the international revolution there may be several defeats of separate revolutions.
>
> (quoted in Mason and Smith (Eds.), 1970)

Leon Trotsky likewise predicted (in his well-known *The Revolution Betrayed*) the possibility of restoration of capitalism in the Soviet Union if the more advanced economies remained capitalist.

5 Interestingly, architects of the U.S. labor's foreign policy during the Cold War regarded themselves as internationalists—anti-communist internationalists. They cooperated

closely with the CIA to break left-led strikes (for example in France in 1949) and overthrow leftist governments (for example in Guatemala in 1954). *Business Week* described the AFL-CIO's global operations, such as its International Affairs Department in Washington and its American Institute for Free Labor Development in Latin America, as "labor's own version of the Central Intelligence Agency—a trade union network existing in all parts of the world." (*Business Week*, May 15, 1966; as quoted in Brecher and Costello 1994: 150; and in Sims 1992).

References

Bello, W., Cunningham, S. and Rau, B. (1994). *Dark victory*. London: Pluto Press.

Blodget, H. (2013). America today: 3 million overlords and 300 million serfs. *Business Insider*, April 10. Retrieved from www.businessinsider.com/wealth-and-income-inequality-in-america-2013–4?op=1 (accessed June 26, 2013).

Braverman, H. (1974). *Labor and monopoly capital*. New York and London: Monthly Review Press.

Brecher, J. and Costello, T. (1994). *Global village or global pillage: Economic reconstruction from the bottom up*. Boston, MA: South End Press.

Bronfenbrenner, K. (Ed.) (2007). *Global unions: Challenging transnational capital through cross-border campaigns*. Ithaca, NY: Cornell University Press.

Cohen R. B., Felton, N., Van Liere, J. and Nkosi, M. (Eds.) (1979). *The multinational corporation: A radical approach, papers by Stephen Herbert Hymer*. Cambridge, MA, Cambridge University Press.

Cooke, S. (2012). Theory and practice in the Occupy Movement. *Global Research*, January 11. Retrieved from www.globalresearch.ca/index.php?context=va& aid=28596 (accessed August 4, 2013).

Daly, H. E. and Cobb, J. B. (1994). *For the common good: Redirecting the economy toward community, the environment, and a sustainable future* (2nd edn.). Boston: Beacon Press.

Danaher, K. (Ed.) (1994). *50 years is enough: The case against the World Bank and the International Monetary Fund*. Boston, MA: South End Press.

Finger, B. (2013). Economic recovery from below: Notes on the insufficiency of "taxing the rich." *New Politics*, *54*(2). Retrieved from http://newpol.org/content/economic-recovery-below-notes-insufficiency-taxing-rich (accessed August 2, 2013).

Flanders, L. (2012). A new era for labor? Creative defiance from factory to street. *CounterPunch*, May 16. Retrieved from www.counterpunch.org/2013/05/16/ a-new-era-for-labor/ (accessed August 6, 2013).

Fraser, D. (1991). *Labor will rule: Hillman and the rise of American labor*. New York: Free Press.

Freeland, C. (2011). The rise of the new global elite. *The Atlantic*, January–February. Retrieved from www.theatlantic.com/magazine/archive/2011/01/the-rise-of-the-new-global-elite/308343/ (accessed August 8, 2013).

Friedman, T. (2010). The fat lady has sung. *New York Times*, February 20. Retrieved from www.nytimes.com/2010/02/21/opinion/21friedman.html?_r=4& (accessed July 25, 2013).

Fukuyama, F. (1992). *The end of history and the last man*. New York: Free Press.

George, S. (1994). The new world order: Development or exploitation. *International Union Rights 1*(6), 10–12.

Gorz, A. (1967). *Strategy for labor; A radical proposal*. Boston, MA: Beacon Press.

Hadas, E., Hutchinson, M. and Currie, A. (2009). American wages out of balance. *New York Times*, November 10. Retrieved from www.nytimes.com/2009/11/11/business/11views.html (accessed July 25, 2012).

Hossein-zadehh, I. (2012). Occupy Wall Street at a crossroads. *Global Research*, January 20. Retrieved from www.globalresearch.ca/occupy-wall-street-at-a-crossroads/28765 (accessed August 4, 2013).

Johnson, D. (2010). President Obama says "made in America" At heart of US recovery. *Seeing the Forest*, August 4. Retrieved from www.seeingtheforest.com/archives/2010/08/president_obama_2.htm#.UfGclqzznIg (accessed June 25, 2013).

Johnson, D. (1993). U.S., Mexican unions are teaming up to organize. *Labor Notes 174*, 8–9.

Juravich, T. (2007). Beating global capital: A framework and method for union strategic corporate research and campaigns. In K. Bronfenbrenner (Ed.). *Global Unions: Challenging Transnational Capital through Cross-border Campaigns*. Ithaca, NY: Cornell University Press.

Klein, N. (2007). *The shock doctrine: The rise of disaster capitalism*. New York: Metropolitan Books.

Konczal, M. (2011). Labor share, long-term trends and financial crises. *wordpress.com*, October 20. Retrieved from http://rortybomb.wordpress.com/2011/10/20/labor-share-long-term-trends-and-financial-crises/ (accessed August 5, 2013).

Krimerman, L. and Lindenfeld, F. (1992). *When workers decide: Workplace democracy takes root in North America*. Philadelphia, PA and Gabriola Island, BC: New Society Publishers.

MacShane, D. (1992). *International labor and the origins of the Cold War*. Oxford: Clarendon Press.

Mason, D. and Smith, J. (Eds.) (1970). *Lenin's Impact on the United States*. New York: NWR Publications, Inc.).

Moody, K. (1994). Pulled apart, pushed together: The North American working class and the labor movement in the U.S. (Unpublished paper).

Obama, B. (2010). President Obama provides progress report on national export initiative, announces members of the President's Export Council. The White House, July 7. Retrieved from www.whitehouse.gov/the-press-office/president-obama-provides-progress-report-national-export-initiative-announces-membe (accessed July 28, 2013).

Obama, B. (2009). Speech by President Obama on U.S. economy. The White House, April 14. Retrieved from www.america.gov/st/texttransenglish/2009/April/20090414142247eaifas0.3019068.htmlk (accessed June 20, 2012).

Riehle, D. (1993). Labor Party advocates gathered in Chicago consider call for convention of a U.S. Labor Party. *Bulletin In Defense of Marxism*, November–December (111), 12–13.

Rippert, U. (2013). Europe on the eve of mass working class struggles. *World Socialist Web Site*, May 7. Rterieved from www.wsws.org/en/articles/2013/05/07/pers-m07.html (accessed July 27, 2013).

Schor, J. (1991). *The overworked American*. New York: Basic Books.

Shuman, M. (1994). *Towards a global village: International Community Development Initiatives*. London and Boulder, CO: Pluto Press.

Sims, B. (1992). *Workers of the world undermined: American Labor's role in U.S. foreign policy*. Boston: South End Press.

St. Clair, J. (2013). The silent death of the American left. *CounterPunch*, May 24–25. Retrieved from www.counterpunch.org/2013/05/24/the-silent-death-of-the-american-left/ (accessed August 5, 2013).

Thompson, D. and Larson, R. (1978). *Where were you, brother? An account of trade union imperialism*. London: War on Want.

Trotsky, L. (1977). *The transitional program for socialist revolution*. New York: Pathfinder Press.

Tugal, C. (2013). The end of the 'leaderless' revolution. *CounterPunch*, July 10. Retrieved from www.counterpunch.org/2013/07/10/the-end-of-the-leaderless-revolution/ (accessed July 12, 2013).

Waterman, P. (Ed.) (1988). *The old internationalism and the new*. The Hague: International Labor Education, Research and Information Foundation.

Weitzman, M. (1984). *The share economy*. Cambridge, MA: Harvard University Press.

White J. (2012). Michigan's right-to-work law. *World Socialist Web Site*, December 13. Retrieved from www.wsws.org/en/articles/2012/12/13/pers-d13.html (accessed July 25, 2013).

Yates, M. (2009). *Why unions matter* (2nd edn.). New York: Monthly Review Press.

Yates, M. (1994). *Longer hours, fewer jobs: Employment and unemployment in the United States*. New York: Monthly Review Press.

Zacune, J. (2013). Privatizing Europe: Using the crisis to entrench neoliberalism. Working Paper, Transnational Institute (TNI), March 13. Retrieved from www.tni.org/sites/www.tni.org/files/download/privatising_europe.pdf (accessed 23 June, 2013).

Zweig, M. (2012). *The working class majority*, Ithaca, NY and London: Cornell University Press.

Index

Alexander, J.B. 113, 127
Allegretto, A.S. 78, 81
Andrews, A. 12, 14, 15, 24
Andrianova, S. 130, 133, 134, 141
Arie, S. 123, 127
Atwater, T. 116, 127
Augar, P. 20, 25
bail out 16, 69, 77, 126, 135, 152
Baker, D. 34, 38, 42
Bank for International Settlements 161
Baran, P. 102, 108
Basu, D. 106, 108
Beams, N. 11, 25
Bellamy-Foster, J. 42, 48, 62, 90, 99, 101, 106, 108
Bello, W. 150, 156, 167
Benyon, H. 140, 141
Bezemer, D.J. 5, 7, 10, 25, 48, 50, 51, 54, 55, 62
Bigelow, G. 52, 53, 60, 62
Blaug, M. 14, 25
Blodget, H. 78, 81, 144, 167
Braverman, H. 157, 167
Brecher, J. 167
Brenner, R. 48, 62, 90, 99, 101, 102–3, 106, 107, 108
Bronfenbrenner, K. 151, 162, 167
Brown, E. 73, 74, 82, 130–2, 135–6, 141
Campbell, D. 61, 62
Chossudovsky, M. 44, 62
class/social classes/class struggle 2, 7, 16, 21, 28, 32, 33, 34, 35, 36, 37, 38, 39, 41, 55, 56, 60, 63, 67, 68, 76, 97, 98, 144–6, 147, 148, 149, 152, 153–7, 162, 165
circular flow 4, 5, 10, 45–6, 47–8, 50, 51, 90, 99
classical economics 53–7
Cohen R.B. 155, 167
Cooke, S. 153
Cumbers A. 139, 141
Danaher, K. 164, 167
Daly, H.E. 164, 167
debt cancellation/relief 6, 110, 111, 113, 114, 116, 118, 120; in Argentina 122–5; in Babylon 112–13; in Bronze-Age Mesopotamia 110–13; in Iceland 120–2; Jesus on 110, 115, 118; Jubilee and other Biblical passages on 114–20; in Pharaonic Egypt 113–14; Rationale for 111, 114, 119, 120; in Sumer 111–12
debt deflation 22–3, 100, 103, 104, 105, 107
Dennis, B. 120–2, 127
derivatives 17, 19, 23, 24, 70, 77; rationale for 65–6
distribution 8, 9, 49, 53, 78, 88, 97, 143, 158, 159
Dumenil, G. 101, 105, 108
Epstein G. 67, 82
Federal Reserve Bank 16, 19, 47, 67, 72, 77, 131, 138; and financial bubbles 16–18, 77; history of the 72–3; independence/dependence of the 72–3, 137; and inequality 77–9, 138; ownership of the 72, 131
fictitious capital 2, 5, 6, 13, 51, 66, 76, 77, 84, 85, 87, 88, 90, 107, 120
financialization i, 3, 27, 28, 48, 70, 86, 100, 101–2, 104
financial innovation (s) 2, 17, 19, 50, 64–5, 69, 85
financial institutions 18, 23, 47, 69, 71, 77, 123, 126
financial sector: growth (parasitic) 5, 48–50, 67–70, 132; impact on inequality 6, 68, 76–8, 80; impact on politicians/ policy-making 70–2, 74–6, 79–80
Finger, B. 67, 71, 92, 143, 158, 167
Fisher, I. 21–3, 25

Flanders, L. 163, 167
Fraser, D. 166, 167
Fraser, S. 49, 62
fraud 13, 24, 26, 44; fraudulent asset price inflation 20; fraudulent compensation of financial speculators 138; fraudulent debt/money creation 1, 5, 121; fraudulent mortgages 137
Freeland, C. 154, 167
Friedman, T. 147, 167
Galbraith, J. 12, 47, 62
general equilibrium 3, 4, 8, 10, 44, 45, 51, 99
George, S. 157, 167
Giles, C. 9, 10, 25
Goldman Sacks 19, 20, 23, 24, 25, 160
Gorz, A. 166, 167
Gowan, P. 16, 20, 25, 36, 86, 100, 129
Graeber, D. 9, 25
Great Depression 2, 7, 21–2, 27, 28, 34–5, 65–6, 73, 104–5, 144
Great Recession 11, 23, 34, 99, 100, 101–7, 144, 146
Greenspan, A. 12, 13–15, 17, 25, 77
Gray, B. 24, 25
Griffin, B. 23, 25
Hadas, E. 147, 168
Harding, R. 5, 7, 48
Heilbroner, R. 47, 62
Hilferding, R. 90–3, 108
Hossein-zadeh, I. 153, 168
Hudson, M. 48, 52, 54, 62, 74, 75, 77, 82, 111, 112–14, 117–20, 137
Hunt, K.E. 55, 56, 57, 58, 59, 62, 94, 97
Hyman, R. 139, 141
income inequality 49, 78–9, 97, 144
International Monetary Fund 11, 25, 154, 165
Jevons, W.S. 56, 58, 59, 62
Johnson, D. 146, 150, 168
Juravich, T. 149, 168
Kalecki, M. 102, 108
Kalur, J.S. 32, 42
Kaufman, F. 19, 25
Keen, S. 10, 25, 61
Kennedy, M. 132, 141
Keynes, J.M. 21, 22, 25, 34, 46, 50, 96; on Great Depression 21–2; and the New Deal 34; and "liquidity trap" 96
Keynesian economics 1, 4, 8, 22, 27–9, 31, 33–5, 38–9, 40, 42, 44, 46, 50, 63–4, 96; demise of 28–30, 31–3; and the diagnosis of the financial crisis 27–8; and the theory of "liquidity trap" 46, 50, 96–7; growth and/or employment in 4, 36–42; solution/response to financial crisis 27, 36–42; myths and illusions of 4, 27, 33–6
Kindleberger, C.P. 64, 82
Klein, N. 79, 82, 148
Kliman, A. 101, 104–5, 107, 108
Konczal, M. 159, 168
Kotz, D.M. 28, 58, 103–4, 107, 108
Krugman, P. 34, 35–6, 39, 42, 80
labor theory of value 54–5, 56, 57, 59, 87
Lapavistas, C. 88, 108
Bottom of Form
Lenin, V.I. 93–9
Liberto, J. 74, 82
Lietaer, B. 131, 132
MacShane, D. 166, 168
Magdoff, F. 101, 108
mainstream economics *see* neoclassical economics
Martens, P. 33, 43
Marx, K. 84–90
Marxian views of financial crisis: Marx's view of 84–90; *see also* Marx, K; Hilferding's view of 90–3, 108; *see also* Hilferding, R; Lenin's view of 93–9; *see also* Lenin, V.I.; contemporary Marxist views of 99–107
Mettenheim, K.V. 134–5, 141
Mishel, L. 80, 82
Mohun, S. 109
Moody, K. 157, 159, 168
Nasser A. 31, 32, 40, 43
Nelson, R. 15, 24
neoclassical economics 4–5, 8, 14, 27, 44–5, 47, 50–1, 53, 56, 57, 84, 89, 90, 99; and money supply/credit 45–51; ideological foundations of 53–60; and mathematics/science 59–60; and real world developments 51–3; science or religion 3, 12–15, 44, 60
neoliberal economics: explanation of the financial crisis 1–2, 3–4, 8, 9–11, 28, 31, 35, 44, 46, 70, 71, 79, 85, 96, 123, 148, 164; faith-based nature of 11–15; and financial bubbles 15–20; response to the financial crisis 8–11; as a never dating prescription 20–4; *see also* neoclassical economics
Occupy Movement 152, 153, 167, 168; response to the crisis 152–3
Obama, B. 33, 35, 39, 40, 145, 146, 147
Okun, A. 32, 43
Palley, T. 31, 43

Phillips, K. 50, 62
public banking 128, 131, 134, 135, 138, 140; advantages over private banks 129–35; and the case of the Bank of North Dakota 130–1; in Brazil 134–5; in China 134–5; definition of 128; and democratic control/management 138–40; in France 131–2; in Germany 136; in India 134–5; as a public utility model 135–8; Rationale for 128–9; in Russia 134–5; in Sweden 136; U.S. experience with 71–2, 135–6
Quantitative Easing 19, 24, 77; and financial bubbles 24, 77; and inequality 77–8
Reeves, J. 70, 82
Reich, R. 39–40, 43
Riehle, D. 156, 168
Rippert, U. 144, 145, 168
Roberts, P.C. 74, 82
Ross, M. 23, 26
Schor, J. 158, 168
Schultze C. 32, 43
Shaikh, A. 27, 29, 43, 100, 106, 109
Shuman, M. 168
Shutt, H. 43
Silber, W.L. 42
Sims, B. 168
Snyder, M. 24, 26
speculation 2, 5, 16, 18, 19, 23, 47, 51, 69, 88, 89, 90, 102, 134
St. Clair, J. 159–60, 168
Steindl, J. 109
Stiglitz, J. 43
supply side 21, 28, 33, 36, 39, 79, 138, 140
surplus value 2, 57, 58, 71, 84–5, 87–8
Sweezy, P. 108
Taibbi, M. 20, 26
Thompson, D. 166, 169
Toporowski, J. 10, 26, 29–30, 64, 65–6, 69–70
Toussaint, E. 110, 111, 113, 126, 127
trade unions 144, 148, 150, 151, 154, 157; response to the crisis 144–8; international 148–52
Tremblay, R. 77, 83
Trotsky, L. 166, 169
Tugal, C. 153, 169
value added 87, 88
Vickery, W. 52, 62
Washington's Blog 24, 26
Waterman, P. 169
wealth inequality 41, 78, 80, 132, 144
Weeks, J. 63, 68, 83, 85
Weisbrot, M. 123, 125, 127
Weitzman, M. 169
White J. 169
Wray, R. 43
Yates, M. 149, 157, 169
Young, A. 133, 142
Zacune, J. 80, 81, 83, 164, 169
Zweig, M. 157, 169